A PLAN of the … UPPER CANADA, according to … which has passed the two Houses, and reserved for the Signification of the Royal Pleasure.

B

Surveyor General's Office, Upper Canada 28th August 1799.

For the Acting Surveyor General
(Signed) Chewett & Ridout

N.B. The names of the Townships are taken from a Plan in the Engineer's Drawing Room Quebec

Copied in the Engineer's Drawing Room Quebec by Lieut. Wm. Hall Rl. Artr.

43.10 / 9.55

Gother Mann
Col. Command. Rl. Engrs.
Quebec 3d. Nov. 1800

Ottawa River
The Midland District
The District of Johnstown
The Eastern District
Cy. of Carleton
Co. of Russell
Co. of Prescott
Co. of Glengary
County of Stormont
County of Dundas
County of Grenville
County of Leeds
County of Frontenac
County of Hastings
Incorporated Counties of Addington
Lenox
Kingston
Co. of Prince Edward
Newcastle
St. Regis
Lake St. Francis
Pointe au Bodette
River St. Lawrence
ONTARIO

Eastern District
1 Lancaster
2 Charlottenburg
3 St. Regis Indians
4 Cornwall
5 Kenyon
6 Roxburg
7
8 Mr. De Longueuils Seigy.
9 Alfred
10 Plantagenet

Eastern District
11 Clarence
12 Cumberland
13 Glocester
14 Cambridge
15
16 Osgoode
17 Mountain
18 Winchester
19 Finch
20 Osnabruck
21 Williamsburg
22 Matilda

District of Johnstown
23 Edwardsburg
24 Augusta
25 Walford
26 Montagu
27 Marlborough
28 Oxford
29 Gower 30 Nepean

District of Johnstown
31 Elizabethtown
32 Yonge
33 Lansdown
34 Leeds
35 Bastard
36 Kitley
37 Russel
38 Burgess
39 —

Midland District
…ittsburg
…ingston
…ortland
…oughborough

…rnesttown
…redericksburg
…dolphus Town
…ichmond
…amden

…arysburg
…ophiasburg
…meliasburg
…ohawks
…hurlow
…idney
…ungerford
…untingdon
…awdon

Home District
61 Murray
62 Cramahé
63 Haldimand
64 Hamilton
65 Percy
66 Alnwick
67 Hope
68 Clarke
69 Darlington
70
71 Whitby
72 Pickering
73 Scarborough
74 York
75 -
76 -
77 Markham
78 Whitchurch
79
80.
81.
82
83 Flamborough
84 Beverly
85

District of Niagara
86
87 Newark
88 Stamford
89 Grantham
90 Louth
91 Clinton
92 Grimsby
93 Saltfleet
94 Barton
95 Thorold
96 Pelham
97 Binbrook
98 Ancaster
99 Glanford

District of Niagara
100 Caistor
101 Gainsborough
102 Bertie
103 Willoughby
104 Crowland
105 Humberstone
106 Wainfleet

District of London
107 Rainham
108 Walpole
109 Woodhouse
110 Charlotteville
111 Walsingham
112
113 Windham
114 Townsend
115
116 Burford
117 Norwich
118 Dereham

District of London
119
120 Blandford
121 Bleinheim
122 Houghton
123 Yarmouth
124 Southwold
125 Dunwich
126 Aldborough
127
128
129 Dorchester
130
131
132

Western District
133 Orford
134 Howard
135 Harwich
136 Raleigh
137

District Western
138 Dover
139 Chatham
140 Camden
141 Moravian Village
142
143 Romney
144 Tilbury
145 Rochester
146 Mersea
147 Gosfield
148 Maidstone
149 Sandwich
150 Colchester
151 Malden
152 Huron's Land

THE BALDWINS

AND

THE GREAT EXPERIMENT

* *

THE BALDWINS AND THE GREAT EXPERIMENT

* *

R. M. and J. Baldwin

Longmans

Longmans Canada Limited
55 Barber Greene Road
Don Mills, Ontario

Set in 10/12 Baskerville
Paper: 60 lb. Library Book

Printed in Canada by The Alger Press Limited

"You have commenced a great experiment.
It is for your honour that you shall, if possible,
remain to work it out."

Lord Stanley to Sir Charles Bagot, 1842

CONTENTS

PART III
THE PEACEFUL REVOLUTION, 1838-1858

ILLUSTRATIONS

A NOTE OF GRATITUDE

During four years of hard, but intensely interesting, research my wife and I have worked on this book as a team in every sense of the word – we have composed and written together, wrangled, argued and rewritten together and we only hope that those who read this book will have half as much enjoyment from it as we had in writing it. When we had finished, the realization that we had become involved in it more or less by accident came as rather a shock.

Driving back from Toronto to Ottawa after a brief holiday in 1962, we were passing Newcastle when I remarked to Joyce that our family had first settled in that area but that I had never taken the time to find the place. Intrigued, she suggested that we stop and explore. It was our good fortune to be directed to old Mr. Lovekin (the late James Lovekin), a direct descendant of the family that had befriended the Baldwins when they arrived in Upper Canada. Following our afternoon with Mr. Lovekin, during which we explored Baldwin's Creek in Clarke Township, we received an invitation from his son to the unveiling of a plaque to mark the site of the first homestead of the Baldwin family in Canada; this was erected by the Ontario Archaeological and Historic Sites Board, sponsored by the Durham County Club and the Newcastle Chamber of Commerce, and unveiled in June 1963 by the Honourable Leslie Frost. It was during this ceremony that we realized how little was known of the early life and family of Robert the Emigrant and that if this material was not located soon, it might disappear forever. Might it not be fun to retire early and do something about it? It took two years to put our idea into practice but in October 1965 we sailed for Ireland to begin our research.

During the next four years we met with the greatest help and understanding. In Cork, where we spent most of our six months in Ireland, we became particularly indebted to Mr. Daniel O'Keeffe, Librarian of University College, who located so many copies of the *Volunteer Journal* for us, and to his friendly and helpful staff; also to the college authorities who permitted our researches there, and to Professors Pender and Roche and others of the History Department for suggestions and advice; to Mr. Patrick Madden, Head of the County Cork Library; and to that other fine local historian, John T. Collins. While in Dublin, we spent an unforgettable few hours in the boiler-room of Trinity College, sitting on a packing-case discussing responsible government with Professor McDowell, a most profitable session laid on by Professor Moody, Head of the History Department; nor shall we forget the kindness of the staff of the National Library of Ireland in assisting us in getting additional copies of the *Volunteer Journal* and other documents.

Just outside Carrigaline we found Knockmore where the original house, Summer Hill, was burned down but where the present, smaller house stands on the same site; here the present owners, Mr. and Mrs. R. Chambers, received us with the greatest kindness. Among the many others in Ireland who were both kind and helpful we would like to thank Mr. Basil O'Connell, the noted Irish genealogist, for permitting us to use extracts from the yet unpublished Deasy Papers, Mr. and Mrs. Worth Newenham of Coolmore (which is still occupied by the same family as it was in Robert's day), and Miss Gwendoline Baldwin, a distant but dear relative, who directed us to Miss Rosemary ffolliott of the Genealogical Office in Dublin. In England, Mr. Peter H.

Tresidder of Penzance supplied us with information about Greatwood and Great Weir, as did Mr. Neil G. Treseder and Geoffrey Wilson, M.P., of Truro.

Back in Canada in 1966, we found that the bulk of the letters and papers that we needed were in the custody of the Baldwin Room, Metropolitan Toronto Central Library, and we are most grateful to Miss Edith G. Firth, head of the Canadian History and Manuscript Section, and her staff, as well as to the staff of the Public Archives of Ontario for making available to us copies of documents, thus enabling us to work on our book in Ottawa. There the staffs of the Public Archives of Canada and the National Library were tireless in helping us.

We are greatly indebted to Professor G. de T. Glazebrook for his kindness in reading part of our manuscript and for his suggestions, also for a morning spent with Professor Donald McDougall; to our friend, Professor Anthony Adamson, who guided us through Dr. William Warren Baldwin's sallies into architecture and supplied an illustration of St. George's house (but any shortcomings in this chapter are our own); to Mr. Jim Lovekin, who took us to Port Hope to show us the early housing development started there by Dr. Baldwin; to Mrs. D. Forster; and to so many others who helped and encouraged us, including members of the family, especially R. E. Y. Baldwin of Niagara, Miss E. Baldwin of Orangeville, Hamilton Cassells, Q.C., and the late Miss Suzy Robinson of Toronto. Above all, our very grateful thanks to our editor, Helen O'Reilly, for all she has done.

And finally, our gratitude to the subjects of our research for providing a political thread that led us through the lives of father, son and grandson and which proved such an exciting one to follow.

R.M.B.

Ottawa,
July 1969.

Part I

FROM CORK TO YORK
1741 - 1816

THE BALDWINS OF CORK AND YORK

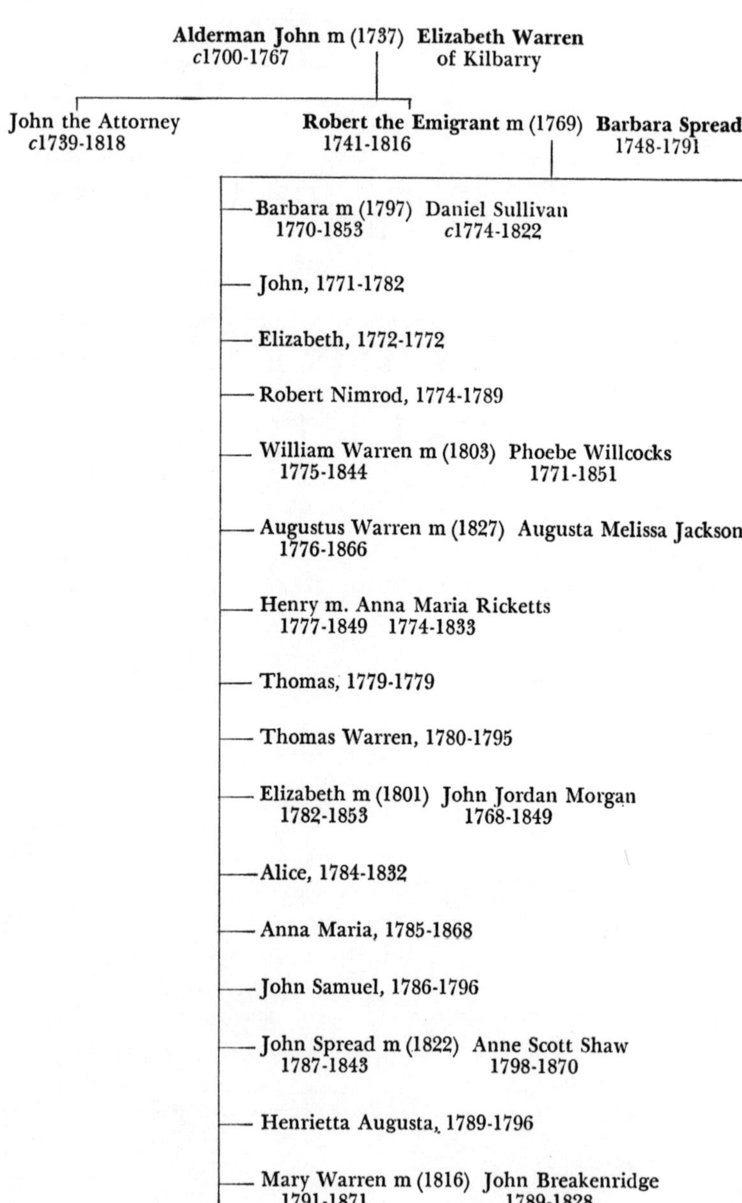

Alderman John m (1737) **Elizabeth Warren**
*c*1700-1767
of Kilbarry
John the Attorney
*c*1739-1818
Robert the Emigrant m (1769) **Barbara Spread**
1741-1816
1748-1791
Barbara m (1797) Daniel Sullivan
1770-1853
*c*1774-1822
John, 1771-1782
Elizabeth, 1772-1772
Robert Nimrod, 1774-1789
William Warren m (1803) Phoebe Willcocks
1775-1844
1771-1851
Augustus Warren m (1827) Augusta Melissa Jackson
1776-1866
Henry m. Anna Maria Ricketts
1777-1849 1774-1833
Thomas, 1779-1779
Thomas Warren, 1780-1795
Elizabeth m (1801) John Jordan Morgan
1782-1853
1768-1849
Alice, 1784-1832
Anna Maria, 1785-1868
John Samuel, 1786-1796
John Spread m (1822) Anne Scott Shaw
1787-1843
1798-1870
Henrietta Augusta, 1789-1796
Mary Warren m (1816) John Breakenridge
1791-1871
1789-1828

* *

1

THE IRELAND OF ALDERMAN JOHN

The Baldwins who arrived in Upper Canada in 1799 came of a family that had lived in the west of England for a number of generations prior to coming to Ireland in the reign of Elizabeth I. They accompanied the Herberts, whose kinsmen they were, although they did not follow the Herberts into Kerry, but bought land about five miles north-west of Bandon in County Cork and settled there. By an indenture made "the two and twentieth day of February in the year of our Lord according to the computation of the Church of England 1612 and in the year of the Reign of our Sovereign Lord James . . . Thomas Baldwin bought from Gyles Maskelin of Colatrim the lands of Lisnegatt," also a water or grist mill with other adjoining lands, and his brother, Henry Baldwin, purchased Mount Pleasant (Curraghvordy) and Mossgrove (Garrancoonig).

By direct descent these lands finally came into the possession of cousins Henry and John Baldwin, the latter known to his family as Alderman John. He was born about the year 1705, an individualist and certainly a colourful figure in a colourful age. Dominant, impulsive, ambitious, he had the typical Irish tastes for speculation and good living. An anecdote told in later years to his grandchildren paints a vivid picture of a provocative and irritating man who liked to call the tune in conversation, and who "never answered to a form of impertinence till he had whistled 'Lillibulero'," an old Irish nursery ballad and a song popular in Ireland from the time of William III. Alderman John had broken with tradition, for while most of his uncles and cousins were country gentlemen, by 1723 he had become apprenticed to Theodore Van Sevenhoven, a Dutch merchant of Ballencurra, Cork.

Ireland in the eighteenth century was a land of contrasts. A land of the very rich and the very poor; of large estates and pitiful hovels; of wealthy merchants and tithe-ridden tenant-farmers; of one fifth Protestants with political rights, and four-fifths Catholics with none. But, with all that, a countryside full of soft beauty, and with fine harbours full of ships.

The very rich were the owners of the great estates, for wealth was measured in acres, and the work of these wide acres was done by tenants and labourers. Many of the owners of these fine tracts of land in Ireland found it was more comfortable, more entertaining, and more fashionable to live in London or Bath. This absenteeism played 'merry hell' with the economy of Ireland. The money-drain in rents to England* of over a million pounds sterling each year left the country poor and prevented many improvements in agriculture. The tenants also suffered, for as long as rents were forthcoming the absentee landlords were not worrying very much how these were being collected, or of bettering the conditions of people they hardly ever saw. Finally, when it became profitable, these wealthy owners did not hesitate to fence large tracts of land for sheep and cattle and to evict their tenants.

Behind the landlords and their way of life was the Irish land system which had developed over the years by conquest, redistribution, rebellion and confiscation. Great numbers of Irish landlords had been dispossessed, many had been killed or fled the

* Hely Hutchinson, Secretary of State for Ireland, calculated the sum remitted to Great Britain for absentee rents in 1783 at £1,227,480 and in 1797 at £1,500,000.

country.* The land system had become a gigantic layer cake, with all the icing, in the form of rents, near the top; and with the burdens of heavy rent and the payment of tithes falling on those at the bottom. At the lowest level were the vast majority, the poor and illiterate, the cottiers and labourers, the majority of whom were Catholics; and hanging over and all but smothering them were the tithes. These tithes were enforced taxes on crops and produce in support of the Protestant church and clergy. They were corrosive in men's minds, as they bore heavily on the poor and were so unjust towards the Catholics, who thereby contributed a major share for the support and upkeep of a religious faith which they abhorred.

The all-important question of religion in Ireland was to be a razor's edge on which the fate of the country hung teetering in uneven balance, uneven because, under the penal and other laws, most of the Catholics had been reduced to mere tenants at will (holding their land at the landlord's pleasure). For the cottiers, who, under the Irish custom of cottier-tenure, rented their cottages and small plots annually at a rent fixed each year by public competition, life was even less secure and more miserable.

The penal laws could roughly be divided into those laws which prevented Catholics from acquiring property, and those which excluded them from certain livelihoods and occupations. In the first group were the statutes whereby Catholics could not buy freehold property nor hold a lease of over thirty years, nor own a horse worth more than £5. As the franchise was extended only to those who owned freehold land assessed at forty shillings and over, this excluded most Catholics from the right to vote.

Sandwiched between the rich and the poor were the small landowners and merchants. They were in a very literal sense the middle class. They spent their lives working in Ireland and they had a very big stake in the country's future – their all. They

* Many of these political refugees joined cavalry units abroad, notably in Austria, and risked their lives to visit Ireland to see those they loved; they were known as "the Wild Geese" and it was for one of them that Eileen Dobh Ni Conaill wrote her lovely *caoine,* "Lament for Art O'Leary," when her husband was betrayed and slain during such a visit in 1773.

had contact daily with the tenant-farmers, the cottiers, and the labourers, and sometimes with the very rich. Most of the landowners were Protestant, but a large number of the merchants were Catholic. All the forty-shilling freeholders had the vote, so they exerted a greater influence on Irish affairs than their numbers would imply. During the latter half of the eighteenth century this was the group that stood a chance of bringing the various elements together. And for a brief period the political opportunity was to present itself.

The Baldwins were part of this predominantly Protestant middle group. The Corporation Book of Cork shows John Baldwin, following his apprenticeship in 1723, making steady progress in business and municipal affairs. Early in 1728 he was admitted a Freeman of Cork; as such he was now permitted to carry on his own retail business, and might even inherit that of his master. Late in 1730 he was elected one of the two sheriffs and became a member of the city council during that year of office. On April 30, 1735 he became an alderman and a permanent member of the city council. In February 1737 he married Elizabeth Warren, younger daughter of Robert Warren of Killbarry, a wealthy and highly respected landowner; in October of the same year he was elected Mayor of Cork.

The country surrounding the city then would have been much as Chief Justice Willis describes it: " 'Tis very rough country till we arrive within five miles of Cork where it is well improved and wooded, and adorned with several gentlemen's seats . . ." On entering Cork, he continues, "The river Lee runs across it from which are cut two great canals . . . Ships of tolerable burden come up to the town and merchandise is brought up by lighters and other vessels to most of the merchants' doors." For many of the streets of today were the ship-laden canals of yesterday.

Cork "of the white sails,"* a noisy, prosperous Irish Venice, had become the centre of Ireland's rich provision trade; and "for packing and salting and barrelling of beef this city gives place to no other in Europe." In addition, by the middle of the century a number of allied trades flourished. At Douglas on the southern Liberties (suburbs), Huguenot weavers had established

* A line from the lament of Eileen Dobh Ni Conaill for her husband, in Frank O'Connor's translation.

a thriving sailcloth industry; large quantities of tanned hides and tallow were exported annually; Cork became noted for its butter; and wool was a rich trade and even continued, in a clandestine manner, after crippling restrictions were imposed, because Irish products were threatening British trade.

Alderman John and Elizabeth his wife lived on the outskirts of Cork at Cold Harbour, a choice location for merchant shipping, situated at the junction of the River Lee, and so commanding the water approaches to Cork. "The spreading Lee that like an island fayre encloseth Cork with his divided flood" – so Spenser, writing his *Faerie Queene* in his house near Cork two centuries earlier, saw this sail-filled harbour. John's house, with its own quay, served also as his place of business, and it was here that his two sons, John and Robert, were born – the latter on August 21, 1741.

Alderman John's sons received a good classical education, as was the fashion for the young men at that time. John, like his father, lived in the city and studied to become an attorney but Robert loved the country, a preference probably fostered by his mother who had been brought up on the large Warren estates of Killbarry and Warren Court, the latter one of the fine old houses that stood until 1921, when it was burned down during the "troubles."

No doubt many days of Robert's boyhood were spent riding over the vivid green fields of the Warren lands; he would have passed and repassed the mill and the tannery, of which the ruins are still visible beside a nearly dried-up stream; and he would have ridden over with his mother to the next estate of Mount Pleasant where his Aunt Alice (his mother's sister) lived with his Uncle Henry and their children, the Baldwin cousins having married sisters. The house was large and austere, having been a fortified farm, built for defence in the early days, but it faced a long slope down to a small lake and there was a lovely walled garden with fruit and flowers and under the shady trees periwinkles grew in profusion. One of the basic conflicts all through Robert's life was the tug of war between town and country. When he had the choice he lived in the country, but other considerations kept pulling him back to the city for the family business was, of course, in Cork.

That business was suffering from the general decline in Irish trade during the seventeen-fifties. Alderman John had always had business ties with the Netherlands; now this connection was to prove the final straw, for a large Dutch estate that owed him a considerable amount of money became bankrupt. All he was able to recover were two old oil paintings known in the family as "The Hermit" and "The Hen and Chickens." The first was thought to be a painting of the head of St. Jerome, and the second showed a farmyard – and must also have shown some hens and chickens! This last was initialled G. D. H. and is thought to have been painted by G. D. Hondecoeter whose "Hen and Chickens in a Landscape," dated 1652, hangs in the gallery of Rotterdam.

In 1759 Alderman John, "having met with misfortune," left Ireland for the Isle of Man, his intention being to sail from there to the West Indies and so make his fortune. He went alone, for his wife refused to accompany him, and both John and Robert stayed with their mother in Cork. But the Alderman instead went to London – to escape his creditors? To try to drum up trade? To enjoy the bright lights? Perhaps it was a combination of all three; but he left his sons, young men of eighteen and twenty, to run his business, look after the family lands of Lisnegatt, and no doubt to remit a substantial share of the profits, badly needed in Ireland, to their father in England. There was also their mother to provide for who, it is said, never lived to see her sons out of difficulties.

The last we hear of Alderman John is a line in the *Cork Chronicle* of December 21, 1767 – "Died lately in London, John Baldwin Esq., one of the Aldermen of this City."

* *

2

ROBERT, FARMER AND SENESCHAL

So for a time Robert worked with his brother in the city. The state of the family business made it necessary for the two brothers, so dissimilar in temperament, to pull together. Robert, who loved the country, now found himself in the role of a merchant. His brother John, "inheriting some part of his father's disposition for speculation . . . applied his means to building houses. He was moreover a man of much taste and ingenuity . . . and indulged himself also in the construction of pleasure boats: a very favourite and fashionable amusement with the young men of the city who could afford the expense." It was no hardship for John to live and work in the city.

Robert, while preferring country pursuits, enjoyed the amenities of Cork. A few surviving letters from his friends lift the curtain of silence which must obscure the events of two hundred years ago. One such was written by Will Verlin, a young and promising attorney from Cork. It begins: " 'Pleasures are ever in our hands and eyes, And when in act, they cease; in prospect rise' – An odd manner this to begin my answer to your agreeable and long wished for epistle; the lines quoted above are out of your favourite author Pope." He is writing from London and goes on to describe the delights of Ranelagh, saying: "I could wish you with our little Society transport yourselves there, this evening I intend going."

This little society of which Robert was a part enjoyed and patronized horse racing and the theatre; for Will wrote, "I am so sorry we shall not have a better set of players to go to Cork this summer than we had here." Cork had a good theatre where comedians from Dublin performed during the Summer Assizes, "and a month or two longer as they met with encouragement."

This letter of Will's also unfolds a little drama.

About seven miles from Lisnegatt, "and four miles east by west of Macroomp [Macroom] is Forrest, the pleasant seat of William Spread Esq., where is an handsome house, good gardens, large orchards, fish ponds and a great number of trees planted." The Spread girls, Anna Maria, Barbara and Henrietta, attended Christmas parties and other gaieties in the vicinity; so it is not surprising that Robert fell in love with one of them. This was Barbara, a charming vivacious creature, "with a lovely smile." At this time, 1763, Barbara was only fifteen, and Robert a dashing young country squire of twenty-two.

The fact that Barbara's father had died when she was two, and the guardianship of the children had been entrusted to an uncle, certainly did not help this romance. When Robert asked for her hand, he was not yet established either in farming or in business, and was understandably turned down. But from what can be gathered the uncle made Barbara write to Robert herself rejecting him. Not knowing what was behind this refusal, Robert was deeply hurt.

So he began to court Martha P. (her surname does not appear in the letters), no doubt one of the "little Society", for Will Verlin writes: ". . . and as you say you love the girl proceed and may happiness equal to your most sanguine wishes attend you, her manner of behaviour to you incomprehensible – possibly your Friend Samuel may be the bar to your happiness. – Try her once more, though you may be repulsed the first attack, yet on a vigorous second attempt you may carry the citadel." And he goes on to say, "Let my little Mary [Will Verlin's fiancée] prepare your little Martha for the R'encounter and you will find you will succeed."

Evidently Robert acted on this advice for it is recorded: "R. B.

was engaged for a year and a day, that is they were to be bound not to marry till that time was passed, and then they were at liberty to break or keep the engagement." This arrangement clearly indicated that Martha and Robert were not very sure of their feelings towards each other. And before the year and a day was up, Martha P. married Samuel Stedman. So Will Verlin's challenge, "If possible I wish we could be married about the same time and we'll play the first Boy for a hundred ducats," was not to be taken up.

But Robert does not appear to have been heartbroken for on September 7, 1769 this notice ran in the *Cork Evening Post:* "Married last week at Moviddy Church [the parish church of Forrest] Robert Baldwin of this city, merchant, to Miss Barbara Spread." Thus Barbara did not marry until after her twenty-first birthday when Robert was twenty-eight.

After a few years the Baldwin brothers were able to come to an arrangement satisfactory to both. John, now a Freeman of Cork, remained in the city, practised as an attorney and carried on what was left of the business. Robert was able to return to the country, to live at Mossgrove and farm his own and his brother's share of it and of the plowlands of Lisnegatt.

The house at Mossgrove was typical of the Irish country house of the period, a solid, squarish, medium-sized Georgian affair with dormer windows on the third floor. It stood facing south, perched half-way up the sweep of a hillside among some trees. It is somewhat decayed and run down now, but was probably very comfortable at the time Robert occupied it, with its large, high-ceilinged rooms and roaring log fires.

It was at this time that Robert and his uncle Sir Robert Warren came more and more into contact. No doubt Robert joined the Hunt of which Sir Robert was master. On many occasions he would ride over to Warren Court and up the long avenue of trees to the big house with its pine woods and lake. There would be days after planting and harvest when fine fishing was to be had in the Bandon River, and the woods between Lisnegatt and Mount Pleasant were well stocked with game.

Robert had some capital from his mother's marriage settlement and felt that by improved methods he might be able to make a success of farming. He appears to have had good ideas on farm improvement when such ideas were all too uncommon in Ireland. For it was estimated that, in spite of greater soil fertility, the average crop per acre was smaller than in England. Also the quality of Irish crops was inferior owing to the imperfect understanding by many farmers of the system of rotation.

Land in Ireland, which was constantly changing hands during the eighteenth century, was mostly leasehold. So Robert was to find farming for a living a very different proposition from running the family estate. Now, with rent to pay, it was vital to make a profit.

Strong family ties have always been a Baldwin characteristic, so what more natural than that, when Robert decided to farm on his own, he should lease a farm from his first cousin Herbert Gilman, whose mother was Alderman John's only sister. Their property, Russell Hill, was near Lisnegatt about four miles east of Bandon on the way to Cork.

Then, fired with enthusiasm, Robert leased more land, this time a larger farm belonging to an Edmund Roche and here he laid out considerable sums on improvements. As to the terms of this lease, no deeds can be found; but in 1816 Robert's son William wrote of this venture, "He inconsiderately left himself in Mr. Roach's [*sic*] power, of which the latter availed himself to my father's considerable loss." This setback of Robert's was due in large measure to the land system, and was typical of many of Ireland's troubles. In the case of Mr. Roche, Robert had come up against the massive powers conferred on Irish landlords by law, with the frightening insecurity of tenure which made many tenants merely tenants at will. This had the effect of stagnating most farm improvement in Ireland, for unscrupulous landlords would give verbal permission for improvements to be made and then evict the tenant when they were completed, as actually happened in Robert's case.

This was the beginning of Robert's own financial troubles, added to those which he inherited from the Alderman, his father; such a setback, so early in his career, was one from which he never really recovered. He retained his interest in Lisnegatt, but he had now crossed the magic line between freehold and leasehold and he had further added to his land holdings by taking the lands of Knockmore. He had leased Knockmore, five miles south of Cork in the Parish of Carrigaline, on a 999-year lease from the Widow Day. This was before he lost Roche's farm but was a wise move for he and Barbara with young Barbara were able to move to Knockmore to live. He also leased two other small farms, Munroe and Ballea, giving him in all about 420 acres, although he himself farmed only Knockmore, as he let the other two farms to undertenants.

The house that Robert and his family now occupied on Knockmore was called Summer Hill. Here is a description of it, typical of houses owned by gentlemen farmers of modest means.

Picture the usual austere squarish grey house with a handsome fanlight over the front door, the rooms high-ceilinged with tall windows giving plenty of light. "On the ground floor [there were] two parlours, a hall, two closets and a counting house." There was a small cellar and coalhouse, but the kitchen was large, twenty-six feet by sixteen, equipped with boiler and ovens. "The second floor contained six lodging rooms [bedrooms] with a fire place to each." There was also a large closet (linen cupboard) and there were good garrets overhead. The out-offices consisted of stabling for twelve horses, a lofty barn fifty feet by eighteen in the clear, with a large liney (lean-to) and other outbuildings.

The house and demesne of Summer Hill then comprised 220 acres of choice land in a rough triangle with Ballinrea Cross at its apex to the north, and the house and a tiny lake, formed by a dammed-up stream, a little to the south. This little stream formed part of the north-west boundary, and then emptied into the Owenboy, a small swiftly-flowing river at this point. It passes through a picturesque miniature gorge below Ballea Castle and round to Ballea Bridge, and forms the western boundary of Knockmore. The Ballea property, which Robert also leased, lay to the west of this river. The eastern side of Knockmore was bounded by the old Cork Road from Ballinrea Cross past Summer Hill to Carrigaline. Half-way along this stretch there was, and still is, a lane on the right leading downhill to St. Roanog's Well, which dates from Roman times.

Robert and Barbara lived happily here, and by 1775 there were five children. Barbara, the eldest, had gone as a baby with her parents to Summer Hill; John, who was born in 1771, died when he was eleven. Local lore has it that one son was drowned in the little lake near the house, and apparently this was the tragedy which surrounded the loss of this eldest son. Of the other children, a daughter died shortly after birth, but Robert Nimrod lived until he was fifteen. William Warren, the fifth child, was born on April 25, 1775. This growing and closely knit family was a happy one, and to say the marriage of Robert and Barbara was amply blessed with children would be an understatement—for they were to have sixteen. Not all survived, which was not unusual in that day and age.

Robert was well liked and respected and held in high esteem in the Parish of Carrigaline. But after a few years, crop farming became less profitable because of the English Corn Laws and the resulting swing to grazing in Ireland. Robert, who had insufficient capital to follow suit, began to feel the pinch financially. Possibly as a mark of approval, and also perhaps as a subtle way of offering financial help, Lord Shannon appointed him seneschal of the manor.

The duties of seneschal approximated those of a rural magistrate or justice of the peace, and in this office it was Robert's duty to hold Court Leet. Courts Leet were special courts of record which lords of certain manors were empowered to hold annually or semi-annually. In this office the holder was entitled, by the system of the manor, to fourpence a year from every house. But, we are told, "This he never exacted."

Besides the Court Leet, which was seldom held, Robert presided over the Court Baron, or Manor Court. This sat every three weeks with a jury to try cases of ten pounds and under, and Robert's register of this court was rendered twice yearly to the judges of assize in the City of Cork. "There never was an appeal carried before them from the Manor Court of Carrigaline during his occupancy of that office."

The good relationship of Robert with his tenants and the villagers of Carrigaline, and their reaction to his kindness in not exacting his yearly fee, is underlined by the following incident, recounted by his son William Warren: "He invited the inhabitant labourers to come to him on a certain day to grass a piece of unsubdued land on the summit of Knockmore. He prepared bread and milk in abundance and a piper into the bargain." The bread and milk would have been sumptuous fare for the poor cottiers, even in summer, for their regular diet from May to August would have been a little corncale or cabbage sprinkled with salt, and some days a draught of sour milk; while in the winter they ate potatoes.

William Warren continues: "On the morning of the day appointed the hill was covered with men, with their "graffons" [mattocks] on their shoulders. They immediately set to work and easily finished the business in the evening. The day ended with music and supper on the field, and all returned to their homes happy and much pleased with themselves for having rendered this return." This event, added William, was "well-remembered by reason of the delight it afforded me and my brothers in those days."

Robert, in not exacting his fee, was doing the poor cottiers a real service, for in a shocking sense the cottiers were a way of life in Ireland. This had not always been the case but was due in no small measure to three main causes: a frightening dependence on the potato as the only staple food of the poor; a terrible rise in the cost of living accompanied by very little increase in wages; and scandalous wholesale evictions of cottiers and tenants to provide grazing.

In regard to the first of these, in the sixteenth century the poor in Ireland had eaten not potatoes but porridge, much as the people of Scotland. But in 1585-86 Sir Walter Raleigh brought back the potato from the New World and it is claimed that it was grown for the first time in the Old World at Yougal, near Cork. Gradually the practice of eating potatoes became general among the poor all over Ireland. The Reverend J. Mockler, in his report of 1775 to the Dublin Society, estimated that one acre sown to potatoes could support a family of eight for a year, whereas it would require two acres of grain. Equally important was the fact that the potato would grow where grain would not, and that grain was subject to tithe, and the potato was not, except in Munster. Thus the results of a serious potato famine (and there were a number, varying in severity) could be catastrophic and turn what started as a blessing into a curse.

As to the cost of living, the report compares the conditions which obtained fifty to sixty years before in the Mallow area (fifteen miles north-west of Cork) with the situation then existing in 1775. In the early years of the century, food prices were low, for beef sold at five to six shillings a hundredweight, butter at nine to ten shillings a firkin (a keg containing nine gallons), and wool at four and sixpence a stone (fourteen pounds). A medium-sized farm was sufficient for a plow of six horses and employed seven or eight labourers. Land was cheap and a cottier could get a small cottage and garden for ten shillings per annum and the grass for a cow or a collop of sheep (six sheep to a collop) for a further ten shillings. Also his breakfast and dinner were provided by the farmer.

But in 1775, the report states, the rent of a cabin and small garden and the price of all the necessities of life were four or five times greater. Rents were now thirty to forty shillings per acre, while wages had risen only to five or six pennies a day. The cottiers worked in the fields for pitiful wages without any additional payment in kind, had no meals provided, and suffered the insecurity of competing annually with other cottiers for their hovels, of which there was a scarcity. They could no longer afford wool, and what is more, few of the women of that generation knew how to weave.

So we have the poor and the very poor. The first were exemplified by the tithe-ridden tenant farmers who still had something to lose, the second by the cottiers and labourers living in hovels who had nothing to lose. And as prices rose their lot became worse. About 70% of the population during the eighteenth century were in one of those two categories.

During their first ten years at Summer Hill, Robert and his family lived quietly and happily, although it was a time of growing unrest for Ireland. Between 1776 and 1780, four more children had been born to them. Besides Augustus Warren, who was born in 1776 at Russell Hill, there were Henry, born in 1777; Thomas, who was born in February 1779 and died the same year; and Thomas Warren, who arrived a year later.

Robert was a busy man at Summer Hill, in fact there is plenty of evidence to show that he worked hard and conscientiously at all the different projects which he set himself. Among other things he would supervise the feeding and grooming of the horses; there was stabling for twelve horses at Summer Hill, and most of the family rode and hunted. On many days he was about the farm overseeing the planting, or planning for the clearing and preparing of land on the summit of Knockmore. On other occasions he would ride into Cork, five miles away along the Carrigaline Road and over the hills.

These journeys into Cork could have presented a hazard, for

secret societies had sprung up among the desperately poor and abused cottiers and labourers, who, in an effort to try to stop the enclosures and evictions, to raise wages and abolish tithes, formed themselves into armed bands. They could not get amends by lawful means, so they resorted to terror, mutilation and murder. There were the Whiteboys in Leinster and Munster, the Steelboys in Antrim and the Oakboys in Ulster. Their grievances were social and economic rather than religious, for their terrorist activities were carried out in most cases against the landlords and their agents (although the Whiteboys in some places were also roused against their own clergy for demanding financial support for Catholic churches).

Robert would have been safe enough in his own area, where he was known and respected; but he would travel armed, as all gentlemen of property did in those days. For coming out of Cork in the evening there was the danger of meeting small gangs of Whiteboys or a footpad.

These armed bands of Whiteboys and others grew to such proportions that means to protect property were taken; and as early as 1773 Volunteer units were formed, one in particular by Sir Vesey Colclough at Enniscorthy. These units have sometimes been called anti-Catholic, and in the sense that by far the larger proportion of the bands they fought were recruited from among cottiers and labourers who were Catholics, this is true; but it is also true that most of the Oakboys in Ulster were Presbyterians. At one point the Whiteboy outbreaks reached such a pitch that "A desperate skirmish took place between 30 of the Volunteers and upwards of 600 Whiteboys near Inchegelagh, Co. Cork; in which three of the latter were killed, two drowned trying to escape across the river and nine taken prisoners."

Life at Summer Hill was certainly not all work and no play. Robert enjoyed parties and entertaining his friends and relations just as he had done when he was younger. His hospitality was not lavish, but open, and there was always a welcome for a friend. It was a happy time for the children too; writing many years later, in 1836, Anna Maria Spread sent this message: "I beg Mr. B. will have the goodness to give my affectionate love to my cousins . . . and assure them I do not forget the many happy days passed in their society at their Father's house at Summer Hill."

About 1780 Robert took on another duty. While continuing

to farm Knockmore, he lived for about three years at Coolmore House, a very large estate on the other side of Carrigaline on the lower reaches of the Owenboy river. "During the minority of the heir William Worth Newenham Esq. . . the Guardian of this heir wished Robert to live in the mansion [while the heir was being educated], in order to protect and maintain it. Though the writer [William Warren] was at the time a very small boy, he recollects that there was retained on the place a woodranger in charge of the Park and a gardener in care of the garden, hot-house and greenhouses [as well as other servants]." Robert had the use of the garden, the pastures, and the park – "as well for venison as for pleasure."

During the next politically turbulent years, Robert and Barbara had six more children: Elizabeth in 1782, Alice in 1784, Anna Maria in 1785 (in each generation family given names predominate), John Samuel in 1786, John Spread in 1787, and Henrietta Augusta in 1789.

Robert Baldwin, "the Emigrant,"
who came from Cork, Ireland, to York, Upper Canada, in 1799.

VOL. III.] *JOHN* AND *ROBERT BALDWIN's* [No. 59

VOLUNTEER JOURNAL; Or, INDEPENDENT GAZETTEER.

T H U R S D A Y, JULY 22, 1784.

From the DUBLIN EVENING POST.
TO THE PEOPLE.

BE patient, my virtuous countrymen, be patient, yet be firm, never was the calm of prudence more necessary to direct the spirit of fortitude. At the first view, I doubt not but it will appear to many that reiterated insult calls for the valour of Irishmen, to vindicate unequalled wrongs, to avenge unequalled insolence. But I trust, a little consideration will convince you, that the surest mode of obtaining full redress, is by persevering in moderation, and joining to the courage of the soldier, the wisdom of the philosopher.

It is some time ago since a minion of the court, even in the very Senate, dared to threaten us with the suspension of civil jurisprudence, and the introduction of martial law; and from that hour to the present every effort has been made use of to give an open for such a measure, by exciting clamour, by propagating confusion. Thank heaven your conduct has not yet defaced the glory of your ancestors, and I sincerely trust that violence and arms will be your last resource, the means exerted not to offend the state but to preserve your liberty.

I thought it necessary for me, because I consider it the duty of every Irishman, to offer to your consideration whatever appears for the advancement of the general good, and the attainment of perfect freedom; and however the mercenary tribe of ministerial hirelings may endeavour to propagate fallacious rumours of popular frenzy and rebellion in embryo, I am bold to say, that an insurrection an-

His Majesty on his passage to one of the theatres had the window of his chair broken by a stone which a woman disordered in her senses had thrown at him—this assault from the very nature of it endangered the Royal life, yet the woman was quietly arrested—delivered over not to an hireling army, but to the peace officers who attended, and upon examination her insanity appearing she was given up to her friends without further molestation. Compare the conduct of your king with that of his representative; his Majesty personally and dangerously attacked, not straining the laws of his country, not invading the constitution of his kingdom but acting consistent with the rules by which he governed his people, and behold a public tumult created by the attendant of the Viceroy, the peace broken, the police of the city insulted, and a gentleman narrowly escaping with his life, because he dared to sit after paying a crown for his admission in one of the boxes of the play house.—Well might riot be prophesied, well might disturbances be foretold when the very footlayers had riot & disturbance in their contemplation; nay, her Grace wisely kept at home—why? because her presence would ill have suited the scene that was to be performed.—Can ye my countrymen, can ye longer doubt, but every scheme is planned to urge you to forget your moderation, that by some unguarded stroke ye may lay a foundation for the evils now in store for a long injured island? fall not, all not into the snare. Let the indignant Majesty of the people behold with contempt the infamous policy of a faction, and conscious of your rectitude, persevere in virtue. Implore your Sovereign to rid you of a man who promotes disorder—who countenances rioters in his train; your King is graci-

the prices of tea so low as to take off that most powerful incentive, cheapness.

If the coalition had continued to bless the nation in office, Mr. Fordyce, heretofore so well known, was to have had a formal appointment in India.

Extract of a letter from Tiverton, Devonshire, dated July 7.

"The old game is now playing over again between the merchants and the working weavers of this place. The looms are all stopt: the merchants only pay the poor labourers 4s 6d. for making a duroy (six days hard work), for which heretofore they paid 8s. 6d. The poor starving labourers are driven to violence and outrage, and it would have ended tragically but for the arrival of a detachment of the 40th regiment of foot from Taunton. These poor creature are greatly pitied, because oppressed."

A gentleman who travelled from Southampton to London on Tuesday last, has favoured us with the following authentic account of the storm which fell on Wednesday evening. The southern limit of the tempest appears to have been about two miles on this side of Basingstoke, from hence upwards beyond Hook the rain was from nine until after ten o'clock almost a volume of water; and the thunder and lightning the most tremendous that imagination can conceive, being incessant, loud and extremely vivid. Many houses were flooded; and at Hook the lightning was so strong as to be distinctly seen playing round the candle like a moth. Great injury has deen done to the grain, and many cattle killed. The storm was also violent at Farnham. The consternation of the people round the country was very great, during this battle of the elements.

Edinburgh, July ... There are several

which was instantly in flames; fortunately, by the timely assistance of the neighbourhood, the adjoining buildings were preserved.

D U B L I N, July 17.

Yesterday, at the quarter assembly, the Sheriffs and Commons agreed to support the Lord Mayor and Board of Aldermen in the reward of two hundred pounds for prosecuting to conviction the persons who assaulted Mr. Sheriff Kirkpatrick in the execution of his office; and the citizens and common council have resolved to support the civil power, at the risque of life, to maintain the police of the metropolis.

By a gentleman just arrived from England, who had passed through Chester on his way here, we are informed, that the fair at that place, which ended on Saturday last, had been very much frequented during the week, insomuch that the place was full of company. The linen manufacturers from the North had plentifully assorted the market with fine linens; and the buyers from the different parts of England, were greater than was ever remembered at any former period at that place.

Yesterday, one of the unhappy wretches who escaped on Thursday from the new gaol, was taken out of the sewer in Pill-lane suffocated. Two others were yesterday evening in a state of the most extreme misery under King's-street, where the inhabitants handed them bread thro' the gratings; a guard soon after arrived with a number of labourers, to deliver them from their very uncomfortable situation.

Notwithstanding the pleasing LULLABY that the hacks of administration hold forth to their masters of a decrease in the Volunteers, they may now be convinced of the contrary. The reviews through-

the perpetrators of it themselves very much bewail. A Mr. Esdaille, an engraver of this city, went up to the Tenther-fields, in the Liberty, to take a sketch of that ground for an engraving of a man tarring and feathering in it, which he was employed to make for one of our Magazines.—Seeing him pencilling down something in his hand, the rumour went about that it was one of those nefarious tribe of Rutland's paragraphers, who have so frequently belied and wantonly abused the people. Upon which they laid violent hands upon him, and used him in a most severe manner, before the mistake was discovered: and nothing could equal the distress of these deluded people, when alas! they saw the effects of their precipitate rashness.—It is hoped however it will not prove fatal to that ingenious artist.

BELFAST REVIEW, 1784.
TUESDAY, 13th July.
MOCK ACTION.

The business of this day was conducted in a stile of military perfection that reflected very great honour upon the Exercising Officer who planned, and the collective body of Volunteers who executed it.—Indeed the excellence of all concerned was the more strikingly displayed, because the action was performed without the formality of a matured plan; the Commander threw out the general outline but a few hours before, the officers under his direction improved upon circumstances as they arose with an ability, which to a military eye could not fail to mark them out as finished leaders.

The object was the attack and defence of the camp.—The Belfast Battalion, Ulster Regiment, Belfast Volunteer Company Ballymena Fusiliers, Belfast troop and four pieces of artillery belonging to the

The Old Spadina House

* *

3

THE VOLUNTEER JOURNAL AND REFORM

The outbreak of the American War of Independence in 1775 made a tremendous impact on Ireland, ideologically and economically. Events in America were reported in the Irish press and followed with avid interest. Many respected politicians openly expressed sympathy for the American cause and the American colonies.

But in 1778, when England's arch-enemy France and later Spain entered the war, there was a great political and sentimental turnabout. "Irish sentiment which had strongly opposed the British Government on America somersaulted into loyalty once the French entered the arena." As Britain became increasingly involved in the war, with armies fighting in the East, in Europe and in America, the garrisons first in England and then in Ireland were drained almost to a man. Now Irish shores were left virtually unguarded, particularly since British naval resources were stretched to breaking point. Thus fears of a French landing on the coast of Ireland were very real indeed.

Irish public opinion was uniting in the belief that Ireland must and should protect herself. There was an attempt made to introduce a Militia Bill, but because of the condition of the Irish treasury this was never implemented. Also many Irish parliamentarians favoured instead the formation of independent companies on a limited scale, and recruited at the local level. What more natural than that the idea of Volunteers, which had been used before, should now be used on a much broader scale? So people all over Ireland began to associate together to form these Volunteer corps. This citizens' army was drawn from all walks of life, but mostly from the middle class. Some units were formed by country gentlemen with their tenants, some by merchants, and others by groups of the people themselves. It was in fact the first volunteer civil-defence corps to be formed on a large scale in the eighteenth century. All the Volunteers served without pay; they selected their own officers and submitted with a will to military discipline and regular drilling.

The Catholics had obtained some welcome relief in 1778 with the passing the the first Catholic Relief Act. In order to gauge the viewpoint of this middle group, here is a quotation from the letters of a Catholic member of the community, Richard Deasy, who was a contemporary of Robert's and lived in the same general area:

> It was after 1780 that the Catholics dared even to aspire to the honour of becoming volunteers, for in that year on the rumour of a French Fleet being in Bantry Bay, they offered their services to the authorities in Corke [note the old spelling]. And on the panic produced by this rumour, they were given out arms; but when it was found there was no French Fleet and no danger to be apprehended, they were ordered to return them, and so, with indignant feelings, they reluctantly complied.
>
> At that time such was the Volunteer zeal that I recollect a shopkeeper in Clonakilty, not having the slightest prospect of admission in the corps there, actually had himself enrolled in one in Mallow, which then also began to admit Catholics. He had to ride forty miles to parade and drill and so much back again and all for the pleasure of having arms and wearing military dress to the annoyance of his prejudiced protestant Townsmen.

Robert, as a genial gentleman farmer, by environment and association, but even more by his spirit of public service and his belief in the aims of the Volunteers, was drawn into this movement. In 1778 he joined the Muskerry True Blue Dragoons, a unit within the Volunteers. This Munster cavalry unit was under the command of his uncle, Sir Robert Warren, and Robert became an active member. One can picture him riding to parades in his colourful blue and silver uniform–"Blue lappelled, edged white, silver epaulets, white jackets edged blue, furniture goats skin." The Volunteers, while they were never declared illegal, were never legally recognized. In the beginning they were a convenient method of protecting the Irish shores without expense to the Government; later the Government was to realize that they had become a potent political force. Nobody in Ireland appeared to pay any heed to the question of legality. After all, the Volunteers, comprising a sizeable force which was to grow to approximately forty-thousand men, supported law and order and protected property. What more could any government ask?

The Volunteers were ready and available for defence. But Irish trade and morale had again reached a dangerously low ebb, and shocking economic conditions were a primary source of trouble. If the Irish farmer was bedevilled by rising rents and excessive tithes, then the Irish merchant and trader was bedevilled by grievous bans and restrictions on trade and export. One after another, as they became a threat to British interests, Irish manufacturers were deliberately restricted and snuffed out, until the provision trade in the south, and the manufacture of linen in the north, as well as wool, were the only ones of importance left.

First the linen trade fell victim. Because of the war, Ireland's best market, America, was cut off, throwing thousands of Irish weavers out of work. Then in January 1776 restrictions were placed on the export of certain provisions, and in 1778 a United Kingdom Order in Council was passed forbidding the export of any provisions from Ireland. As a result, beggars stalked the streets and Ireland was faced with financial ruin.

Nearly everyone in Ireland was adversely affected in some way. Parliament did not have sufficient funds even to implement the Militia Bill. Large and small landowners were very hard hit by the embargoes, many merchants were ruined and even some banks failed. Thousands were out of work and the poor now suffered even more from rising prices and extreme want. No circumstances could have united Irish opinion so solidly.

But the Irish Parliament could only initiate and pass its own laws subject to the approval of the King and his Ministers at Westminster, and the Irish House, with its three hundred members, was a mockery of representation, with 124 members nominated by fifty-three peers and about ninety more nominated by fifty-two commoners. In some boroughs there were only half a dozen voters while in others there were twice that number; four-fifths of the population, being Catholic, were excluded altogether, although the Catholics now had some rights.

Feverish efforts were made by the Lord Lieutenant and the Irish Government for trade concessions from Britain. When these began to fail, opposition to the Government was spearheaded in the Irish Legislature by a very able group of men who became known as the Patriots. Their aim was first to win equitable trade concessions and then, perhaps their main object, to make the Irish Parliament more independent of the British, and more receptive to the wishes of the Irish people. But they had no desire or intention to sever the connection or break away from Britain, and the same sentiments applied also to the Volunteers.

It would be a mistake to think of the Patriots as a compact group or as a political party. They were not. At this early period there were very few political guide-lines for them to follow, and they had no agreed political policy. They were a loosely knit group of extremely intelligent men whose ideas and sentiments were similar. Among their number were such men as Denis Daly, Hussey Burgh, Barry Yelverton and G. P. Bush, and possibly Hely Hutchinson. Without any doubt the most brilliant members of this group were Henry Flood, sometimes referred to as the most able man in Ireland, and Henry Gratton, his equally brilliant political pupil who had gained the leadership of the Patriots by 1779. Both Flood and Gratton were also colonels in the Volunteers, and most of the Patriots were members, including Lord Charlemont, their able Commander-in-Chief. It was not surprising that the Volunteers soon made their presence felt in politics.

Robert would attend parades and exercises, but he would also attend meetings where discussion developed into the framing of resolutions. These resolutions would be printed in the local press, together with a brief report of the meeting itself. At other meetings delegates were elected, and these delegates represented the unit and put forward its resolutions at the Volunteer conventions up to the national level. In this way Robert and his fellows had a direct say and a very forthright one.

The question of free trade for Ireland came to a head in 1779. Irish views had been made abundantly clear to the British Government and pressure had been put in the form of widespread boycotts of British goods. In February 1779 Edmund Burke was extremely outspoken in the British Commons. He deplored the narrow policy towards Ireland, and said it was such a policy that had lost America and would yet lose Ireland, "not by rebellion or invasion but by political and commercial death."

Now everyone waited for the British Government to act, but Lord North seemed mesmerized, incapable of action. Exasperation and tension mounted. The Patriots waited until the Irish Parliament met in October 1779. Then the storm broke; it was led by Gratton and Hussey Burgh. Grattan was brilliant and devastating. Both impaled the Government by proposing amendments to the address to the King, the final text of which read, "That it was not by temporary expedient, but by free export, that the nation was to be saved from impending ruin." But the answer came back promising nothing.

The Volunteers, by now very much a political force, entered the national scene in dramatic fashion. On November 4 a mammoth review was held in Dublin to commemorate the birthday of William III. We are told that they paraded with great precision and finesse, that they were fully armed and quietly marched through the streets and filled College Green, near the Parliament Buildings. They had notices affixed – as one account stated – to the mouths of their cannon: "Free Trade or This!" Other signs said "Short Money Bill," "Relief to Ireland," and similar slogans.

In Parliament Grattan carried a motion refusing any new taxes, and another granting only six months' supply.

At last, in December, the British Parliament gave way and in 1780 Irish exports were free; but free trade was not enough.

And 1781 was to be a year of considerable Volunteer activity. Henry Flood, who had been eclipsed by Grattan, left the government ranks and was challenging the leadership of the Patriots. Then in February 1782 there was a mass convention of the Volunteers in Ulster. Their delegates met at Dungannon in a church, and their findings became known as the Dungannon Resolutions. Two of these will suffice to show the spirit of the delegates.

(a) That the claim of any body of men, other than the King, Lords, and Commons of Ireland, to make laws to bind this kingdom, is unconstitutional, illegal, and a grievance.

(b) That the powers exercised by the Privy Councils of both Kingdoms, under, or under colour or pretense of, the law of Poynings' are unconstitutional and a grievance.

These and other Dungannon Resolutions, in which incidentally Grattan had had a hand, were enthusiastically adopted by the Volunteers all over Ireland. Thus Protestant public opinion throughout the country was heartily in favour of the emancipation of the Irish Parliament.

But in the very nature of things it was the united front of the Volunteers and the influential leadership in the persons of Lord Charlemont, Grattan and Flood, which impressed and carried the greatest weight with the Parliament at Westminster.

At this point it was again events outside Ireland which decided the issue. In March, the British Ministry of Lord North fell. Rockingham, Charles James Fox and Edmund Burke came to power, with the Duke of Portland as Irish Viceroy. In addition, the disaster at Yorktown in America made English politicians anxious to avoid trouble in Ireland.

There followed the repeal by the British Parliament of a number of acts odious to the Irish, both Catholic and Protestant, and the enactment of statutes establishing Irish Parliamentary sovereignty. For the first time in centuries, the Irish Parliament was a reality and not a shadow.

Once again the pull of events was drawing Robert out of the country and back to the city. It was his brother John who started things this time. As a result of the growing interest among the people in politics and the Volunteers, he hit on the idea of starting a semi-weekly newspaper in Cork to be called the *Volunteer Journal* (not to be confused with a radical paper of the same name, printed in Dublin, eighteen months to two years later). The eighteenth century was the great age of Irish printing, and John was fortunate in persuading Phineas Bagnell, who had edited the Cork *Evening Post* from 1757 until 1773, to join him as a partner.

The first issue of the *Volunteer Journal, or Independent Gazetteer,* Vol. I, No. 1, appeared on Thursday, November 7, 1782. It was a well-printed newspaper appearing on Mondays and Thursdays. It covered four quarto sheets of four columns each (five columns after April 1, 1784). Separating the title was a large device depicting Britannia and the Maid of Ireland clasping hands under the motto *Quis Seperabit.*

The aims of this paper were given in a brief editorial entitled "To the Public" which stated in part: "The Devise and the Title will best explain our political creed. We wish at a humble distance to keep in view the glorious conduct of the Volunteers. . . . We shall sedulously preserve our paper independent of party faction and carefully distinguish between liberty and licentiousness."

Phineas Bagnell retired from the partnership after six weeks and John purchased Bagnell's share in the *Volunteer Journal,* bringing in Robert to replace him. Thus on the day after Christmas 1782, Robert became a partner with John in this challenging new venture. They were without experience, but that did not deter them; they were without much capital, but that did not stop them – for what they lacked in these matters they made up in enthusiasm. Their printing press was situated at No. 9, the Long Quay, now Patrick Street, and the building is now occupied by the *Cork Examiner.*

Events in Ireland were being closely watched in Great Britain, and the brothers obtained good coverage of Irish, British and world news. At its peak the *Volunteer Journal* had a circulation of some eight thousand copies and sold in London, Bath, Birmingham, Edinburgh and some other cities. It was also circulated in Dublin, Limerick, Waterford, Belfast and every principal town in Ireland. Even Charles James Fox seems to have read it, for William Warren recorded in his Memorandum in 1816: "It was said to have been favourably spoken of by Mr. Fox for the spirit and talent with which it was conducted."

The coverage which the two brothers set themselves to maintain was an interesting one. As far as was possible within the limits of the four quarto sheets (printed on both sides) they followed this pattern. Each copy usually contained news of Volunteer activities on the local and national level. There were reports from Dublin on the proceedings of the Irish Parliament; and, by special service from London, on those of the British House of Commons. Nearly every copy contained American or Plantation (West Indian) news as well as other items of foreign interest. Space was given to news of interest in Cork, with some mention of social events: a fashionable marriage, the visit of Mrs. Siddons, a charity ball; and also information on the popular Irish lotteries. Side by side with news about footpads and drownings in the canals were the arrivals and departures of ships, and details of cargoes for sale. As Cork was a city of merchants, where the provision trade predominated, there was a list of food and commodity prices under the heading "The Assize of Bread." There were advertisements and at times a humorous item or two.

All the credit for the smooth running of the printing press which they had bought, the clear type and the good typesetting must go to John, who was creative, and also mechanically minded. No doubt the good advice and experience of Phineas Bagnell, while he was a partner, was also of considerable help. But on the selection of material it is possible that Robert, with his first-hand knowledge of the Volunteers, had the last say.

We have only to follow the Volunteer activity, as shown in the *Volunteer Journal* from January to September of 1783, to realize that a crisis was building up. First there was a flurry of Volunteer activity. In February, Lord Charlemont held a large provincial review of the Volunteers at Phoenix Park in Dublin. Then in the south there were the meetings of the Munster Volunteer Delegates, held in Cork. The Muskerry True Blues, Robert's unit, were no doubt represented, and the *Journal* had good coverage of the resolutions framed at this meeting. One of these was of considerable importance as it called for the reform of the indigent boroughs (rotten boroughs), thus starting the Volunteers on their demand for parliamentary reform. This resolution went forward and was taken up on the national level.

In September of 1783 the presses were humming as Volunteer activity, this time in the cause of parliamentary reform, worked up to a new pitch. The *Journal* brought out a special issue in the form of a broadsheet, distributed to all subscribers. It was entitled "The Dungannon Meeting", and it described the convention held on Monday, September 8, 1783, of more than five hundred Volunteer delegates, representing 278 corps.

Fifteen resolutions were proposed by the Ulster Association, and these were unanimously adopted by the meeting, as were the findings of the Munster, Leinster and Connaught Armies which followed. From these resolutions and findings the aims and wishes of the Volunteers all over Ireland became clearly defined. Briefly, they were: more frequent, possibly annual, elections; wider suffrage, but this was to be extended only to "those likely to excercise it for the public good"; reform within the Irish Parliament itself, as its very existence "must become precarious when it shall lose the confidence of the people to whom it originally owed its creation and from whom alone its powers were derived"; the Constitution to remain because "every approach to those fundamental principles tends to a renovation of, not an innovation in, the constitution." But the most explosive and the one most likely to be stoutly resisted by landlords and parliamentarians alike was:

> Resolved unanimously, that the Majority of the House of Commons is not chosen by the people – but returned by the MANDATE of Peers or Commons, either for indigent boroughs where scarcely any inhabitants exist, or considerable cities and towns where the elective franchise is vested in a few, who are thus suffered to place the highest trusts of society – *against the interest and the will of many,* in the hands of men, who seldom act as if they considered themselves accountable for their conduct to the people.

Two important questions still had to be resolved. Were the Irish people really going to control their own Parliament, and if so, how? And were the Irish Catholics going to have their full voice in that Parliament? The alternatives, which were not recognized, were disunity and rebellion.

* *

4

THE BREATH OF PARLIAMENT

In the Irish Parliament there had been a sour note. In the Commons, Grattan and Flood started a feud which developed into one of the greatest verbal donnybrooks in the records of parliament. Both were masterly orators and experts in debate. Each was convinced he was right. Nothing pleases an Irishman more than a good fight, so the Irish House sat back, spellbound, quite content to watch and listen.

The tragedy was that each of these honourable gentlemen had one end of the same stick. Grattan had backed the cause of the Roman Catholics, realizing full well that they must be brought into a united Parliament. On the other hand, Flood, and most of Volunteers, wanted parliamentary reform. Both of these were necessary and urgent. It was like the ageless problem of which came first, the chicken or the egg. The one would inevitably have brought about the other. Complete and full emancipation of the Catholics would have given them seats, and this would have led to parliamentary reform. And parliamentary reform, if it meant anything at all, would have recognized and provided a place for the Catholics.

So it was that Flood and Grattan belaboured, belittled and abused each other, to the confusion and division of their followers and the delight of their enemies, because the majority of the Irish Parliament were determined that they would resist and stay in office at all costs. They had, after all, everything to lose by dissolution or a change in franchise, and they were not going to vote themselves out of power.

People in Ireland were aroused by these hot political issues. They were argued in the streets, debated in the coffee houses and reported in the press. But it is the four or five articles in the *Journal,* relating to parliamentary reform but unconnected with the Volunteers, that would seem to be significant. First, because they would not have been included unless Robert or John or both had been interested in the subject; and second, because it shows that others in Ireland were also vitally interested in these ideas.

On the front page of the *Volunteer Journal* of December 8, 1783 there is an article signed "Marius" which says, in part: "The first thing to be considered is to settle the form of representation on such footing as to preclude for ever from the executive power, all probable means of procuring a corrupt majority in the House of Commons." Although Marius goes on to advocate the remedy of wider representation, the two significant phrases are "the executive" and "a majority in the House of Commons." Up to this point there appears very little, if any, thought of curbing the powers of the executive, or a link between the executive and a majority in the House.

We now come to the first clear definition of ministerial responsibility. It occurred during the debate in the British House of Commons on the question of parliamentary reform. On March 7, 1783 William Pitt was the chief speaker. For a time, discussion centred on the responsibility for the American War, the resignation of Lord North, and the fall of his Government. Then the following statement was made in the House and was fully reported in the *Volunteer Journal*:

> The House having once taken a dislike to the war, soon got rid of it, by that famous resolution which put a padlock on the Sword of Great Britain. Where was then the influence of the Crown? Why did it not avert this blow? Why did it not keep

a Minister in office, in spite of the voice of Parliament? It was impossible for such influence to interfere, for it did not exist; while he enjoyed the confidence of Parliament he continued in office; when he lost that confidence, he was obliged to cease to be a Minister; the breath of Parliament made him, the breath of Parliament unmade him – for he was at once the proof and the victim of the power of Parliament.

Here are two more extracts, the first from Monday, April 5, 1784 (Vol. III, No. 28) :

> As His Majesty had dissolved the parliament of Great Britain, merely because, the people asserted, their sentiments disagreed with the sentiments of the House of Commons, a correspondent is of opinion, that we should petition His Majesty to treat this parliament to similar discipline; as it is plain, the voice of Ireland is not spoken by our virtuous senators.

The second is an editorial "To the People" from Vol. IV, No. 65, of Monday, November 28, 1785, signed Fitzpatrick:

> I do therefore, with great freedom, admit, that the Chief Governor or other Minister of the day, is to consider the voice of Parliament as the voice of the people. But in order to render the voice of Parliament the voice of truth, it is necessary that the communication I have, should exist between representatives and the electors, otherwise the reason falls to the ground and the constitutional idea is destroyed.
>
> Can we have an higher authority that what I urge is just, than Mr. Pitt himself, the present Minister of England and the declaration of Majesty from the regal throne? By the advice of Mr. Pitt the monarch dissolved the British Parliament, and when he assigned the reason, and it is worthy of attention of every man who regards the constitution and liberty of the nation, it was because Parliament did not deliver the sentiments of the nation.

Grattan and the Patriots, in obtaining free trade and legislative freedom, operated outside the administration. It was as if the leader of the Opposition introduced amendments and legislation, and then by brilliant eloquence, burning patriotism and political logic dominated Parliament and forced through this legislation. In this we must not underestimate the active role played by the Volunteers, or the militant mood of many of the Irish constituents. The success of the Patriots was more remarkable when we remember that they were dealing with an Irish Parliament filled with placemen and nominees who normally voted with the Government and, in the case of the placemen, were dependent on the Government for their positions.

The Patriots now believed that they had won self-government for Ireland; in fact they had won only legislative freedom. At no time did they advocate the choosing of their own Chief Minister. In point of fact it was usual for one to come over from England with the Lord Lieutenant of the period. In addition the posts of Chancellor and Secretary of State were government appointments and were looked on, even by Grattan, as more or less permanent. Finally, if defeated in Parliament, the government of that day was neither forced nor expected to resign.

If the Patriots had advocated these things they might have been on the way to getting responsible government. That is why the extracts taken from the *Volunteer Journal* and quoted above are of interest and importance, for they either suggest or imply a number of these points. They were obviously of importance to Robert and John and may have been written by one of them, for all these articles were given a prominent place in the paper.

But to go back a little, in contrast to the Patriots, who were mostly M.P.'s, it was the Volunteers and their supporters who, after their successful meeting at Dungannon, were determined to go a step further and to put the question of parliamentary reform to the test. Early in November of 1783 their delegates assembled in Dublin for a national convention. They had the power, they had the public backing. But a third force now entered the political arena which could tip the scales against them. This was the British Government, which had been viewing the situation with growing alarm. Under the system of patronage they exercised some control over the Irish Commons, but what the situation would be in a reformed Parliament, none could tell. Moreover, they were not at all averse to regaining control of Irish affairs, which they would do if the influence of the Volunteers could be quietly eliminated.

In November, 1783, Charles James Fox, the British Secretary of State, wrote that if any points were conceded to the Volunteers then Ireland was lost forever. He sent certain instructions to Lord Northington, the Lord Lieutenant of Ireland.

We have a dramatic picture of the events of November 10, 1783, as the 160 delegates from the Volunteer Associations all over Ireland assembled at the Exchange in Dublin. The Earl of Bristol, Bishop of Derry, was the chief delegate, and he appeared among them with great pomp and ceremony in his coach drawn by magnificent horses and a mounted detachment of dragoons. From the Exchange the delegates proceeded to the Rotunda, through ranks of gaily uniformed Volunteers, lining the streets with arms presented and colours flying.

Lord Charlemont was elected chairman of the convention – fortunately, in the opinion of Lord Northington. Mr. Flood, although unwell, attended. The Earl-Bishop proposed that a committee of one member from each county should draw up a plan of reform, which was afterwards to be submitted to the convention. This was agreed to.

The next day when the meeting assembled, the seeds of dissension that Lord Northington had been instructed to sow with much diligence for the purpose of embarrassing the proceedings began to be apparent. The following quotation, Northington to Fox, November 17, 1783, is sinister and significant: ". . . the next step was to try by means of our friends in this assembly, to perplex its proceedings and to create confusion in their deliberations, in order to bring their meeting into contempt." For instance, George Ogle, M.P., claimed that he had a letter written by the Catholic peer, Lord Kenmare, stating that "the Catholics were not making any request for the right to exercise the franchise." This threw the meeting into confusion and not only split the vote on this resolution but split Catholic opinion. Kenmare denied having written such a letter but the harm was done. Ogle was later admitted to the Irish Privy Council. Thus Fox and his advisers deliberately planted seeds of distrust between Catholic and Protestant.

What were the Volunteers going to do under these circumstances? This was their moment in political time. The Lord Lieutenant watched. He had played his hand cunningly. The British Government watched uneasily. The Irish Parliament watched with anger and apprehension, while the Irish people watched spellbound as this drama was played out, for the stakes were high.

Either the Volunteers had to move forward and give the Irish Parliament a determined push and win their objectives, or they had to leave the matter to the Irish Parliament, which meant no settlement at all. They ought to have had a continuing program for their reformed Parliament, one which could catch the imagination of the Irish people, but they had none.

What the Volunteers desperately needed were friends in Parliament. But they had virtually no friends except Flood, who stood alone. He wanted only a Protestant, not a united, Parliament. What they needed even more was leadership, but men like Charlemont and Grattan had been alienated, Charlemont because of his fears of an open break with Britain, and Grattan through the question of Roman Catholic emancipation. In spite of his great popularity in the years 1780-82, Grattan had been expelled by the Dublin Independent Corps of Volunteers in December of 1783 because of his attitude towards reform and the fact that he had refused to attend the convention.

The Volunteers were not prepared to overthrow their Government, still less to upset the constitution or to sever links with the Crown. So at the end of November Flood introduced a Bill in the Irish Parliament to establish wider representation. It was soundly defeated.

Discouraged and divided, the Volunteer delegates decided to take Lord Charlemont's advice and submit the convention's plans for reform to their county meetings all over Ireland. What they did not realize was the fact that once they and the other Volunteers left Dublin, their political power was virtually at an end, and their days were numbered.

Naturally the Volunteers tried to make a comeback. They were strongest in Ulster, but how hard the battalions everywhere worked and how they enlisted the support of clergy, freeholders and others all over Ireland can be gauged to some extent from the *Volunteer Journal* of March 4, 1784. A full page and a half in two wide columns appeared, interspersed with banner headlines: THE BILL OF RIGHTS BATTALION (at Ballymoney), THE COUNTY OF MAYO MEETING, THE LONDONDERRY MEETING and THE COUNTY MEETING OF THE CONNAUGHT VOLUNTEERS. All four reports included the resolutions of these bodies together with their addresses to the Earl of Bristol, with his replies. The Mayo meeting expressed the feeling of the "Gentlemen, clergy and freeholders." Two resolutions will illustrate their feelings and aspirations:

> Resolved: That our loyalty to our Sovereign, and attachment to his person and family being founded upon sacred principles of the Constitution, and established in those of honour and fidelity can only terminate with our existence.
>
> Resolved: That a Parliamentary Reform in the Representation of the people is necessary.

With the results of the meetings very much the same all over Ireland, Flood once again submitted reform legislation to the Irish House; but without the physical presence of the Volunteers there was little chance of success, and the motion was rejected. Flood now left for England to seek election as an Irish member in the British House. But it was men like George Ogle and the former Patriot Barry Yelverton, once active Volunteers but now the Privy Councillor and the Attorney-General respectively, who helped to deliver the *coup de grace* in the Irish Parliament: "Let the Volunteers whom they respected return to their occupations . . . and leave the business of Legislation in those hands where the law had placed it."

Nothing could have been more frustrating to Robert and John, and nothing more financially disastrous, than the decline and fall of the Volunteers. The initial success with the *Journal* which the brothers had enjoyed, their hopes for the future and their faith in the rightness of Parliamentary reform and in the final vindication of the aims of the Volunteer movement, were all bound up in this frustration. It was a bitter pill and it took time to swallow.

As a result of the gradual disintegration of the Volunteers (the force officially came to an end and was disbanded with the passing of the Arms Bill in 1792), subscriptions to the *Journal* began to drop off alarmingly. Then in 1785 a government stamp tax was imposed on all periodicals, which cut further into the very narrow margin of profits. Bad debts also became more frequent, so Robert, the junior partner, finally left the paper in

June, 1785, to return to his first love, the country.

But during the years Robert had been with the *Journal,* the second period in his life in which he had worked with his brother, he "never intermitted his agricultural labours on Knockmore or Munroe." This meant that he had to hire extra help, and this in turn meant that he became over-extended. Living in Cork for part of the time also added to his expenses.

Barbara, on the other hand, had not been left to manage alone at Summer Hill. Henrietta Spread, an unmarried sister, lived with her and the nine surviving Baldwin children, three having died; three more children were born during the next four years.

The years following his return to the country were trying ones for Robert. Politically, the Ireland that he loved seemed to be crumbling about him. He had been proud to be a member of the Volunteers, who had seemed men of destiny. Those ideas which had seemed to hold such promise when reported in the *Journal* were being lost in the bickering and bitterness of a divided people. When his personal affairs continued to crumble, Robert's disillusionment grew. His debts and expenses were increasing, which was tragic because after the passing of Forster's Corn Law in 1784 considerable prosperity was enjoyed by numbers of farmers.

In 1786 he took out a thousand-pound mortgage on the lands of Ballea, Munroe and Knockmore, with his uncle Sir Robert Warren. But even with the help of this mortgage Robert was not able to take advantage of the general prosperity, and in 1788 he became bankrupt. Sir Robert Warren being Robert's chief creditor, his bankruptcy was not allowed to press as "heavily as such disasters generally do." The family continued to live at Summer Hill, but after this nothing seemed to go right for Robert.

* *

5

ROBERT THE EMIGRANT

The next blow the Baldwins sustained was the death in 1789, at the age of fifteen, of their eldest surviving son, Robert Nimrod, a delicate boy who had been apprenticed to Ben Lawson, a merchant of Cork. But an even greater blow fell on June 20, 1791, when Robert's wife Barbara, his boyhood sweetheart, died shortly after giving birth to Mary Warren, their sixteenth child. They had been a devoted couple. Barbara was "a most amiable and excellent woman of sound understanding," her son William wrote of her, and added, in a burst of understatement, "she fulfilled all her duties in a most exemplary manner." Robert was left desolate and a most lonely man after her death.

That same year Robert's fourth son, Augustus Warren, then fifteen, entered the merchant navy and went to serve his apprenticeship with John Rackham, Master Mariner. Robert now had ten children at home to bring up and educate and he had only his eldest daughter, Barbara, now twenty-one, to manage the household (with three children under five years), after his sister-in-law, Henrietta Spread, married John Barter of Cork in 1792. To his credit, and possibly with further help from his uncle Sir Robert Warren, he continued the education of William Warren, now his heir, in spite of so much financial and domestic trouble. Of all his many sons, William must have shown the most promise and about 1794 he entered the celebrated medical school of Edinburgh University to study for his degree.

The choice of university was a wise one. The Edinburgh Medical Faculty enjoyed a world-wide reputation, established under the first Alexander Munro, in the fields of surgery and anatomy. There were three generations of Alexander Munros at Edinburgh and William would have trained under the second, and most famous, of these. There were other men of note on the faculty, and in after years William often spoke of Dr. John Rutherford "with much regard and respect." This same John Rutherford had been a classmate of Alexander Munro at Leyden University, and on coming to Edinburgh he became professor of the practice of medicine and introduced clinical teaching. He was also the maternal grandfather of Sir Walter Scott.

Also in 1794, Augustus returned to Cork under unusual circumstances. Having received most cruel treatment as a ship's apprentice, he made his escape, but while journeying through Cork to get home he was picked up by the press gang. An entry in the *Cork Remembrancer* refers to this practice: "A hot press commenced at Cove [Cobh], and in the city of Cork and every seaman who could be met with was impressed." The family must have thought, with some justice, that this was the last straw. But fortunately events turned out well in the end, for after this rather violent introduction to a naval career Augustus Warren rose to be an admiral.

There is an account of this incident in the Murney Diary.* Augustus happened to be taken on board the flag ship and, upon declaring who he was, "the Admiral said to him, 'Well Sir, and what objection have you to serve His Majesty?' 'I have none, Sir, but my father does not wish it.' 'Your father is a fool, Sir.' So he sent him home to get permission." The Admiral, a friend of the family, made him "enter as a common sailor – gave him the bounty of £6 – and then the next day, his commission."

At Edinburgh, William did well and, in time, became friends

* The unaccountable name given to the recollections of Mary Warren (Baldwin) Breakenridge, written by her daughter in 1859 "from her Mother's own words." (See Bibliography.)

with some of the members of the Speculative Society of Edinburgh. This society was, and is, a famous and exclusive one; Sir Walter Scott was a member, and the Duke of Edinburgh is one of its present members. It was formed in 1764 and on December 6, 1796 William Warren had the honour of becoming its 302nd member. Each new member was expected to read a paper, and his was an essay on "Happiness."

To this happy period as a member of the Speculative Society he owed an increasing interest in liberal ideas and in debating. He was among men highly trained in their various professions of medicine, law and the arts, but who were also widely read and articulate on many other subjects. William at this time also developed his appreciation for fine architecture and his preference for urban rather than rural living. During his formative years at school in Ireland, and even more while he was back from Edinburgh on his university holidays, he became conscious of the political feelings of his father, and of the political developments in England, Ireland and Europe. Politics was a favourite topic for discussion both at the university and at home.

William Warren Baldwin graduated as a doctor of medicine in June 1797. No doubt he arrived home full of enthusiasm to set up in practice and contribute to the family finances, but during his absence three further blows had fallen. Thomas Warren had died at fifteen of yellow fever in Jamaica where he had probably gone as an apprentice, and at home John Samuel, aged ten, and six-year-old Henrietta Augusta had also died – and Robert Baldwin was considering emigration.

This was not altogether surprising. For one thing, his own affairs were in a shocking state and, for another, he was most unhappy about the political direction in which the country appeared to be heading. In reaction to the French Revolution, reform had become an ugly word and even George Washington felt that matters had gone far enough. In Ireland the political storm which had been gathering for a decade was accelerated by the recall of Lord Fitzwilliam in 1796 when, according to Richard Deasy, the sudden change in the disposition of the Catholics was so alarming that:

> the Government soon commenced hostilities for the purpose of forcing the arms and weapons of every kind out of the

hands of the people or driving them into premature and unaided rebellion. To attain one or both of these objects the measure of "free quarter" was adopted, and troops and yeomanry were quartered in every parish. Nothing was better adapted to produce what the Government wished.

For some time now emigration fever had been prevalent in Ireland, especially in Cork. In fact, Hugh Hovell Farmar, a neighbour and intimate acquaintance of Robert's, had been trying to interest the Honorable Peter Russell in Upper Canada in a joint land and immigration scheme, under which Farmar would enlist settlers from Ireland, while Russell would obtain grants of land in Canada. Moreover, men like William Willcocks and Richard Lovekin and their families had already emigrated to Upper Canada, or were about to do so. In fact it was this very H. H. Farmar who, when Robert was inclined to seek better things in some new country, inspired him to choose Upper Canada.

So in 1797 Robert finally resolved, contrary to the advice of his uncle and his many friends, to leave Ireland the following year. With his usual generosity Sir Robert Warren, who was his chief creditor, "wholly discharged him of his debt." This meant that Robert was able to take with him sufficient funds from the sale of his property to start again, with some degree of comfort, in the New World.

Robert's talk of emigration probably decided Barbara, his eldest, that the time had come for her own life. For six years, as her sister Alice wrote years later, she had "supplied the place of a most excellent Mother at a time of life when the occupations she had to attend to were very different from those that would have been agreeable to a young woman. When in Ireland I was too young to feel the full force of the obligations we were under to her." Now, in February 1797, she married Daniel Sullivan of Bandon; she was twenty-seven.

After Barbara's marriage Robert went on with his preparations, having made up his mind and set his face firmly to go, and young Dr. Baldwin, instead of hanging out his shingle, had, as one of his sisters recalled, "much to undertake and perform to assist my father in making ready for America – so large a family and so many put-backs was a serious thing." So, at fifty-seven years of age, Robert Baldwin set out for America with two sons and four daughters: Dr. William Warren, aged twenty-three; John Spread, eleven; Elizabeth, sixteen; Alice, fourteen; Anna Maria, thirteen; and Mary Warren, just seven. He left behind his eldest child, Barbara Sullivan, in Bandon; Augustus Warren, then twenty-two, who was serving in the Royal Navy on the high seas; and Henry, twenty-one, who had entered the British merchant service.

Robert obtained passage on the *Lavinia* sailing in convoy, probably in mid-October 1798, from the Cove of Cork for Halifax and New York. He had put his affairs in order and sold his property, but took with him many of his treasured belongings including silver, china and glass. Among these were one very large and beautiful Cork glass decanter holding approximately a gallon, his father's snuff-box with the Cork coat of arms, and a magnificent gold turnip watch with three outer cases. "The ship in which the family sailed from Cork in company with about 200 sail under convoy, proved unseaworthy. After being three weeks out, the vessel sustained very severe weather and they were driven into Passage."

Here they were back where they started, for this is the name given to the narrow channel with its shipyards which joins Cork to the Grand Harbour. Robert and his family remained during the refitting of the ship in the John Baldwins' large comfortable house in Ballintemple in the south Liberties of Cork.

After six weeks they again set sail, this time with a convoy of a hundred ships. "After some days the Captain let fall that he was a Bonaparte man, and fearful that when he landed in England the passengers would complain of him, he wished to take the ship into Lisbon. This was stoutly resisted by my father and the sailors rose *en masse* and declared if he did not carry them into Falmouth they would put him under hatches, so for Falmouth they steered." So Robert and the sailors were mutineers! Then once again they were pursued by bad weather, and the diary says, "the weather became so frightful that I and my sisters were lashed to the deck while every man on board was ordered by turn to the pumps."

After a narrow escape from the rocks off the Scilly Isles, they reached Falmouth on the coast of Cornwall, and had scarcely docked, when the ship sank. "The Customs House Officers seized everything seizable, such as wine, porter &c, which added to the losses already sustained of provisions and stores which were thrown overboard during the gale."

Nearly all families who set out to emigrate at the close of the eighteenth century encountered adventures and hardships. Each had a spice and originality all its own, and the adventures of the Baldwins were no exception. At this time, the French fleet was an almost constant threat and often broke the British blockade. Consequently British merchant ships sailed in convoy, often preferring the seasons of bad weather as being safer. And when the French fleet was not there, then the privateers took over and exacted their toll. (According to a footnote in the Murney Diary, this actually happened to Robert's friend William Willcocks, when the vessel he had chartered was seized and taken to Bordeaux as a prize.)

The family stayed in England for seven months, and although Mary Warren writes that she remembers very little of their stay (which is not surprising as she was then only seven years old), she mentions the kindness of a family she calls "Trisidor of Greatwood." Greatwood was an estate on the Carrick Roads owned, at the time Robert and his family were stranded there, by a John Tresidder. Not far from Greatwood was the village on the sea called Great Weir, about two miles by water from Falmouth; here Robert and his family stayed. At first the reason for this prolonged stay may not be apparent, but during these months Robert had to find extra money, since the passage money already paid for the voyage on the *Lavinia* was a total loss. This entailed raising additional funds from Cork, and supplies also had to be replaced. No doubt they were all determined not to embark again on the horrors of a winter crossing.

In the spring of 1799 the Baldwins were ready to set forth again. It seemed they might have a better chance of a passage by journeying to the Isle of Wight. But again misfortune overtook them. They had actually got all their baggage, a considerable amount for seven people, on a small vessel bound from Falmouth to the Isle of Wight, and some of the family had even taken tea on board, when Elizabeth was "taken ill of intermitting fever" and it was left to William Warren, as a doctor, to decide if his sister was able to travel. He decided that she was not able, and all the baggage was brought ashore. Robert must have wondered if his dream of the New World would ever come true.

Falmouth was one of the ports from which the Admiralty maintained a "Packet service." These packets were the mail and despatch carriers. They were usually fast ships, often under sealed orders, and though armed, had orders to avoid combat. They sailed at short notice. Under these circumstances it took time and adroitness to arrange to have money, stores and provisions ready, as well as the family of seven, with their baggage, at the time of sailing.

About May 1799 Robert heard of a King's Ship, the *Grantham* Packet, about to sail from Falmouth. Quoting Mary Warren, "He paid his money, fifty guineas for himself, fifty for my brother William Warren, and fifty for John Spread, and how much for my three sisters and myself I cannot say."

The *Grantham* was a twenty-gun ship and sailed with a convoy. But she sailed at such short notice that she carried off the family luggage before they could get on board, much to their consternation and to the regret of the captain, who lingered as long as he could. He actually lay to under the cliff where he was out of sight of the authorities. The passengers becoming impatient, it was determined to put it to a vote whether or not they would wait any longer. The vote was carried in Robert's favour, and soon the family came on board, probably by fishing boat and boatswain's chair, for Mary Warren recollects being seated in a chair, hoisted up to the yardarm first and then let down on deck.

One of the people who voted to wait for the family was a young American lawyer, John Jordan Morgan, from New York. Having been recently widowed,

> he had come to Falmouth from Lisbon, where he had been for the recovery of his health after yellow fever. He had waited in vain at Lisbon for a ship going to New York – and at length found it best to come to Falmouth and embark in the *Grantham*. He had been waiting like all the other passengers for the ship's orders and they came to him so suddenly at four o'clock one morning that he was perfectly unprepared – and had no money out of the Bank. He was in great distress and knew not what to do, – when the landlord

said to him "Well, here are so many guineas" – the housekeeper lent him five guineas and among the household they made up his fifty guineas in time for him to go on board and took his note, – which of course was cashed for them at ten o'clock when the Bank opened. This was an act of generosity to a perfect stranger never forgotten by him, to the honour of the English people.

There is little doubt that John Morgan was staying at the Green Bank Hotel in Falmouth, for in 1688 Falmouth was chosen as the packet station because of its location at the entrance to the English Channel, and more than thirty ships would gather there. Situated as it was on the harbour with the ships sailing from the Green Bank Quay, the hotel became the rendezvous for the captains of the packet ships; gold-braided and tricorn-hatted, they would gather in the Packets Coffee Room and over toddy and porter would discuss winds, tides and actions at sea. In contrast, Greatwood was situated more than three miles up the Carrick Roads, which accounts for many of the difficulties encountered by Robert and his family in getting aboard.

Once they were on board, Robert's bad luck seemed, for the time, to have ended. The voyage in the *Grantham* was a calm and pleasant one, until one day a cry came that a French fleet was to be seen on the horizon. Great was the consternation! Soon the deck was covered with guns, swords and ammunition. The ladies retreated below and the gentlemen brought them their watches and money for concealment in their ample clothing. But all was well. On a closer approach what had looked like sails was a large school of whales, spouting in the sun.

Later, as the ship neared Halifax, she was pursued for three days by H.M.S. *Boston,* a British frigate, who supposed her to be French. Of course, when she came near enough to see the *Grantham's* colours, the chase was ended. Later the family was to learn that Robert's son Augustus was a lieutenant on board the *Boston*.

The *Grantham* landed at Halifax and remained several days in harbour. There the family saw, for the first time, Indians and their squaws paddling about in their canoes.

Mary Warren describes an adventure which apparently made

a great impression on her, as she remembered it for nearly sixty years. It started at Halifax when the captain took on board a quantity of money, mostly in Rix* dollars. Specie of all kinds was in short supply everywhere and particularly in North America. Due to the great scarcity of coin, the Bank of England suspended cash payments in 1797, and then released Spanish dollars (pieces of eight) held by the bank, for circulation in the colonies. These were counter-marked at the mint with a small oval bust of George III, or in some cases with the initials G.R. only. These Rix dollars the Captain counted on the cabin table and put into bags, each marked with the amount it contained. The bags were then put into a locker in the inner cabin.

A young French woman also came on board at Halifax. She complained of being very delicate, and after much entreaty she was allowed to sleep in the only cabin, which was already occupied by Robert's daughters.

When the ship arrived at New York, Robert kept the family on board for a few days, while he made arrangements for transporting them to Canada. The evening after their arrival he and Mr. Morgan took Elizabeth and Anna Maria to the theatre. Alice, the invalid sister, now fifteen, stayed aboard to take care of John Spread and Mary Warren. The mate was left in charge of the ship as the captain and most of the sailors had also gone ashore.

Soon Alice observed with consternation that the Frenchwoman, who had also remained aboard, was making stealthy trips into the inner cabin where the money was kept. When the woman saw that she was observed she tried to reach the ship's side to throw something overboard, but Alice bravely contrived to prevent her and to call the mate. He and the watch seized the woman, who stoutly resisted, and the captain and the gentlemen were sent for.

The woman kept declaring her innocence, but she was searched and a $1,000 bag with a large amount still in it, was almost immediately found. Robert, furious with the woman for placing his daughter in this unpleasant position, took her by the shoulders and shook her, whereupon dollars fell from her in a shower. She still continued to argue, when William leaned

* Specifically Rix dollars were Dutch rijksdaalder, but the term was widely used for all silver dollars.

over and took off her cap, and down fell the remaining money. The thousand dollars was all complete.

She was sent ashore and the captain vowed he would have her hanged if he set eyes on her again. Alice was the heroine of this little drama and her courage and determination were often to be demonstrated during the pioneer period of their life in Upper Canada.

Robert and his family reached New York in early June 1799 and stayed there while he made financial and other arrangements for their journey to Upper Canada.

In this connection it should be remembered that in those early days much the best and safest route to Upper Canada was by the Hudson and Mohawk rivers to Lake Ontario, and not by the longer and more hazardous route up the St. Lawrence to Montreal and on to York (Toronto) via the rapids and Kingston.

In his memorandum William Warren says, "From New York, shifting into schooners, sloops and bateau, with some labour, great fatigue and exposure to the heat of the sun and to the stings of flies [we proceeded] up the Mohawk River and through the then unsettled Genessee country to Oswego."

Robert himself has told about the cost of this journey and other interesting details, in a letter written a few years later to an Irish friend and prospective emigrant. He tells him that the journey from New York to York cost him $139, and he breaks the figures down in this manner: New York to Oswego, $83; Oswego to York by schooner, $26: heavy luggage sent by bateau, probably around Lake Ontario, $30. He goes on to say that the bateau, properly packed with the heavy luggage at the bottom and the feather beds on top, will provide, with an awning, a pleasant mode of travel. He adds that two families or a group could travel for the same, thus cutting the cost. He even suggests they might wish to buy their own bateau and retain it.

The diary gives us a few more details of their trip: "From Oswego they crossed Lake Ontario to the (Island) then the Peninsula, opposite Toronto, which was a 'Carrying place of the Indians,' and at night they crossed the Bay of (Toronto) then York arriving at that celebrated town," on July 13, 1799.

* *

6

ROBERT, FARMER AND MAGISTRATE

In 1799 York consisted of less than seventy houses. For the most part these formed a horseshoe along the curved shore of the bay, from the Don Valley on the east to York and Peter Streets on the west. The diary says, "There was no church, – school house, . . . there was not even a Methodist Chapel." The northern boundary was Queen, then called Lot Street. The trail leading north to Lake Simcoe was a narrow corduroy road hacked like a sword thrust through thick woods as it left York – this was Yonge Street. The garrison lay about a mile west of the town with thick woods between.

This little town may have seemed wild in those days, with wolves paying an occasional visit and carrying off a lamb or two, and the roads in the spring being almost impassable. It may have seemed "little more than a village" to girls just arrived from the hustle and bustle of Cork and New York.

But life in this little town had its compensations and its charms, while its natural resources lay at its very doorstep. There were fine stands of white pine, already reserved for the Royal Navy; there were great oaks on the hilly slopes back of the town site, splendid catches of salmon were to be had from the Don River, and good farm land and town lots were sound, marketable real estate. In 1799 there were two potasheries in York, for potash, made by burning trees felled in clearing the land, was exported; indeed much of Irish glass then depended on it.

Robert and his family received a welcome from the Russells, who were expecting them, as letters had been passing concerning Robert between Hugh Hovell Farmar in Ireland and the Honourable Peter Russell in York. William Willcocks and his family welcomed the immigrants by inviting them to stay, which they did while they were in York. This was the Mr. Willcocks whose chartered vessel from Cork had been "diverted" to Bordeaux, but he was now established as a merchant. He became a magistrate, and later a judge, in York.

The Honourable Peter Russell was the son of Captain Richard Russell and Elizabeth Warner of Skibereen, County Cork. He was educated at Cambridge and served in the British Army during the American Revolution as secretary to Sir Henry Clinton. Later he was posted to General Simcoe's staff, coming to Upper Canada in 1792 when the capital was Niagara-on-the-Lake, and was Receiver General under Simcoe. At the time the Baldwins arrived in York he had been President of the Council and chief administrator for three years. He lived with his half-sister, Elizabeth Russell, in an attractive one-storey house with two wings facing the bay.

The house was comfortable, well furnished and, for that period, luxurious with its shining engraved silverware and polished mahogany. Little did these weary travellers dream that some twenty-two years later this very silverware, the house, and much of its contents would belong to William. All he wanted at this time was to set up his medical practice as soon as possible, while his sisters longed for a home and the fun of furnishing it.

Without doubt their stay would have included a visit to Peter Russell's farm, Petersfield, on the outskirts of the town. This was being run by that admirable couple John and Sophia Denison; there would have been Pompadour, that fascinating old rogue who worked, when he did work, for Peter Russell and John Denison. He was a free Negro, but his wife Peggy was still a slave and belonged to Russell.

Peter Russell had very kindly procured 1,200 acres each for Robert and his son William Warren. He had enough influence with the Surveyor General to get them "a most eligible location." But after remaining a few days Robert took one of those impulsive steps that were characteristic of him. He had come to a new land and was determined, and apparently impatient, to get his family and himself settled as soon as possible.

Among his former acquaintances from Cork, now in Upper Canada, was Richard Lovekin. He had taken up lands in the Township of Clarke, about fifty miles east of York, in the county of Durham near the village of Newcastle. When Robert arrived, Mr. Lovekin invited him to go there and see that part of the country. As a result Robert bought a thousand acres at a dollar an acre, "broken front Lots 29-30 and 31 in the said Township," on Lake Ontario adjoining the Lovekin property. By this impatience and eagerness to get settled he risked offending Peter Russell.

The financial mix-up which followed was typical of Robert. Peter Russell writes:

> And without consulting either Mr. Willcocks or me he gave Bills on New York, where he had left all the money he brought to this country, to two Brothers in Trade in this Town, tho' strangers to him even by character, to be paid in cash when his Bills were honoured. The consequence was what might be expected. One of the Brothers received and went off with the money, and he has been at law ever since with the other for its recovery. In the meantime he has been deprived of the means of putting a comfortable House over his Head or even of taking up the land I got him an order for.

As soon as possible the Baldwins moved down to Clarke. They travelled in open bateau, and at night pitched their tent on the shore of Lake Ontario. The journey generally occupied two days, but sometimes longer. When they arrived Robert named the river mouth Port Patrick, but the neighbouring people later called it Baldwin's Creek. On the land was a small log hut, with a bark roof and a chimney made of stock (framework) and clay; the chinks between the logs were stuffed with moss, and there was only a ladder up to the loft above. Only ten acres of the land were cleared. To this rough cabin Robert brought his two sons and four daughters. Consequently, winter found them very miserable with an unfinished log hut, no stove, and only a great open fireplace for both heating and cooking. One corner of the room was boarded off for the four daughters, where they slept on beds laid on the floor. Robert had brought his family into the bush without sufficient money to improve the cabin, very little furniture, and no proper stove. But in fairness to him it should be pointed out that he had arrived in Upper Canada during the summer when the climate was at its best, and could not be expected to know the severity of the winters.

The men of those days were utterly unconcerned with the vital problems of housekeeping, and Robert was no exception. These problems were multiplied tenfold when applied to pioneer life in the bush, particularly with a father getting on in years and set in his ways. The brunt of the house and farm work fell on the shoulders of three young and inexperienced girls who were the real heroines of these early days in Upper Canada.

The first years at Clarke must have been grim ones for this family fresh from Ireland and unaccustomed to the ways of the bush. Winter came earlier than in Cork and it caught them unprepared, but they made the best of it. In their draughty little cabin the men, who slept in the loft, had to go down on cold nights every few hours to replenish with great logs that one and only fire.

William was ready to practise his profession as a doctor; but his father was now fifty-eight, labour was scarce, and his brother John was only twelve years old. William, who had a tender conscience, soon realized that here he must stay, at least for a time. But he was frustrated by not being able to live in town and make his way in his chosen profession. As his sister wrote of him, "The poor Doctor with more genius to be a painter or poet gave himself up to assist his father on the farm."

But during this time an added bond of affection grew up between William and his younger sisters; and some of the frustrations and hardships would have been forgotten during the long winter evenings when he read aloud to them or played the flute. "The younger ones of the family have reason to remember him [William] with the affection and gratitude of a father rather than a brother."

As the family became known, the Baldwins were drawn into taking part in the affairs of the district. On August 27, 1800 Robert received from General Hunter, the new Governor of Upper Canada, the commission of Lieutenant of the County of Durham and was also appointed a magistrate. As Lieutenant of the County and with it Colonel of the Militia he had the nomination of all the militia officers to be appointed from time to time as the county became populous. As second in command, William received his commission as Lieutenant-Colonel.

As magistrate Robert presided at the Court of Quarter Sessions, or magistrate's court, and as well dealt with many administrative duties outside the courts, from roads to acting as registrar, for couples would come to him to be married.

But the Colonial Secretary in England had frowned on General Simcoe's project of county lieutenants, stating that it was not to be encouraged by a parent state and that the Governor must keep all power consistent with the constitution in his own hands. So the office of Lieutenant of the County was later abolished.

The importance of the local justice of the peace in the early administration and development of Upper Canada was very great and one leading authority describes their role as "all pervasive." This was entirely owing to the fact that magistrates had been given the direction of most of the local affairs in rural areas in Upper Canada. It was no accident, for the controls and direction set up by John Graves Simcoe, the first Governor of the province, stemmed from his distrust of local assemblies, and even more from his distrust of the large numbers of American settlers. Many of these men and their families were now flocking into the province in search of grants of good land. (They should not be confused with the United Empire Loyalists, who had come earlier and were loyal to the British Crown.)

Now these American-born settlers were airing their republican sentiments and clearly had no attachment to Britain or British institutions. Some of them who lived in the Newcastle area were described in a letter written in 1800 by William Warren to a relative in Ireland:

> The greatest discontent reigns among the people, who came to this Province almost naked and hungry but now [are]

Dr. William Warren Baldwin,
whose career included the practice of medicine, law, architecture, and politics.

The first house designed by Dr. Baldwin and built for his friend, Laurent Quetton St. George.

> comfortable and independent . . . . these people, the immigrants from the United States would, had they the least prospect of success, to-morrow attempt to overthrow the order of things in this country.

So, in accordance with the laws introduced under Simcoe, rural districts, as they became settled, were brought into the official scheme of things. In the District of Newcastle a statute (42 Geo. III C2) dated July 7, 1802 established a Court of General Quarter Sessions to provide for the administration of justice and placed the management of all local affairs in the hands of the district magistrates. This last provision meant that even the local members of the Assembly (Parliament) were paid by the magistrates from taxes which they raised locally and gives some idea of the control of local affairs exercised by the Governor in Council. The powers of the Governor were in turn reinforced by the Alien Act, which gave him power to deport any undesirable persons.

Even in 1802, when they were set up, the Courts of Quarter Sessions (they met four times a year, as the name implies) gathered with all the pomp and majesty that could be mustered in those country areas. Thus not only was justice done to the best ability of the court, but quite as important, justice was *seen* to be done.

The original minutes book of the Court of Quarter Sessions for Newcastle District survives. It was faithfully kept from its inception, and clearly shows the many administrative as well as judicial duties which fell to the lot of the local magistrates. It also provides a splendid cross section of the rural life of the time. Robert and his fellow magistrates were kept busy indeed.

Here are some items taken from this early minute book of 1802-1810.

> "April 10, 1804 to the Sheriff: To cash paid John Ogden Sr. for making Constables staves three shillings and ninepence." But Mr. Ogden Sr. perhaps kept one of the staves, for at the next quarter sessions we find him up for assault, in this example of how a court session was conducted.

The King vs John Ogden Sr.

Upper Canada District of Newcastle

The General Quarter Sessions on the peace, holden at Hope in and for the said District. On the tenth day of July in the Forty fourth year of the reign of our Sovereign Lord, George the Third by the grace of God of the United Kingdom of Great Britain and Ireland King defender of the Faith. Before Timothy Thompson, Alex Chisholm, Robert Baldwin, Leonard Soaper, Richard Lovekin, Elias Smith Sr., Joseph Keelor, Benjamin Marsh, Elias Jones and Asa Burnham Esquires, Justices of our said Lord the King, assigned to keep the peace in the said District, and also to hear and determine divers felonies, trespasses and other misdemeanors in the said District committed.

A jury of twelve is chosen and sworn in to try an

Indictment for assault and challenging to fight.

The Prisoner on his arraignment pleads guilty. The Court set a fine upon the Prisoner of twenty shillings and the costs of the prosecution and that he find security for his good behaviour for twelve months, himself in fifty pounds and two sureties in twenty-five pounds each:

John Ogden in £50

David Turney (the older) £25

John Nanatts £25

Conditioned that the said John Ogden shall keep the peace and be of good behaviour for twelve months.

Regarding the rates and taxes in the year 1804 it was ordered "That one penny in the pound be collected the ensuing year."

Then the payment of the local member of the Assembly: "The Magistrates in Quarter Session Assembled in the District of Newcastle 10th April 1804, Order that the sum of Forty-five pounds, ten shillings be collected in the County of Northumberland to compensate David McRogers for services as member of the House of Assembly for the years 1801, 1802, 1803 and 1804. [Signed] Tim Thompson, Chairman"

This was done to catch up on the back payments to Mr. McRogers. New procedures were used later, and these provided that a member was eligible for ten shillings for every day he had attended the House and also for travelling time. This was to be paid to the member out of a special levy, to be made by the magistrates after receiving the necessary warrant, and the warrant was in the form of a letter from the Speaker of the House to the local magistrates, stating the number of days their member had attended.

There was a Deputy Collector of the Port of Newcastle, and he "Did seize a four-handed [oared] batteau and six barrels of salt, said to be the property of Bass Chard, on suspicion that it came from the United States of America and had not been entered at either of His Majesty's Custom Houses in the Province." The seizure was made August 12, 1804 at the River Trent. On October 11, Bass Chard was duly summoned before the court and as "he hath nothing to say nor can say anything in his own defence," he was found guilty. The goods were forfeited to be sold at public auction and the money (not in excess of twenty pounds) to be distributed according to law. Salt was an important commodity in those days, particularly in the preserving of food, and had to be imported.

In 1804 wolves were a menace. "Ordered: That the Treasurer of the District of Newcastle that the sum of One Pound be paid to George Davis of the Township of Hope for a Wolf Certificate formerly granted to him by W. Baldwin Esq. which certificate appears to the Court to be lost by fire. April Sessions 9th April, 1804. Alex Chisholm, Chairman."

And in the matter of welfare: "Ordered: That the Treasurer do pay the sum of fifteen shillings to Thomas West to purchase some wine, he being deprived of the use of his limbs and not having the means of obtaining it."

As William said of his father at this time: "His appointments are all honour, but no profit." Indeed these activities of Robert's entailed considerable expense for they left him less time to devote to his farm, and all the chores now devolved on other members of his family, especially William, who stayed at Clarke until after the harvest and until such time as he had to fetch supplies for the winter from York. He was in York staying at the Russells' in September 1800, and on one occasion went with his host and Joseph Willcocks (a relation of William Willcocks who had arrived from Dublin that March) for a walk "to Sugar Loaf

Hill it is a Beautiful place." This would be Russell Hill, for writing some years later about his brother Augustus Warren, William says, "he has bought Miss Russell's 200 acres the old sugar loaf lot." The other "sugar loaf" was, according to Dr. Scadding in *Toronto of Old,* "a most singular conical hill, like an immense Indian tumulus for the dead." It was across the Don River from Drumsnab, now 5 Castle Frank Drive, and could not be called beautiful.

At the end of September, when his supplies were ready, William returned to Clarke, going by "canoo" from the island very early one morning. He must have had quite an adventurous trip, for Joseph Willcocks wrote to him on October 9:

> I congratulate you on the many hair breath scapes you have had during your Late daring and adventurous voyage along the rugged coast of Ontario – daring indeed it was, for no man in his senses besides yourself would undertake such a voyage in such a vessel and with such rigging for if your vessel continued to leak during the remainder of your Journey as she did at the inception of it I am sure she would have kept a good pump in play . . . and as for your rigging except my silken ropes, a good Irish spider would have made as strong, but my fears for you soon subsided when reverting to the old addage, that a man who is born to be hanged will never drown.

It was during the summer of 1800 that John Morgan wrote to Robert and to William, asking Robert for the hand of his daughter Elizabeth, and begging William to escort her to New York as Morgan's doctor would not permit him to take the long journey to Upper Canada. He also suggested that Mary Warren should accompany them to be a companion for Elizabeth and to continue her own education.

So two weeks after his return to Clarke from York, William with eighteen-year-old Elizabeth and nine-year-old Mary was back in York on the first leg of their trip to New York. Here they stayed with the Russells until November 4. During this time they managed a visit to the Russells' farm accompanied by their host and hostess, Peter and Miss Elizabeth Russell. On another occasion William and Elizabeth went to the garrison with Mrs. D. W. Smith, wife of the Surveyor General, and the same evening they and Miss Russell had tea with Mrs. Smith and her husband. Later William attended and sat with Joseph Willcocks, who had contracted a fever; and evidently the doctor sat up with him the following couple of nights.

Then on Monday the weather turned mild with the coming of Indian summer, and on Wednesday November 4, "Dr. and the Miss Baldwins left Mr. Russ to go to Niagara [by schooner] and thence to Whitestown." This time they did not follow the summer route as they had done on the journey to Upper Canada, but took the winter route via Niagara, the Finger Lakes and on to Albany. On arriving at Niagara they were delayed until they found a party going through the forest trails for travel was so hazardous and uncertain at this time that travellers waited and went through in parties, "much as a caravan does over the desert." While they waited at Niagara they visited the Falls, which they came upon through the dense forest, "And which was infinitely grander then in its primeval state."

While in York William had been able to raise only a hundred dollars, "that sum being barely adequate to the unavoidable expenses of your Daughter's Journey," and according to Mary Warren the delay of three weeks at Niagara had gone far to exhaust this amount.

After a few weeks they finally started and proceeded as far as Canadaigua, where William discovered to his consternation that their funds were insufficient to complete the journey to New York. It took a whole month, during which time William and the two girls waited in great distress and want, until further funds reached them. Then when another party was formed, they set out once again, this time by sleigh as winter had set in. They crossed Lake Cayuga over a bridge two miles long, and after that somehow lost their way. This could easily happen in the dusk, particularly if snow was falling to obliterate earlier tracks.

Then to add further to their misfortunes the sleigh overturned and their money, being in silver and gold coins carried in small bags, was lost for a time in the snow. After a feverish search in the semi-darkness they recovered the money, but by now they were quite lost and wandered about trying to find their path, until at length by the moonlight they observed smoke, and hurried towards it. As they neared an encampment, dogs began to bark and an Indian approached them to whom they explained their plight. "He proved to be the chief and very politely invited us into his wigwam." This invitation they gladly accepted. Afterwards Mary Warren often spoke of that, to her, delightful night in the bark wigwam, "with the blazing logs on one side and the hole at the top." As she lay on her bed of hemlock boughs and bearskins, she saw the stars twinkling down on her.

The Indians were very hospitable, giving them shelter and food and seeing them on their way. The rest of the journey was through more populated areas and seems to have passed without incident. No further mention is made until their arrival at Albany, where it appears the weary travellers were met by John Morgan. Here Elizabeth was trotted off to a dressmaker, and was amazed to learn how the fashions had changed. For "the open gown with the long train," all the rage when the family left Ireland, had now been replaced by the round gown!

William and his sisters, with John Morgan, finally arrived in New York about the first of February. The girls stayed with Mr. and Mrs. Delancy (John Morgan's mother and step-father) in Cherry Street; and on February 12, 1801 Elizabeth and John Morgan were married by the Reverend Mr. Pilmore (Philmore?). And after a brief rest William returned home to Upper Canada, having acquired a brother-in-law and lifelong friend who was a fine American in every sense of the word. The friendship which grew up between them and between all the members of the two families was of the greatest value to the Baldwins through the years, culturally, socially, and politically.

* *

7

DR. BALDWIN, THE LAWYER

William Warren arrived back in York March 11, 1801 and again stayed with the Russells before returning to Clarke on March 16. During this time he visited friends and the William Willcocks family more than once. He was determined, as on his return home from Edinburgh, to practise as a doctor, but "finding the settlement at Clarke not likely to call for the practice of his profession – he removed to York."

Joseph Willcocks from Dublin, a cousin of the Willcockses from Cork, became one of William's friends. He was a man of some education, and Peter Russell, in his capacity as Receiver General, had appointed him his private secretary.

Joseph kept a diary during the period 1800 to the end of 1802. It is racy and revealing and gives us a fine picture of York, the activities social and otherwise which occured during this time, and the families concerned. Among these are many interesting facts and annecdotes about William, as he and Joseph were part of the same circle of friends and relations. William was perhaps a too serious young doctor; Joseph a rather likeable, odd, wild Irish bachelor, hard-eating, hard-drinking, party-loving, a man of moods and violent temper. William kept an eye on Joseph at parties and treated him when he was sick, which was often.

An entry in Joseph's diary for September 1800 (before William Warren went to New York with his sisters) describes a picnic on which Joseph went "with Mr. & Mrs. Russell, Mr. & the Miss Willcocks Mr. Weeks and Dr. Baldwin. We left York at 10 oClock reached the Humber in Mr. Jarvis's boat at half past 12. Walked about for an hour dined at half past 1. We had for Dinner a piece of Cold roast Beef. Cold Ham cold chickens and Hot stewed Wild Ducks. We all arrived safe home at 5 oClock in the evening. The Humber is a Beautiful River navigable nearly 2 miles for Large ships & at the Upper end is a Government Saw Mill." But work was not forgotten for one evening "Dr. Baldwin was sent for to the Gaol to see Mrs. Cameron" (the wife of the jailer). Then on another occasion William spent the night at Mr. Russell's farm where he and Joseph Willcocks, with Franklin, Mr. Russell's man, sat up all night watching for a wolf which had the previous night killed two sheep. They did not see the wolf.

On the fifth of October, 1801, Joseph Willcocks and William Warren, whom Joseph refers to as "the Doctor", with two other passengers, set out in Joseph's boat. After a pleasant voyage they reached Baldwin's Creek that evening, but, being no sailors, they left the boat at anchor outside the small harbour with all their luggage on board except for their cloaks and the extra food they had brought. In the morning a very heavy storm blew up and swamped the boat, but in the end, fortunately, all their things floated ashore. They were soaked to the skin recovering them. Lake Ontario is cold at the best of times and must have become extremely chilly by October. After this, they had for dinner boiled fowl, cold beef and potatoes. In the evening, as the waves still ran very high, they drank tea and husked some Indian corn.

The next day they threshed in the barn, and later a man came over to assist them in the slaughter of one of the cattle, presumably for beef. After dinner the Doctor, Joseph, and young John Baldwin went in a "canoo" to bring Joseph's boat into the creek. But as they were attempting to weigh anchor, the Doctor fell overboard, and Joseph fell into the bottom of the boat. But soon after they had the craft safe in the little harbour within the creek. Later, Mr. J. Lovekin, a firm friend and neighbour, called in, and after tea they celebrated their many wettings, and as Joseph puts it: "Mr. B. and I got drunk."

On the morning of the eighth, Joseph saw and killed a deer in the lake, near the house. They threshed in the barn before breakfast, and again before breakfast on the ninth, as well as in the forenoon. For dinner they had cowshead, soup and beefsteaks; then they threshed in the afternoon. When they returned to the house they drank some "whisket" punch, and Joseph retired to bed after tea. On other evenings they often had pancakes for supper.

The business of carrying the wheat to the mill was an arduous one. So on Monday, October 12, after emptying Robert's boat, they went to the home of Mr. Beate, another neighbour, who gave Joseph a quarter of dried (smoked) venison. Finally they set out by boat for the mill early in the evening, and reached Captain Bates's where they lay over that night, being completely soaked by the waves.

The next day the party continued to the mill, killing a deer on the way. They carried it with them and dressed a quarter for their dinner. Then they got the corn (wheat) ground, and left at nine o'clock that night. This time they lay over at Captain Sloaper's, finally reaching Robert's house, with the grain, about twelve noon the next day. For their dinner they had roast venison and snipes and after tea the Doctor played the flute.

Another day Joseph walked over the land and saw Mr. J. Lovekin. Later he and the Doctor read aloud to the Misses Baldwin Addison's play *Cato,* which was admired for its advocacy of constitutional reform. Meanwhile Robert inspected a cow, which had been sent over from Burks, but did not buy the animal. Supper that evening was venison and tripes, while the Doctor again read aloud after tea.

In November 1801 there is mention of a dinner at Captain McGill's at which the Surveyor General, Mr. Smith, was present, and from there at eleven o'clock William went with Joseph Willcocks to see Mr. Deaves on board the *Kendrick.* Mr. Deaves was on his way to Niagara, and from there back to Ireland, and William took the opportunity of asking him to take letters back to his cousin John in Cork, and to others of his Irish friends.

Later in November William joined the celebration at the

garrison, "to see the Union flag hoisted and the Guns firing. Col. Shaw afterwards took us to the Mess where we got wine and cakes." This would have been the first time that the new Union Jack, celebrating the parliamentary union between Ireland and Great Britain, had been flown in York.

In June 1802 we find the Doctor was living with the Willcockses on Duke Street. William Willcocks, now sixty-six, was a first cousin of Peter Russell. He was a colourful, flamboyant opportunist with a highly developed flair for speculation and for acquiring land.

Not only had he passed through a spectacular bankruptcy in Ireland before he first came to Upper Canada in 1792, but having been promised a township near Whitby, he returned to Cork for settlers. Back in Ireland in 1793 to 1794, he could not resist running for Mayor of Cork. He was elected, but in consequence of this delay he lost his township.

In Upper Canada he had settled with his family in York, where he acquired considerable property, much of which passed to the Baldwin family through his daughter, notably the Spadina and Millbrook properties. The household on Duke Street comprised William Willcocks, his wife, a son Charles, and three daughters; it was the ladies of the family who supplied its character and ballast. The daughters were Maria, Phoebe and Eugenia. Maria, the eldest, remained unmarried but she capably and efficiently carried out the duties of housekeeper for the Executive Council (possibly the nearest thing to a career woman in those days) and was universally liked; Phoebe was to become the able and intelligent wife of William Warren; but poor Eugenia died shortly after marriage in 1802 to Augustin Boiton de Fougères, a French royalist in Upper Canada.

It was one of William Warren's sisters, who was certainly in a position to know and yet under no obligation to say, who paid these ladies their highest compliment.* Writing some years later of her brother William Warren, she said, "He made a most happy choice in a wife. She was a blessing to him and to many. Her excellent understanding and mental attainments were of the greatest consequence and assistance to him. And I really think her [Phoebe's] Mother and Sisters were the best women I ever knew. They were Equally prudent and benevolent."

* In an unsigned letter believed to have been written by Anna Maria.

From entries in the diary of Joseph Willcocks it seems that the Misses Willcocks used their accomplishments to advantage, "Bought worsted at Allan's for Stockings. Sent it to the Willcocks's to be [k]nit." And again, "Maria & Eugenia Willcocks came to the Office to see me about altering my Cloaths." They may even have kept a small shop, for on one occasion Joseph "Called at Mr. Willcocks bought two pairs of black silk stocking for 2 lbs 2s, N.Y.C."

Joseph, in his capacity as private secretary to Peter Russell, had been given rooms at Russell Abbey as his house was called. He had on occasion taken Miss Russell sleighing on the ice on the bay and had driven her over to visit friends. In the evenings Joseph sometimes joined the family at cards or would go with them visiting. With the Doctor and his father, Robert, coming up from Clarke during those first few years to stay at the Russells' or the Willcocks's, it was a happy group. Certainly in July 1802 it seemed tranquil enough.

Joseph wrote: "Was so extremely Ill untill this day that I was unable to write . . . . Took Bark yesterday & find myself much better today. The Governor left us to go to Quebec . . . . Mr. & Miss Russell the Dr. & myself spent the Evening at Mr. Smith's [the Surveyor General]. Mr. [Justice] Allcock proposed my going to Quebec to the Highlands with him for a few days."

Then on Friday, July 25, "Went with Mr. Russell & the Dr. to the Farm to Weigh Hay. Had about 17 Ton. Returned to Dinner & had Roast Beef, hash, and pancakes. We walked a little after Dinner." Then the following Tuesday Joseph "Left York for Niagara for the recovery of my health. I did not return untill the 15th of August. One of the sailors fell over board and was drowned on our return to York." August 15 was a Sunday and everything was much as usual. "Arrived at York [presumably after a night crossing] called at Capt. McGill's and Mr. Jarvis's. Had for dinner roast beef, bacon and cabbage. Went in the Evening to the Chief Justice's with a package from Mr. Russell. The W's [Willcocks] spent the Evening with us."

But sooner or later Joseph with his temperament was bound to get into trouble. On Thursday, August 19 Joseph wrote: "Miss Russell and I differed." On the Saturday William was drawn in, for "Doctor Baldwin told me in the evening that Mr. Russell insisted on Miss Russell's informing him what letter she received, meaning a letter I wrote her, and that she told him. Mr. Russell did not speak to me that Night." Breakfast the following day does not appear to have been very cheerful, for again Mr. Russell was not speaking and Miss Russell did not appear; and William was charged with the unpleasant duty of telling Joseph that Mr. Russell was dismissing him. Joseph consulted the Doctor and asked him to tell Mr. Russell that he would not dine there, "Lest it should be the means of keeping Miss R. from quitting her Room." Joseph, having walked to the farm, found on his return that William had brought him some "victuals from Eugenia Willcocks," and also his account with Mr. Russell to the thirtieth of September. On the Monday, with William again used as the go-between, Joseph was called to Mr. Russell's office, "and Mr. Russell gave me a great deal of severe language and pd. and dismissed me." After his dismissal Joseph hoped to stay with his relative William Willcocks and did so for a night or two. But old Mr. Willcocks had no wish to offend the Honourable Peter Russell and sent him on his way.

By this time Joseph had taken his story to Chief Justice Allcock and William Allan and had much sympathy from them. After a time he went to live with the Chief Justice, who obtained for him the post of sheriff of the Home District in York. So Joseph landed on his feet and during the period 1803 to 1805 was under the patronage and steadying influence of Mr. Justice Allcock.

Among the Baldwin Papers in the Metropolitan Toronto Central Library is a letter dated June 17, 1797, at the time of William's graduation from medical school at Edinburgh. This brief note shows an interest from outside the university in William's medical work:

> Dr. Duncan presents best compliments to Mr. Baldwin and will be obliged to him if he can favour him with coppies of his Inaugural Dissertation for –
>
> Dr. Gahn of Stockholm.
> Dr. Sandefort of Leyden and
> Dr. Wisberg of Gottinger [Gottenburg]

No wonder he had come away from the university with high hopes! Now in Muddy York with its seventy-five houses and 375 altogether too healthy inhabitants, with its two doctors – one the garrison doctor, already established – William was to find it most difficult to scratch a living.

One of his first patients in Upper Canada was Peter Russell. One reason for this was the fact that the two men got on very well together, in spite of the discrepancy in age of some forty years. Peter Russell was a man of letters as well as an able administrator, and both men enjoyed discussions on the topics of the day and other subjects. Good books were scarce and both were fond of reading aloud, sometimes a book, sometimes a play. Russell also had a keen interest in scientific matters which endeared him to William. Joseph's diary shows this:

> Sept. 28, 1800 Returned home [to Russell Abbey] to tea, Dennison and his son George spent the evening with us. Mr. Russell and Dr. Baldwin were striving to fix a microscope but could not do it complete. Mr. Russell read part of Gulliver's Travels. The whole day was very fine weather, bought six salmon for Mr. Russell for a dollar.

But William's only patients, apart from the Russells and the Willcockses, were the more serious fever cases and the result was that he himself contracted a bad attack. His father, writing to Dr. Richard Hill, a family friend in Ireland, on December 2, 1802, says of William:

> I thank God not one individual of my family, from the day I came here to this time, experienced a day's sickness – the doctor [William] excepted. He has returned about three weeks where he has recovered his health and become quite a new man in everything but his liking for the country. Indeed he has some reason, his early and long study has subjected him to violent pain in the chest upon every violent exertion of his arms.

During his recovery at Clarke, William did some soul-searching. He became convinced that he could not live in the country, for having lived in Edinburgh and recently in New York, he felt intolerance and impatience for a community concerned only with farming, for which he had no aptitude or interest. He therefore realized that he had to live in an urban community where he could practise his profession. Robert put no obstacle in his son's way as during his, Robert's, fairly frequent visits to York both the Honourable Peter Russell and Chief Justice Allcock had advised him not to keep William on the farm.

Before returning to York William had made two major decisions. First he determined to marry Irish-born Phoebe, the second daughter of William Willcocks; second to train for another profession, for he realized it would be impossible to support a wife as a struggling young doctor in York.

William appears to have been one of those persons who could assess a need in the community and act on it. Living with Mr. Willcocks, one of the first magistrates of York, and being received with friendship by Peter Russell, he was in a position to realize that in the new colony there was a great need for members of the legal profession. Also his family background provided him with a preference in this direction since an uncle was an attorney in Ireland, and his first cousin, John, with whom he continued to correspond, was also a lawyer. The two cousins, on the friendliest terms, would have compared notes during the time they trained for their two professions of medicine and the law.

The ingenious twist to all this was William's method of calling temporarily on a third profession to finance him during the period in which he was reading law. He put his education to good purpose and opened a small classical school, inserting the following notice in the *Upper Canada Gazette* on December 18, 1802:

> Dr. Baldwin – Understanding that some of the Gentlemen of this Town have expressed much anxiety for the establishment of a Classical School, begs leave to inform them and the Public, that he intends on Monday the third of January next [1803] to open a school, in which he will instruct twelve Boys in Writing, Reading, the Classics and Arithmetic. – The terms are, for each Boy eight Guineas per annum, to be paid quarterly; one Guinea entrance, and one cord of Wood to be supplied by each Boy on opening the School.

In spite of William's busy life in York, the strong family ties continued, and his sister writes of him while studying for the law as "assisting his father and sisters in a most kind and generous manner," and goes on to say, "Well do I remember when I was attacked [with] nervous fever he walked that 40 miles in the heat of summer to Clarke."

William Warren Baldwin was to become an honoured member of the Law Society of Upper Canada. This society was founded at a meeting held at Wilson's Hotel, Newark (Niagara) at 11:00 A.M. July 17, 1797. At first it consisted of only two Crown officials, the Attorney-General and the Solicitor-General, and eight senior barristers all nominated as Benchers. The society grew and by the end of 1800 there were approximately twenty-two members.

We know that, probably in 1802, four new members were admitted by the society and the third on this list was William Warren, making him twenty-sixth on the roll. However, a licence to practise law had to be obtained from the Crown and this after an examination. We are told that the first to be so licensed under this Act, as recorded in the minutes of the Law Society, was William Warren Baldwin on April 6, 1803.

This certificate was obtained from the Chief Justice, Henry Allcock, who examined him on his knowledge of the law; and the certificate stated that "The Court of King's Bench was satisfied as to the ability and fitness of the said W. W. Baldwin to be admitted to practise as a Barrister and Attorney in this Province," and that Lieutenant-General Hunter granted the licence, which bore the official seal.

So as soon as the Doctor had launched into his second profession and felt that he had meagre but sufficient funds to afford this step, he "ventured to marry. I say ventured because he was a man of such strict integrity he feared and abhorred getting into debt."

William Warren and Margaret Phoebe Willcocks were married on May 31, 1803. William was a shy man, particularly in regard to the opposite sex. In a letter to his friend St. George he explains this: "For my own part I have so little skill in the diplomacy of Maître Cupid . . . . it was this ignorance that made me conclude my own matrimonial bargain in such haste, a bargain of which I am so satisfied and so proud that I cannot but think all other men fools or cheats who act otherwise."

After living for a short time with the Willcockses on Duke Street, William and Phoebe moved early in 1804 into a small house on the north-west corner of Palace (Front) and Frederick Streets, where on May 12, 1804 their first child Robert (later to become the Honourable Robert) was born. The little house was to become famous, too; after the Baldwins it was occupied by Joseph Cawthra, who laid the basis of the family fortunes there. Later it was occupied by William Lyon MacKenzie; and it was here that a "Genteel Mob" wrecked his printing office, whence issued the *Colonial Advocate,* and threw the type in the bay. Later the house was destroyed by fire.

We know that William continued teaching, certainly until after young Robert's birth, because it is recorded that on that day all the pupils were given a holiday. Thus for a short period William practised the three professions of medicine, the law and teaching.

* *

8

CLARKE, YORK, AND WAR

Robert Baldwin the emigrant, with his over-developed sense of civic responsibility, never became a successful Canadian farmer but he had a passionate love of the land and of wildlife, and a great enthusiasm for his new country. In a letter to a friend in Ireland he writes:

> To describe the beautiful situation for building on Lake Ontario I am inadequate, suffice it to say that if wood, water and agreeable and rich ground can make it pleasant they are to be found in abundance. Our woods abound with beautiful birds . . . . there are a great variety of delightful flowers . . . In short, my good friend, a man that is not an Epicure may live here as happy as his heart can wish provided he can be satisfied with Beef, Mutton, Pork, Fowls of all kinds, wild and tame, as good as any in the world, fish of different kinds but not as good as Cork Market affords. Vegetables of every sort or kind . . . . as to Venison, this is in abundance. I last week killed three Buck. Two of which weighed two hundredweight each, the horns are nailed up, one eight, the other nine branches

. . . . A four year old doe here is so large as the oldest fallow hind I ever saw in England or Ireland.

Robert had apparently been able to get a certain amount of hired help during the early pioneer period, but now in 1807 it was getting next to impossible to do so. The cabin or house had been enlarged and improved, and more than sixty acres had been cleared. Cattle and other farm animals such as sheep had been purchased, as well as fowls, and a barn had been erected. Possibly this had been done by that picturesque and highly practical pioneer method, a barn-raising bee.

In 1807 Elizabeth and John Morgan brought Mary Warren back to Canada. The country had of course improved during the seven years since William had taken Elizabeth and Mary down to New York in the winter of 1800. But even on their return, where cities now stand, there were vast stretches of forest, with only a few scattered houses; at Buffalo, where they passed a night, there was a solitary inn with its swinging sign, and no other houses to mar the beautiful view of Lake Erie. But one thing was certain – the roads were improving, for we are told that John Morgan drove his own carriage all the way from Albany, although at one time he and Mary Warren had to walk through the woods for ten miles, leading the horses.

Having reached York, Elizabeth and John Morgan with Mary Warren journeyed down as soon as possible to see Robert, going in open bateau. They stayed a month at Clarke, and it was a very happy family reunion. Robert had not laid eyes on Elizabeth since she had set out for New York with William Warren, and he had not seen his son-in-law since 1799 in New York.

There was much to talk over and many plans to discuss. All too soon the Morgans set out to return to New York, but this time, with their usual kind thoughtfulness, they took Anna Maria with them. John Spread also had to leave Clarke; he had been going about on crutches for some time. It seems he rushed into the icy water, when overheated, to get the mail from a passing boat, and had been laid up with rheumatism ever since. Now a place was found for him at York in a store run by one of William's friends, whose name was originally Laurent de Quetton. He was a French royalist who served with distinction in the Catholic and Royal Army of Brittany, but in 1798 emigrated to

North America with the Comte de Puisaye and, coming to Upper Canada, took up lands in the Oak Ridges area north of Markham Township. Scadding tells us that he took the surname St. George to commemorate the fact that he first set foot on English soil on St. George's Day. He possessed a great flair for business and very soon was trading with the Indians and setting up trading posts on Lakes Simcoe and Couchiching. By 1802 he had established a store at York, followed by others at Niagara, Fort Erie, Amherstburg and Kingston.

By 1807 Mr. Russell's health had deteriorated and his half-sister Elizabeth describes in her diary what was apparently a slight stroke.

> Friday 3rd April [1807]
>
> Heward [a member of Peter Russell's office staff] . . . said that my brother had been taken with an oddness in his speech as if he could not well articulate his words, as if his tongue was swelled. He was not so when he was over since breakfast to take his medicine. . . . I sent Mary [the servant] . . . to see how he was. . . . He came over soon after. Found his speech very much altered, but did not seem ill otherwise. Sent for Baldwin but he was in court, but they said that they would send him as soon as he returned. . . . [Having seen Peter, William consulted with Dr. Davidson, surgeon of the 2nd Battalion, Royal Canadian engineers. He returned with William, examined the patient, and:] Told him that his pulse was good and chatted cheerfully to him. Prescribed instead of the blister [that William had prescribed] only hartshorn on a flannel to the back of his neck, white wine whey, and to have his feet well rubbed with flannel when going to bed and wash and gargle with hartshorn and water which he did. The Doctor chatted him into tolerable spirits and [he] seemed pretty well all but his speech. . . . between 11 & 12 . . . Dr. Baldwin returned to tell me that it was right he should be watched tonight & desired to be sent for if he was worse. I told him I would and he went away. He is a poor dear-hearted creature and always fears the worst. Davidson on the contrary is all cheerfulness and good humour.

On January 7, 1808 Elizabeth's diary records: "In the forenoon

Baldwin came and gave Peter the injection." So it is clear that by the end of 1807 Peter was receiving regular injections, and that the giving of injections was by then in general medical use in Canada; but in spite of them the Honourable Peter Russell, who was approaching eighty, died that year.

The final months of 1808 were to be significant ones for Robert. After the departure of the Morgans and Anna Maria, life became quieter, and a good deal lonelier. Robert now decided on a bold throw. During his periodic visits to York he had stayed at the Russells' and had been much impressed by the charm and culture of Miss Elizabeth Russell, Peter's half-sister. In fact he appears to have harboured a secret passion for her. No one could have been kinder to his motherless children. A warm bond of friendship had grown up between the families, and his daughters often stayed with Miss Russell when in York.

Certain considerations prevented Robert from declaring himself to Elizabeth. From 1802 until his death in 1808, Peter Russell was in increasingly poor health. It was obviously her first duty to look after and care for him. The second obstacle was that of age, although fourteen years was not considered such a gap in those days. With the death of her brother, Robert decided to propose; but in the meantime Elizabeth Russell became an heiress. This complicated matters for him, for he did not wish to appear as a fortune-hunter. But being Robert, he tackled the matter head-on, as we see in these extracts from his proposal:

> Permit me to now declare these sentiments which have long lain dormant in my bosom and unknown to mortal but the Bearer who can vouch that it is no sudden thought but was kept secret . . . The moment that announced your being your own mistress also announced your being left sole executrix. This, which to most others would have been a source of exaltation and joy, produced in me a contrary effect. Fearing that the acquisition of fortune may place you beyond my Hope, . . .
>
> Let what ever lawyer you please put your entire fortune beyond my reach by keeping it both now and the disposal hereafter totally in your OWNE power. . . .
>
> Grant me this request, that you will seriously consider this letter before you refuse me and also be convinced that no man on the whole continent of America as disinterestedly and sin-

cerely loves you as the one who ardently wishes to have it in his power to subscribe himself by a still dearer name than that of

Your friend,
R.B. York 3 Nov. 1808

No reply to this proposal appears to exist, but from Robert's tone it can be inferred that he was not too hopeful of success. But if he did not meet with success, he did not seem to incur any great displeasure as had William Willcocks earlier that year. The firm friendship between the families continued, also between Robert and Elizabeth. Later, Robert was the only member of the whole family who knew of the impending marriage of a Miss Thomson, "Miss Russell having confided this mighty secret to him."

Just after Christmas the same year, 1808, Robert, who had been giving a great deal of thought to the possible development at Clarke, wrote a full three-page letter to Quetton St. George. This letter put forward his suggestions, and is interesting because it shows quite plainly that Robert at sixty-seven was not content just to farm, but had progressive ideas for the betterment of himself and the area. Briefly, he proposed "to carry on a pot ash boiling" to pay for clearing his remaining wooded acres, to open a store for farmers only, to erect a mill on his creek in partnership with a neighbour – "you stand well with the Government and can readily obtain a set of mill irons and stones" – and to build a harbour at the mouth of Baldwin's Creek. He goes on gaily: "Romulus laid the foundation of Rome and Baldwin will, please God, lay the foundation of CORKE" (in Upper Canada). But he goes on to excuse himself for his "digression" – "notwithstanding the *very serious* subject of this letter, Small Beer when Bottled in a state of fermentation must Burst or the CORK will fly." St. George, with wide experience, does not appear to have shown any wild enthusiasm – in fact, none at all. But by taking John Spread into his business, training him, and finally taking him into partnership, he did a far greater service to the family.

Mary Warren, who in 1807 had returned to Clarke to live with her father and Ally, was to get her first real taste of roughing it in the bush and describes a number of incidents involving them all.

At the end of that summer the field mice became a plague. They were found in myriads and destroyed everything. Every tree stump that was turned up was infested with them. And "the cat loathed mice as the Isrealites did Quails." The winter killed the mice, which lay dead in hundreds of thousands on the ground, but then a new trouble arose, and one very trying to the women and to those unable to do heavy farm work. White oak staves for casks were found to be marketable and to bring a good price. In consequence every man in the country set to work at this new employment, leaving the women and the old people to get on as well as they could on their bush farms. The man whom Robert had finally been able to hire now followed the general example, and he could get no one else although he offered the highest wages he could afford.

To Alice and Mary Warren, the mice were bad enough; but with the loss of their hired help, worse was to follow. For now Mary Warren, although she was terrified of the animals, was obliged to drag hay up the hill to feed all the cattle and sheep since Robert was now too infirm to do this himself. There was also a pack of nineteen hounds to feed, water to draw, and logs to drag into the outhouse. The three of them worked at that, Robert, Alice and Mary Warren. Robert chopped logs in the outhouse, and the girls dragged them in to supply the great fireplace, which held what we would call a load of wood.

For nearly half this winter Mary Warren was alone with Robert and a little French-Canadian servant girl, as Ally was on a visit to York, staying with Miss Russell. It was during this time that a frightening incident occured. One day just as Robert was leaving to attend the quarter session a rather odd traveller arrived. Mary Warren, who at that time was suffering from whooping cough, was left with her. At night-time she became very alarmed at hearing the woman talking about the "Prince of Darkness" in her prayers. So she and the French girl decided to run to Ebenezer Hartwell's, about three-quarters of a mile across the frozen creek, and beg someone to come and stay with them. Old Mrs. Lovekin and Mr. Hartwell went back with the girls, and on their return they saw the woman hastening to the barn with a lighted candle in her hand, searching for Mary Warren. She was in a great fury, but by degrees calmed down. Mr. Hartwell was obliged to return to his family, but his mother-in-law, Mrs. Lovekin, stayed until Robert returned.

Robert was terribly shocked to find that the person he had left at home with his daughter was a madwoman; he had thought her only an oddity in the few minutes he had seen her before leaving. It was a whole week before they could find anyone going down in a sleigh who would take the poor woman on and rid the family of this frightening visitor.

At the end of this terrible winter, one of the worst on record, Robert lost six fine cows, nearly all the pigs and sheep, and all the geese, which were smothered in the snow or ice-hills on the lake. In the early spring Alice returned to Clarke by sleigh, being driven home by a Colonel Breakenridge of Leeds. Both Robert and Mary Warren were overjoyed to welcome her back.

That summer, 1809, the stave mania was still in full swing and in consequence Robert was unable to get his crops planted. When William Warren with his wife and two sons took a month's holiday at Clarke, journeying there by boat, they were shocked to see how matters had deteriorated. William Warren had been trying for some time to persuade his father to leave the farm, and this time he was able, with the assistance of his wife and sisters, to obtain Robert's promise to move to York the coming winter. He was obviously now too old and infirm to work the farm, and the hardships were certainly too great for Alice and Mary Warren. During this visit to Clarke, Robert's two grandsons were amazed and delighted to see the passenger-pigeons – "the flights of pigeons were remarkable . . . they used actually to darken the air."

In prospect of leaving the farm Robert wished to buy a quantity of furs. There was an Indian encampment on the far side of the creek, and from these Indians he had previously bought some fine skins. One Sunday, soon after he had gone to see his neighbour Mr. Cozens, several Indians arrived at the farm bringing furs and asking for whiskey.

Then occurred one of the most alarming experiences in the lives of Mary Warren and Alice. In Mary Warren's words:

> My sister Alice and I refused, then they became so urgent and insolent and so constantly increasing in number, that we became terrified and sent the French girl to beg my Father to return. She came back in a few minutes more frightened

> than ever, saying that as she passed the camp she saw the squaws hiding away all the knives as they always do when the Indians are drunk. And that they had chased her back. Some of the Indians were intoxicated before they came to the house and their threats were awful.

Although the Indians now numbered about forty, the three intrepid girls continued to refuse to give them any whiskey, and sat firmly on the trap door leading to the little cellar where it was kept.

Then Alice thought of the large family Bible, the two volumes of which they had been reading; she opened these, pointing out the pictures and trying to attract the Indians' attention, while Mary Warren knelt at the other end of the table and prayed to God, loudly and earnestly.

It was a great shock to Robert when he returned and found them in this position. He had brought Mr. Cozens with him, and no sooner did the Indians see him, than one man drew his knife, saying, "Cozens kill my brother, I kill Cozens." At this Robert, to divert them from that idea, was forced to get them the whiskey. Probably nothing else would have saved their lives.

Mr. Cozens then slipped away and called the Lovekins and some other neighbours, and Alice and Mary Warren went into the little inner room while Robert and his friends kept watch. No doubt they were prepared to shoot as a last resort. Meanwhile the unwelcome visitors prepared for a regular orgy. There was a great kettle of food for the hounds on the fire made of bran and potato peelings and all sorts of refuse. This they gobbled up "clean and clever." They drank, danced and sang all night long. Then suddenly in the morning off they went, to the immense relief and joy of the family.

An incident which was typical of Robert occured in June. He felt it his duty, as colonel of the militia, to give a mess dinner for all his militiamen; and this he intended to do to the best of his ability. It was one thing to hold such a dinner in Ireland for a Volunteer unit, and quite another to stage one under pioneer conditions; most likely it never occured to him that his daughters were being taxed to the limit.

This dinner was, for them, "a monstrous chore", two or three hundred men to be fed, "all to be done by three young girls."

They had great sugar kettles full of venison soup, roast meat and pies, and all sorts of good things. "These boors drank terribly and stayed all night." But that was not the end of the party, "About twenty of them stayed to breakfast."

Another factor which added to the labours and discomfort of the young girls was the mode of travel between York and the settlements along the lake shore, which was then the highway. Of necessity, there being no inns, those living on the lake were expected to, and did, extend hospitality to every passer-by who wished to stay, and doors were never locked. A party of fifteen or twenty boatmen might come and take possession of the kitchen and perhaps be stormbound and have to remain several days; all of which added greatly to the labours of Robert's daughters. Of course, it worked both ways; once when William, his wife and children, and his sisters were crossing the bay on their way to Clarke, they arrived at "a house called Aspinwalls" and had to wait there for three days because of a storm.

So again for Robert came the old tug-of-war between town and country, with his daughters on one side (one of them wrote, "The hardships were bearable until the winter came"), and on the other side Robert with his intense love of the country and his philosophy of life: "Something I must do, not to lessen the little I have, and ever to hold fast that blessed satisfaction of Self-Independence while I remain this side the Stigeon Lakes."

At last it was settled that Robert and his family would move up in sleighs to York in December 1809. But to quote William Warren, "Our Christmas circle was not as large as we expected or wished – The want of snow deprived us of the happiness of my father's and sisters' company."

This delay may have been a blessing in disguise, as William Warren's wife Phoebe became very ill and was only beginning to recover by January 23. "She is now recovering daily [having come down to the parlour for the first time the evening before] and is now at a game of whist with her father and mine and Ally. We are now all together."

In January Robert and his family had journeyed up in sleighs, bundled in the furs they had bought from the Indians. By now a military road had been built between York and Kingston, and though this was very rough in places, with a good layer of snow travel by sleigh was often very pleasant.

In York they all lived together, including old Mr. Willcocks, at the house on Front and Frederick Streets where, infirm as he was, Robert took pride in looking after the garden. Old Mr. Willcocks amused William Warren by his attentions to Ally, "Willcocks being quite serious and she rebuking him with much good humour and sharpness." Russell Abbey, where Elizabeth Russell still lived, was nearby and the whole family were continually in and out of her house.

Three years after the birth of young Robert the family went to live in a small house on the corner of Bay and Front Streets. Of Robert as a child we have various glimpses, particularly through Elizabeth Russell's diary. Her judgments are forthright and unbiased, and we get a picture of affectionate and rather indulgent parents, and as a result a somewhat spoiled child. Not only his parents but his grandfather Willcocks and his Aunt Maria indulged Robert. "Willcocks, Maria and little Robert dined with us. He is very noisy and unruly. His grandfather and Maria spoil him by humouring him."

Robert's father William, with fifteen brothers and sisters, had been in no danger of being spoiled; but young Robert for some years held the spotlight, at least with his fond parents, for little Billy died when only five months old and the next child was not born until 1807. Thus for a time Robert was an only child. There is an illustration in Miss Russell's diary of the concern of William and Phoebe for him:

> As we were going [to see the Willcockses] their little maid Jenny came to meet us. I feared something was the matter. She went up to the Doctor and told him that Robert had hurt himself. He ran on . . . What it was he had fallen down and cut his face. Only Willcocks was in the parlor when we went in. . . . Maria then came in with Robert who has a cut just under his eye.

But in fairness to Robert Elizabeth Russell also reports: "I stayed to keep house with little Robert while the Doctor drove his wife to Mr. McGill's and some other places. Robert was very good and played with a little boy, Mackintosh's son, who is about nine years old and lives as a servant with them."

Then in 1808 Robert had his first "picture" taken. A Mr.

Bouker advertised in the *York Gazette* in April and May of that year his "profile likenesses," and according to Miss Russell, "Miss Mary Baldwin and little Robert was taken all at my request."

With the birth of a brother, Henry, and then William Augustus and Quetton St. George, the household settled down to a normal, boisterous and happy family life.

By 1812 the threat of war was so great that "the ladies all met to make a flag* for the 3rd Regiment of York Militia. My mother [Mary Warren] drew the design a wreath of laurel – with the royal colours in the corner and a motto given by Mr. Strachan (now Bishop) "Deeds Speak." My mother showed the ladies how to do the flag and worked a good deal herself. Mr. Robinson (now Chief Justice) used to read the "Battle of Talavera" and other poems to the ladies while they worked. Judge McLean, S. Jarvis, the Boultons and others used to come and inspect the work and General Brock himself came once or twice and approved of the work."

The War of 1812 broke out in June. From Mary Warren we learn: "The reluctance was so great among the people to go to war that the Americans were obliged to withdraw the troops who had been a good while at Fort Niagara because they were so friendly with our people." But with fresh American troops matters took another turn. John Spread, William's youngest brother, was now managing St. George's store at Niagara. In her diary Mary Warren says: "He was taken prisoner and taken down to New York. Here his sister Elizabeth and Mr. Morgan were very kind, got leave for him to visit them – until his liberty caused people to say he was a spy and the government sent him back to Greenbush."

York, with its exposed position on Lake Ontario, became vulnerable to attack, and on April 27, 1813, the American fleet came sailing into the harbour. As Mary Warren remembered it, "nothing could equal the beauty of the fleet coming in – it preserved the form of a crescent while the sails were as white as snow."

With the arrival of the fleet the Baldwin family and Miss Russell, Mr. St. George, Mr. Large (from Cork) and a number

* This flag may be seen today in a case on the wall of the narthex of St. James Cathedral in Toronto; the account of its making is in the Murney Diary.

of friends assembled "to take measures for the flight of the ladies, while the gentlemen went off to fight." It was a bitter pill for Robert when, after hard persuasion, he at last consented to give up the idea of fighting and agreed to accompany the ladies. It was decided to go out to Baron de Hoen's farm about four miles up Yonge Street at what is now Eglinton. Yonge Street was then a corduroy road after leaving King Street, and it passed through thick woods. Miss Russell loaded her phaeton with all sorts of necessities, so that the whole party had to walk: Robert, Miss Russell, and Miss Willcocks; Phoebe and her four small sons; Major Fuller, who was an invalid under Dr. Baldwin's care; and Mary Warren, carrying the youngest boy, St. George, a mere baby, on her back nearly all the way.

When they had proceeded about half-way they heard "a frightful concussion – and all sat down on logs and stumps, frightened out of their wits. They learned afterwards this was the blowing up of the Magazine when five hundred Americans were killed," and that William "was dressing a wounded soldier. He was conscious of a sensation – it was too great to be called a *sound* – and found a shower of stones falling all round him – but he was quite unhurt."

The party at length reached Baron de Hoen's log house; this consisted of two rooms, one above and one below. The gentlemen lodged above, and the ladies below. After three days Miss Russell, with Mary Warren, walked into York, where they were just in time to save her house from being ransacked by the soldiers.

St. George was also in York in 1813, for he was mentioned by Mary Warren as being among the gentlemen who went off to fight at the time of the American capture of York. But by 1814 he was in Montreal and William was writing to him again. Everyone was sick of the war, and many were highly critical of its conduct and fearful of the exposed position of York. Extracts from William's letters reflect this mood, and he must have been unaware of the fine service being performed by Admiral Yeo in blockading the American base of Oswego, which had a vital influence on the outcome of the war. In June William writes, "I wish the War was over – am quite sick of it." And then, what was to him the greatest hardship, "It is very uncomfortable to be divided from my family."

William Willcocks, who had died in 1813, had owned land in the third concession of Markham, situated at the north-west corner of the village of Millbrook, now called Buttonville. It was to this attractive spot that the Doctor, who was concerned for the care and safety of his family, particularly after the sack of York, brought Phoebe and the children, Maria Willcocks, and his father Robert. Millbrook was an ideal place for them, consisting as it did of a farm with a stream, and a pond with a sawmill. Being eighteen miles from York it was far enough away to be safe, and at the same time not too far for William to visit them. Here Miss Russell was prevailed on to join them in July; she had been in a highly nervous state as a result of the war. This rest in the country restored her to health, but when they returned to York they all, including Robert, lived with her, "she not likeing to be left alone."

William's letter to St. George continues: "Was it not for your hospitable invitation I should be at a loss what to do – and still I am dissatisfied and I feel it unreasonable to live on you." This refers to the fact that while the family was at Millbrook, William was living in St. George's house; "William rented his house for a hundred a year." During this year there had been a small rising of American settlers in the London area, and William, who had been on circuit, wrote on June 18, 1814, to St. George in Montreal: "8 or 9 of the traitors have been convicted at Ancaster – I was not applied to in behalf of any of them – so that I staid only a day or two on my way to Niagara, and again on my return – I stayed at Mr. McKays – . . . dont forget a Navy List and if you please the two school books for Robert." Thus, as we shall see, Robert's schooling was not neglected despite the war and the move to Millbrook. The navy list shows William Warren's interest in his brother Augustus and his career; he had distinguished himself in the Napoleonic Wars in the Royal Navy. "Mrs. B– and all my establishment at Millbrook are very well thank God. Maria W– has about her 6 cows, I believe a Dozen Hogs and numerous of the feathered race . . . they are all contented but myself, who live in exile." And in a postscript, "If you could bring me up a pair of Galloshoes I would thank you – I have a long foot."

All the citizens of York became apprehensive when there was an east wind, for this favoured the enemy fleet; and a month later, July 20, 1814, William writes: "I write a few lines by the express to say we are all thank God well and as yet unmolested by the Yankees – but I only say as yet, for at this moment there is nothing to prevent their destroying this place – one would suppose Sir G. Provost still thinks this place unworthy of protection as we have now but about 200 regulars here and the mob of the country Militia – The east wind now blowing puts us in great fear – I put up all my papers last night and kept my horse in to send them off." Then he adds, "Poor Miss Russell is so dejected that it appears like mental derangement." Later, with Miss Russell also now gone to be with his family in the country, William writes, July 31, "If you knew how I feel you would scarcely thank me for this letter; I am so lonely, what to do with myself I know not – all fled to the country not even Cat or dog with me in this house."

It was probably just after the war, while the family were still at Millbrook and Mary was in York with Miss Russell, that a little incident linked up with the past in Ireland occurred, for it was while prices were high and provisions scarce. There was a knock at the door and on the doorstep was Edward Warren, son of Sir Robert of Warren Court, County Cork. Of course he was invited to dine. "There was literally 'nothing' for dinner – poor Miss Russell began to cry. I tried to cheer her saying 'Providence will provide.' Presently a knock came at the door and a boy brought a string of small fish to sell – which dinner was called Mary's Providence!"

Robert continued to live with his son, William Warren, and his daughter-in-law, to whom he became more and more attached. "Indeed her kind attentions to him could not fail to have this effect." And in her household he now enjoyed again many of the creature comforts he had not had since leaving Ireland. So Robert had reached this restful haven among his family, surrounded by love and affection and the merry sound of children which he loved so well. Thus he passed his last years in quiet and content. He died on Sunday, November 24, 1816.

Robert handed on a family tradition both in Ireland and in Upper Canada of fair dealing and of responsible service in municipal affairs. In Ireland he had set an example of loyal and firm support for the Volunteers and for the constitutional reforms which they advocated. In this way he handed on to his son and grandson a lively interest in political reform. Being older and set in his habits when he came to Canada, he did not adjust to pioneer life but tried to live as he had been accustomed to do in Ireland, and in that he was not alone. But he had a splendid appreciation of the countryside, its beauty and its resources; to him Upper Canada was a great land. Some of his descendants were to play a political part in their new country, so perhaps he "builded better than he knew."

Part II

"THE GREAT AND ALL ABSORBING GRIEVANCE"

Robert Baldwin

1810 - 1837

THE BALDWINS OF UPPER CANADA

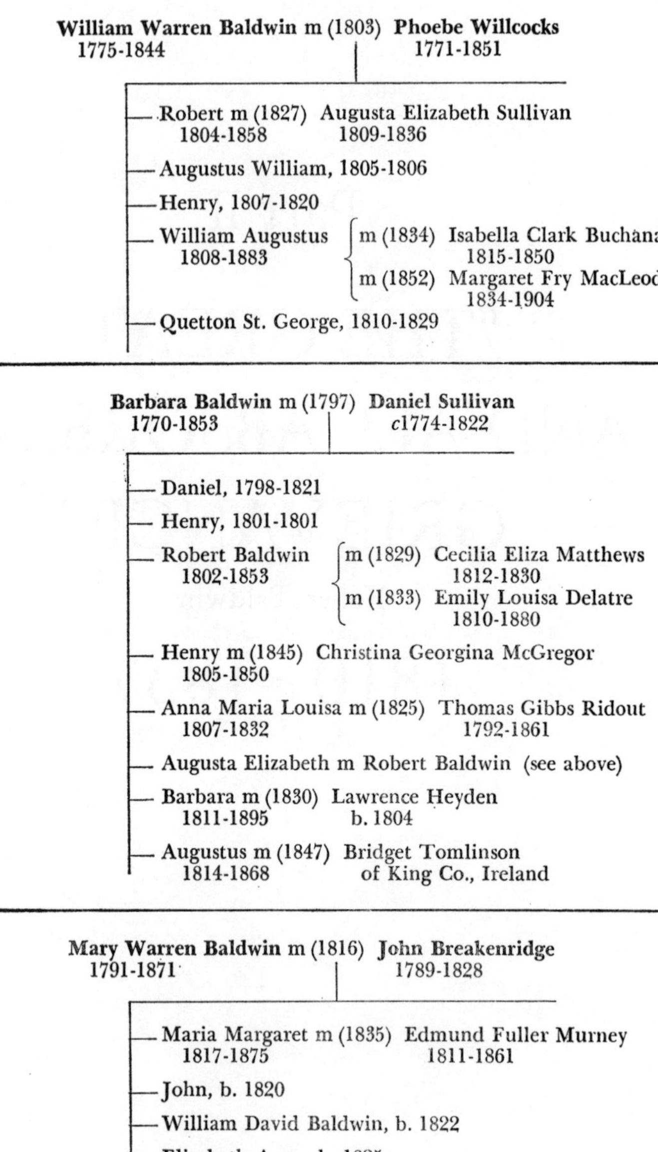

William Warren Baldwin m (1803) Phoebe Willcocks
1775-1844
1771-1851
Robert m (1827) Augusta Elizabeth Sullivan
1804-1858
1809-1836
Augustus William, 1805-1806
Henry, 1807-1820
William Augustus
1808-1883
m (1834) Isabella Clark Buchanan
1815-1850
m (1852) Margaret Fry MacLeod
1834-1904
Quetton St. George, 1810-1829
Barbara Baldwin m (1797) Daniel Sullivan
1770-1853
c1774-1822
Daniel, 1798-1821
Henry, 1801-1801
Robert Baldwin
1802-1853
m (1829) Cecilia Eliza Matthews
1812-1830
m (1833) Emily Louisa Delatre
1810-1880
Henry m (1845) Christina Georgina McGregor
1805-1850
Anna Maria Louisa m (1825) Thomas Gibbs Ridout
1807-1832
1792-1861
Augusta Elizabeth m Robert Baldwin (see above)
Barbara m (1830) Lawrence Heyden
1811-1895
b. 1804
Augustus m (1847) Bridget Tomlinson
1814-1868
of King Co., Ireland
Mary Warren Baldwin m (1816) John Breakenridge
1791-1871
1789-1828
Maria Margaret m (1835) Edmund Fuller Murney
1817-1875
1811-1861
John, b. 1820
William David Baldwin, b. 1822
Elizabeth Anna, b. 1825
Henrietta Augusta, b. 1828

* *

9

DR. BALDWIN, THE ARCHITECT

One of the most intriguing periods in William's life is the decade beginning in 1810. This was a time of consolidation for him. He and Phoebe had now been married seven years, and in that time five sons had been born to them: Robert, for whom the school holiday had been given in 1804; little Billy (Augustus William, who was born in November 1805 and died in April of the following year); Henry, who from the first was delicate, born in 1807, the year that Phoebe's mother, Mrs. Willcocks, died; William Augustus, born in September 1808; and St. George, the fifth and last child, born in January 1810.

When William heard a rumour (which proved false) that his friend St. George was to marry, he wrote, "I therefore must take the liberty of wishing you joy – and many happy years and a *numerous offspring the greatest blessing of human life.*" That William himself was a devoted father is shown clearly in his first letter to young Robert, written while the family was still at Millbrook:

My dear Robert,

When I folded my paper to write to you, I did not anticipate the warm emotion I felt when writing 'My dear Robert' – dear indeed to my heart as all your brothers are, for I know no difference. . . . How kind you ought to be to your good mama who takes such pains to instruct you. You and she will be well pleased to hear, as I am to tell you, that your school fellow George Boulton has left a little Virgil to be given to you, his Sister says she thinks he desired it to be given you as a present from himself, but does not recollect particularly his words. You can explain it. I am myself quite flattered with his attentions to you in this particular, as it gives me reason to think that your manners towards your schoolfellows are such as will gain their esteem. [This letter indicates that Robert had already been at school in York, and during the period at Millbrook was continuing his studies with his mother. William Warren, like his father, had a love of the classics.] Virgil, the author of the book just given to you is the most beautiful of the Roman poets. He lived and wrote in the time of Augustus Caesar, the first Roman Emperor, and was much beloved by him. I should suppose Mr. Strachan will make you read this book next after Cornelius Nepos.

In 1806 William had been appointed Master in Chancery, a post which he held most of his life. He had become a bencher in 1807 and was a judge of the Surrogate Court for the Home District from 1812 to 1836. In 1811 he was treasurer of the Law Society and also in 1815, 1820 and 1821. He was secretary and treasurer of the Society from 1824 to 1826, and again in 1832 and 1836.

But there is ample proof that as a struggling young lawyer in little York he practised both his professions of law and medicine. Indeed there is the well-authenticated account of a case in which he was pleading being adjourned in answer to an urgent call and he absented himself with the permission of the court to deliver a child. On his return, "I have much pleasure in informing your Honour that a man-child has been born into the world . . . and both he and his mother are doing well." At which point the case was resumed.

But it was George Ridout, writing to his father the Surveyor

General of Upper Canada, who paid William the most sincere compliment regarding his medical skill. "Tom and I were taken ill of the same fever which . . . proved so fatal in Whitechurch . . . Had it not been for Dr. Baldwin's skill and attention . . . it would have gone hard with us."

At the time William was working very hard building up his law practice, he was also spending much time on St. George's financial and business affairs, which he managed. St. George realized the advantages of buying his goods in New York and shipping them by this shorter route to Upper Canada, thereby saving time and money. Naturally the war of 1812 put a stop to this, but in the meantime he acquired a very considerable business, a sizeable fortune, and thousands of acres in many parts of the province. It fell to William's lot to administer this estate for his friend, both while he lived in the Canadas and also when he returned to France.

In his first architectural venture in the early days in York, he had undertaken to help St. George build the kind of house he wanted, and for that matter, the kind of house William no doubt dreamed of having. He undertook to draught plans for it and found the work absorbing and satisfying. This fine house for his friend was begun in 1809,* and was situated at the corner of King and Frederick Streets. According to *The Handbook of Toronto,* printed in 1858, this house, probably one of the first private houses built of brick in York, was designed by W. W. Baldwin. It was praised by Scadding, and in our own time Professor Eric Arthur has called it "one that we would wish to preserve if fate had permitted it to survive."

Professor Arthur, in his book *Toronto, No Mean City,* has listed the Doctor as an architect, so there is no reason why we should not use that term here. By definition an architect is a builder or one who draws up the plans for buildings, and William would qualify under both these counts, since he drew up the plans and supervised the construction of a number of public and private buildings. But he received no formal education or training as an architect.

To him, his architectural and planning activities were a crea-

* Most authorities make this date 1807 but St. George seems to have acquired the land in 1808 and Dr. Baldwin was still pricing bricks for it in 1810.

tive outlet most necessary and stimulating to his active mind and surplus energies. In the small community of early York, where those with architectural experience were scarce and where everyone used what talents he had or else did without, each new building which appeared was a source of satisfaction. So what started for William more or less as a hobby turned into a minor but exciting profession.

"The house he built for St. George," to quote a letter from Professor Anthony Adamson, an authority on early Canadian architecture, "had four chimney stacks and probably looked very much like the original Irish house of Summer Hill except for the front porch which was North American." William had lived at Summer Hill for the first twenty-two years of his life and would have been influenced by his memories of its layout and design.

It is quite obvious that he had been influenced also by the fine Georgian buildings, both public and private, in Edinburgh and Dublin. It was the age of fine architecture; the upper library of "Old College," University of Edinburgh, "possibly the finest example of Georgian architecture in Edinburgh," was being built at the time the Doctor was an undergraduate there. In Dublin, "almost a museum of fine classic buildings," the present Bank of Ireland, originally begun as the Parliament House, was under construction. The private houses also showed the stately classic influence of the times. St. George's house in York, which later became the Canada Company Building, has been demolished.

The Doctor wrote often to Quetton St. George. The bulk of their correspondence is of course of a business nature; but among the pages is a line here or a paragraph there that gives interesting titbits of information. St. George, having lived in York during the early years, would know all about the people referred to and William could unburden himself with confidence and candour to his friend, who thereby provided a much needed safety valve for William's feelings. His letters also told how much this witty, gay, likeable Frenchman was missed by his English friends.

December 28, 1809 William wrote to St. George, then in Niagara. "Capt de Hoen was with us he recognized the china Dish that held our Plumb Pudding, and reminded us that it was the twelfth christmas he eat off it . . . We drank your health in a bumper, . . . [Young] Robert & Henry joined in the chorus, & your name went round our table more than once."

The postal service was a problem even in 1810, for in a postscript to his letter of January 8 William writes, "A soldier in your shop promises to take this up to the garrison – perhaps it may overtake the courier."

Here is another side of William's character – January 23, 1810: "I had in a gloomy mood commenced a letter to you; it was not November time, but I am an Irishman and my wife was ill; I may now joke on my past anxiety." On June 23 of the same year he writes in a gayer mood to St. George, who always loved a party and would have known as business rivals all those mentioned:

> Messers J McDonell, Crookshank Wood & Cameron gave a Ball at Brown's house. My father, myself & Ally & Mary went – I came home early that is at one o'clock as became a dull old father of a family – the company continued dancing and feasting till after sunrise. . . . The House goes on slowly – pray John to enquire for me the price of Bricks at Niagara. . . . I expect the ladies will not let you rest till they have an opportunity of trying the elasticity of your floors.

In July 1811 Thomas G. Ridout wrote to his father: "I am so prejudiced in favour of York that I think its the neatest and prettiest place I have yet seen and St. George's house by much the best and handsomest."

The friendship between William and St. George never faltered, as witness these pleasant lines from a letter from the former of July 11, 1810: "I have just hurried from dinner to add a few lines to my last in answer to yours of the 3rd July – there cannot be a pleasure greater than that of opening one's mind to a faithful friend."

Just before Christmas, 1811, Ally went to Niagara to visit John, and her father, William, and Mary saw her off on the schooner. She wrote to Miss Russell:

> John walked [with me] to Mrs. Forsith's – found her sitting on a Black sopha, dressed in Black, her little daughter by

her side, also dressed in Black looking at a Black stove. Mrs. F. received us politely, we drank tea – . . . Dressed half an hour for the Ball before it was time to go, quite happy, danced every set – . . . tea coffy cold meat cakes etc etc for supper . . . I suppose as usual you read, Mary works and Milly sits half smiling in the chimney corner

Then comes a message for the gay St. George, as a ladies' man:

Tell Mr. St. George there was a young lady here very particular in her enquiries about his eye – she had heard he lost the sight of it, I satisfied her fears on that point. Does Mr. Large and my Father often go to see you – I am afraid I am quite forgotten, I never hear from York. Tell my father I am writing to him. Mary forgets a letter would give me pleasure.

"Very late everyone in bed," Ally concludes, and signs herself "Your affectionate friend."

For William the year 1812, apart from the war, must have been dominated by his duel with John McDonell.

John McDonell had studied law at York and had been called to the bar in 1808. He was an ardent member and supporter of the so-called Family Compact and in 1812 he was appointed acting Attorney-General in the absence of Mr. Firth, who was in England and about to be replaced. Writing to his friend Firth, William recounts what took place in open court:

Since you left this [province] I bore much of his [McDonell's] insolence in Court. However at the last Assizes, he used expressions so wanton and ungentlemanly that I appealed to the Ch. J. [Chief Justice] who seemed to disapprove of his words. Mr. McD repeated them twice afterwards in the course of his reply without notice by the Ch. J. – I could bear no more. Lt. Taylor of the 41st was fortunately in court – he is of one of your Inns of Court and has great claim to be admitted to the Bar here – I communicated with Mr. Taylor my determination of calling on Mr. McDonell for an explanation – Taylor would have disuaded me, but proving me resolved – he confessed he thought me right – accordingly in the evening I wrote to Mr. McD stating the offensive words and requiring

> an explanation – he seemed astonished, told Mr. Taylor he did not think he said anything requiring an apology & said he would get a friend to call on Mr. Taylor with his answer – this friend was Mr. D. Cameron who expressed himself much concerned that I should in the first instance have made so preremptory a demand of an explanation as he had no doubt but the misunderstanding might have been settled to our mutual satisfaction without going to this extremity – and that Mr. McDonell could not now think of making an apology – Mr. Taylor said that I could not pass it over that my resolution was fixed and that it only remained to fix time and place as Mr. McD declined explanation and proposed the following morning. Mr. Cameron answered that Mr. McD had public duties to perform which he could not omit, and requested it might be postponed till after the assizes; things remained thus for two days – the Assizes ended on Thursday and Mr. Cameron called on my friend to say that Mr. M would wait on [the] Island at six o'clock the following morning – That evening I employed myself in writing a few lines to my friends and to you amongst them and also my will.

William's will was short, just half a page and typical of the man. It is dated April 3, 1812. In the very brief opening paragraph he says in part, "If I am wrong may the Almighty forgive me – I believe I forgive my antagonist, it is my sincere wish to do so." In the will he left all real and personal property to Phoebe, "my amiable wife . . . unparalleled in all the excellent qualifications of her sex." The will is witnessed by Thomas Taylor and Peter Wheeler and signed and sealed by William.

He also left a tender letter for his wife: "I beseech you to pardon this step which I am about to take, not to indulge a rash or resentful spirit, but to protect me from insults, which as a gentleman I cannot submit to." And he concludes, "I have endeavoured these two days past to fortify myself with perfect resignation to the dispensation of his Divine Providence . . . may he comfort you and preserve you in health and long life – . . . farewell – perhaps for ever."

William continued in his letter to William Firth:

> I went to bed earlier than usual that I might be early awake

> – I slept but little as you may suppose – however I arose at daybreak & Taylor was with me – I was fortunate enough to escape all observation of my own family – we passed Mr. Cameron's house before they set off – we walked they passed across the ice in a sleigh – I stopped at the blockhouse to execute the Will in front of the necessary no of witnesses – and then proceeded to the ground – Mr. Cameron & Taylor made their arrangements & we were placed back to back. I was desired upon first word to face about, the second to fire – upon the word I faced about the word fire followed – but at the instant of leveling my pistol I observed Mr. McD in his place with his arm down, I did not fire but held my hand pointed towards him. When Mr. Cameron called why I did not fire – McD's pistol still down – Mr. Cameron repeated he waits for your fire – I then fired wide – upon that Mr. Taylor proposed shaking hands and Mr. Cameron came up to me with much concern & feeling & said that he lamented I had brought things to that extremity so suddenly that Mr. McD came to the ground with the determination to receive my fire only – I took this as an acknowledgement of his error – we joined hands and thus the affair ended. He has been sufficiently decorous since then.

The incident was closed; but a tribute should be paid here to John McDonell, who as a lieutenant-colonel, aide to General Brock, died gallantly beside his commander in the Battle of Queenston Heights a few months later.

Most of the legal and political problems in Upper Canada centred around land, how it was to be granted and how it was to be developed. There was a superabundance of land, approximately thirty million acres in all. And from the beginning there were far too few settlers and these were scattered in pockets over wide areas.

In the first place land was used to reward those who had fought for Britain; secondly it was used by the Governor and Council as a source of revenue outside the control of the local elective Assembly; thirdly as reserves of Crown land, clergy reserves and Indian reserves; and finally it was used to attract settlers. The use of land as a source of revenue and for clergy reserves was to cause a great deal of trouble.

In the early days from 1800 until the War of 1812 a steady trickle of new settlers was arriving from Scotland, Ireland and Britain, while others came from the United States. These last were sometimes referred to as the "late loyalists" but they came in search of good lands, not for reasons of loyalty as had the United Empire Loyalists. People from the British Isles were looked upon by the Loyalists as farmers, labourers and artisans, as for the most part they were, and also as foreigners, which they were not. During this early period, none of these new settlers had very much, if any, say in the government of the country or the framing of the statutes which directed their affairs. These matters were almost the monopoly of a small clique of Loyalists and earlier settlers which, because of its power and the intermarriage of so many of its members, became known as the Family Compact in derisive comparison to the defensive alliance of 1761 between the members of the Bourbon family who occupied various European thrones. Although the members of the little Upper Canada oligarchy were not a family and had signed no compact, the term approximated the present-day use of the word Establishment and seems to fit very handily the conditions in York.

At this time, the Governor made the appointments to the Executive Council as he saw fit, and not necessarily from any one group. The Legislative Council or Upper Chamber consisted of fifteen sitting members, of whom six were Executive Councillors, and four others held positions under the Crown. In this way the Executive controlled the Legislative Council, and as the latter could reserve or send back any legislation put forward by the Assembly, the cards were indeed stacked. Solidly entrenched around the Governor was the Family Compact. After the War of 1812 they became clearly defined by their control of the political positions and influence, the wealth, and to some extent the judiciary, in Upper Canada. Besides its hold on the Executive and Legislative Councils, the Family Compact controlled about half the elective or popular Assembly. It was only after the election of 1824 that the Reform group had a clear majority.

The rising star of the Family Compact was the brilliant young lawyer John Beverley Robinson, a United Empire Loyalist whose family had come up to Berthier in Quebec from Virginia because of the American Revolution and later had moved to York. Although only twenty-two, he was appointed acting Attorney-General in 1813 while D'Arcy Boulton, who had succeeded William Firth, remained a prisoner in France. On Boulton's return, Robinson became Solicitor-General and in 1818, Attorney-General again. In 1830 he became Chief Justice. As leader of the Family Compact he was, in effect, the continuing chief minister of the Governor and the power behind the throne.

Other members of the little oligarchy were that dynamic, fiery little cleric, Dr. John Strachan; D'Arcy Boulton and his two brothers, all three wealthy and influential lawyers; William Allan, perhaps the wealthiest man in Upper Canada and reputed to be the financial genius of the Family Compact; James Baby, who came from a Quebec family of note and settled in the Detroit-Sandwich area but later moved to York and was a member of the Executive and Legislative Councils from 1792 until his death in 1816; Dummer Powell, who had come with his wife from Boston via Montreal, where he had practised law before coming to York (he was made a judge in the Court of Common Pleas, and some time later became Chief Justice); and Duncan Cameron, a merchant who became Provincial Secretary in 1817, of whom Dr. Baldwin wrote to William Firth in June of 1812: "Mr. D. Cameron a bird of ill omen is again flapping about the Govt House . . . the old bird-lime is still adhesive to the branches of the Administration." There were of course many other members and supporters of the Family Compact as well as a number of border-line supporters blowing hot and cold.

In the little community of Muddy York it was inevitable that nearly everybody should become aligned on one side or the other. By birth, education and financial standing it may appear to some that William should have sided with the Family Compact. He himself realized only too well that it would have been to his advantage, particularly in the early days, to do so. But by conviction he could not and would not; to think otherwise would be to misread his character.

* *

10

THE POLITICIANS OF YORK

Politics in Upper Canada, and more particularly in little York, revolved around personalities, and many of these took issue with the Family Compact on a number of basic issues such as the use of public money, the wretched state of the roads, the lack of schools, and the method of granting land, none of which were receiving the attention they deserved. This was largely owing to a great lack of revenue, but also to the fact that what funds there were, together with the political power in Upper Canada, were vested in the Governor and Council, with the elected Assembly running a poor third. Lacking education, the settlers needed men to speak for them and to stand up for their rights; but it was not from among the more recent settlers themselves that their early champions appeared.

The first of these champions was William Weekes, a barrister who had studied law in the United States and came to Upper Canada in 1798. Early in 1805 he was elected to the Assembly. He found that a "considerable sum of money had been paid out of the provincial treasury without the authority of Parliament or a vote of the Assembly." He succeeded in having a committee appointed (not unlike a royal commission) to look into the state of affairs in Upper Canada. The resolutions of this committee were significant, but in no way breath-taking; they underlined the great need for general education in the province, the terrible state of the roads in all areas, and the very arbitrary methods of granting land. But in October 1806 Weekes was killed in a duel with William Dickson, and his body was hardly disposed of before Mr. Justice Robert Thorpe, a puisne judge of the King's Bench, began to seek election in Weekes's place.

In private life the Thorpes were pleasant and unassuming, but they were not accepted by some members of the Family Compact. Their household consisted of Judge Thorpe, his wife and their seven children, four of whom were girls, and Mrs. Thorpe's sister Miss Featherstone. Elizabeth Russell has a number of entries in her diary concerning them. One such states: "Mr. and Mrs. Thorpe their eldest girl and Miss Featherstone came to return my visit – Gave them cakes and wine. After chatting a while they went away. They seem to be a free-mannered unreserved people and not formal." Dr. Baldwin and his family met the Thorpes on a number of occasions, apart from William's professional contacts with Judge Thorpe in the courts.

But in his public life Thorpe was an unusual character, and his entry into politics not only stirred things up but introduced two new elements – first, the constitutional question of whether a judge could seek election; and second, the political idiosyncrasies and personal ambition of Judge Thorpe himself, who often made political harangues in the court and who, having been Chief Justice of Prince Edward Island, possibly had asperations to become Chief Justice of Upper Canada.

Thorpe was encouraged by a meeting of freeholders, reported in the *Upper Canada Gazette* of November 8, 1806 and presided over by William's father-in-law, William Willcocks, which passed a unanimous resolution requesting Judge Thorpe to stand in the forthcoming by-election for the combined counties of York, Durham and Simcoe.

The Governor, Sir Francis Gore, was probably quite right in his contention that it was not proper for a judge to contest a seat in the Legislature, but there was no legislation in Upper Canada at that time barring him from so doing. The result was that Thorpe went ahead and was elected; he was then summarily dismissed from his judgeship by Gore in 1807 and the election was disputed. Also dismissed was Charles Wyatt, the Surveyor General, who had supported Thorpe. William was on friendly terms with Wyatt, and was to act for him later.

These and other arbitrary actions on the part of the Governor and his Executive raised a considerable storm of protest in Upper Canada. (Later in England Wyatt brought a libel action against Gore for wrongful dismissal and for statements made by the Governor at that time; and in 1816 he obtained a judgment against Governor Gore in the English courts in the amount of three hundred pounds.) In regard to this, in 1815 when William called upon Governor Gore, he was received politely and his Excellency "asked for Mrs. B. and the children and spoke on the subject of Mr. Wyatts suit agt him: hoped I would do him equal justice with Mr. Wyatt; to these words I made no reply – because I thought he ought not to suppose anything else – I trust in God that I may have judgement & penetration sufficient to discover right from wrong – and that I may have resolution to maintain this power – . . ."

(Apparently about 1820, when Thorpe and Gore were living in England as private citizens, Thorpe also brought an action against Gore and was successful.)

These public agitations, coupled with the opinions and opposition of more moderate and responsible men like Thomas Ridout and William Warren, add weight to the view that the Governor and his advisers had exceeded their powers and had acted, to say the least, most unwisely.

In the Thorpe case William was drawn in by his father-in-law, but in the case of Wyatt he became involved because he felt that an injustice had been done, and thus got his feet wet in politics for the first time.

Another champion of the submerged majority was Joseph Willcocks. He was sheriff of the Home District at York, but with the departure of Mr. Justice Allcock for Quebec, Joseph came under the extraordinary influence of Judge Thorpe and as time went on became more and more radical. His attacks on the Governor and his bitterness towards the administration appear to have followed Thorpe's dismissal, and they came to a head when he himself was deprived of his post as sheriff. At that time, 1807, he moved to Niagara, bought a printing press in the United

States and, in September of that year, began editing a newspaper, the *Upper Canada Guardian or Freeman's Journal.* In its pages Joseph renewed the fight for Thorpe and vituperatively attacked the Government.

By now Joseph was quite a popular hero as well as a thorn in the flesh of the Family Compact. So it is not surprising that in 1808 he was elected as a member of the Assembly (for the combined ridings of Lincoln and Haldimand) and he continued to be a member until the outbreak of war in 1812. But this did not prevent his opponents from taking action and from bringing him up to trial before the Assembly. He was alleged to have stated, in September 1808, that certain members had been bribed by the Governor by grants of twelve hundred acres each. Joseph had become an out-and-out radical, although at the trial one of his accusers stated in an affidavit that Joseph Willcocks had been a loyal man down to 1805. Other facts tend to confirm this.

During his trial he was imprisoned in the common jail without even the crudest conveniences, but on his release he was again elected and continued to lead the opposition. In his role as popular demagogue Joseph most nearly resembles William Lyon Mackenzie, who appeared on the scene some fifteen years later. (Willcocks fought first on the Canadian side, and then on the American, before being killed in the War of 1812.)

Finally, but by no means the least important in this list of public champions, was John Mills Jackson, later of Jackson's Point, Lake Simcoe. He had been born in the West Indies and educated at Oxford. In 1806 he came to Canada and settled first on a farm up Yonge Street which he called Springfield. It did not take long before he too became extremely critical of the Government of Upper Canada.

In 1809 while in England he took the step, unusual for a resident of Upper Canada, of publishing a political treatise under the title, "A view of the Political Situation of the Province of Upper Canada." This well-written pamphlet he addressed to the "King, Lords and Commons of Great Britain and Ireland." In it he called on them to examine the dispatches of the Governor and the Journals of the House of Assembly, and of the Legislative Council; he advised them to look into the distribution of Crown lands, and to read the letters of Judge Thorpe and of others. And finally he suggested that a commission should be appointed by the British Parliament to look into these matters.

Although many of Jackson's criticisms were valid and amply supported in his pamphlet, he, like Joseph Willcocks, was something of a firebrand. As such he singed the feathers of a number of influential people in the province, so much so that his pamphlet was branded as a libel by the Government supporters in the Assembly of Upper Canada, who were still in the majority.

One interesting point was that Jackson in this publication was perhaps the first to call attention to the plight of the Six Nation Indians in respect to the very shoddy and ungrateful treatment given to this fine and loyal people. He also showed how a false map had been introduced during the purchase of land from the "Messessagua" Indians, thus defrauding that tribe of some seventeen thousand acres. This too did not endear Jackson to the administration.

William's early involvement in the politics of Upper Canada stemmed from three loyalties: to his father-in-law and his friend Wyatt; to Thorpe as a fellow member of the bar and of the Law Society; and to his principles. As a young man, he had seen in Ireland the attempts of the Volunteers to achieve parliamentary reform blocked by the same arbitrary methods of the Lord Lieutenant, the Castle group, and the Government placeman in the Irish Parliament. To William it was the same situation being played out all over again in Canada. Certainly he enjoyed honours and advancement as well as the next man, but there was a price for these things he was not prepared to pay.

During the War of 1812, Upper Canada had enjoyed a period of prosperity because ready money had flowed to farmers and merchants alike for supplies for the armed forces; these army bills could be redeemed at par and were backed by both Canadian and British governments. But with the end of hostilities the boom was followed all too soon by a bust. The farms had been neglected owing to shortage of manpower. The flow of army bills virtually stopped and there was nothing to take their place, so currency became very scarce indeed and the price of land began to drop owing to this shortage of money and the foreclosure of mortgages.

Three illustrations from William's own letters bear this out. In October 1814 he writes: "I am now planning to sow the three acres of wheat [at his farm at Millbrook] for I dread scarcity in another year which to me with 14 or 15 in family* is a serious apprehension." The scarcity of money was to continue and later William writes, "You can have no idea of the scarcity of money in the country. I went to the Assizes at Dundas and although employed by several there, I brought no more [away] with me than I took in my pocket." In the same letter he tells us how a well-established Niagara merchant bought and paid for his goods (this was James Crooks): "Mr. Crooks told me he had travelled all over the District of London, Niagara and Gore with diamonds of about $6,000 [worth]. He went himself and only brought back $30." Here is a shocker about the sale of land, also in the same letter to St. George: "The Sheriff of Niagara sold 30,000 acres of Lord Selkirk's on the Grand River for £500. This cannot be a just business but such was the sale. The land is worth at least £20,000."

By 1815 William had recovered from his war melancholia, largely because the family was reunited. His law practice was expanding and his salary as Master in Chancery had been increased. With the return of the family to York young Robert again went to Dr. Strachan's, the district grammar school situated in College Square on what is now the south-east corner of Church and Lombard Streets.

William and Phoebe would have liked to see their friend St. George as settled and happy as they now were, and in one of Phoebe's rare surviving letters she writes to St. George on September 11, 1815: "I am glad that you at last confess yourself a convert to my doctrine 'That no real domestic comfort is to be enjoyed without a *good Wife;*' of this truth you know I have been for some years endeavouring to convince you." And then, "I am sorry that York is not to be the place of your residence, but hope that you are not without inducements to spend at least a part of every year amongst us – I suppose now that *Mr. Boneparte* is at rest you will again resume your intention of visiting France next year." Then comes some family news, "the Morgans spent only a week with us. Mr. M. was quite disappointed at not being able to take Henry, who was so weakened by violent bleeding at his nose as to be unfit to travel; he wd not give up hope

* His "family" then included Phoebe and the four boys, his father, his three sisters, his sister-in-law Maria Willcocks, Miss Russell, a domestic or two, and a hired man.

of taking him 'till he had consulted Lee, who was attending the children – he has made me promise to bring him in the winter, as he said he had the Chief Justices leave of Absence for the Doctor during the Session, if Business will permit, I should like the trip very much. . . . As to our little commission for plate (as you know we have not much money to lay out this way) if you think it wd be better executed by lying over 'till you go yourself, I should rather you did so." She signs herself, "Believe me with truth yr sincere friend. Phoebe Baldwin"

In the early days of Upper Canada the experiences of a Home District Judge on circuit were often rugged, but William showed a surprising toughness at times. His journey to New York in 1800 had provided good training. In travelling from York to Niagara in winter the journey often had to be made on foot; the road or track, when it existed at all, was rough and often hard to follow. In *An Irishman in Canada,* Nicholas Flood Davin recalled "on one such journey [in November] Dr. Baldwin lost his way and was compelled to sleep in the woods all night and next day to swim the River Credit which was swollen."

By 1815 conditions were improving. William wrote to St. George in September:

> I returned on Sunday last from the circuit with the Ch. Justice and Mr. Small all well. . . . on the circuit I had but very little business at Sandwich or Charlotteville, but at Niagara a good deal – and you will be pleased to hear that the people at large, the Magistrates and the Grand Jury were all highly pleased at the manner in which the public prosecutions were conducted – I was told by two or three that Mr. Watts, Crooks and Thos Dickson had said they never saw a court conducted with less confusion nor when more satisfactory verdicts were given; this I tell you for your own gratification and not to speak of to others. . . . I meet all my little boys ill with the ague and now write by Robert's bedside, little St. George and Wm. are much reduced by it – Henry very delicate – I am therefore not in high feather just now.

Following the ague Henry did not recover his health, and in January the following year William took advantage of the invitations of his sister Elizabeth and her husband John Morgan to again take a trip to New York, with the intention of leaving Henry with them.

The highlight for Robert during his school years would have been this journey to New York in 1816. Again, as some fifteen years before, William travelled by sleigh, this time with his wife, Robert and Henry. Roads and travel facilities on the six-hundred-mile journey had improved since William's previous trip, and apart from increased costs, he foresaw little difficulty. He wrote to St. George from New York on February 5:

> We arrived here the 28th ultimo – and shall leave this is our intention on Wednesday morning next – the snow has all gone off and has left us in a disagreeable delimma, but go I must and as we leave our little Henry here we are so much the lighter – the journey seems to have improved his health and I hope in God the change of air will be of great benefit to him besides the advantages of an excellent school adapted to his age with the care of his Aunt & Mr. Morgan. – The journey has cost us a good deal but as we thought it necessary, so we submitted to this expense –

The letters in 1816 are full of family news. Mary Warren, William's youngest sister, married John Breakenridge, a law student in William's office. Breakenridge then moved to Niagara with his wife and set up practice for himself. John Spread, William's youngest brother, did not marry until later; he was now living at York in St. George's house and managing the business there; "Anna Maria keeps house for him."

When St. George's trip to France was arranged, William wrote in April 1816: "I would thank you when in England to get me a lawyers silk gown as my salary is increased I must honour the crown – Some Yankees or soldiers stole my old one – Also Russell's *History of Modern Europe*." And then this delightful little touch, "The whole fireside have cried out to say that we hope you will not return hither without seeing Ireland – this land of our forefathers and scene of many happy days. I hope you will also see my brothers Henry and Augustus . . . The House [the Assembly] has increased my salary to £100 per annum. Wm & St George [8 and 6] are to go to school next month."

It was after his father's death in 1816 that William "made a lease of the property at Clarke." This was for a term of years with a Mr. Daniel Arnot and for the benefit of his sisters, Alice and Anna Maria. Now for the first time he called the farm Annarva in Anna's honour for, as he put it: "It was due to her as she partook greatly of the privations, solitude and labour of the early settlement of the family at that place." Again in a letter to St. George of February of that year: "I have got through the business of the Commission between the Governor and Mr. Wyatt with a vast deal of altercation and contention between me and Dr. Strachan – we are nevertheless yet friends."

William's relationship with Dr. John Strachan must have been one of the strangest in his experience. The two men were complete opposites and one might have expected Strachan, the nonconformist son of a Scots crofter, to be the reformer and William, the well-to-do lawyer and property holder, to back the Family Compact; but the reverse was the case. Strachan, who took Anglican orders in 1803 and became the first Bishop of Toronto, had no quarrel with William as a staunch member of the Church and as a man of high principles, for William in his quiet way was a deeply religious person, a faithful and affectionate husband, and a loyal supporter of St. James' Church (later Cathedral), of which he was a pew holder all his life. He sent his boys to Dr. Strachan's school as a matter of course and Robert became head boy there.

In fact, William approved of Strachan as a clever, educated man and a fine teacher but he did not approve of some of Strachan's means in attaining his ends. Strachan was at his best in a tough situation or in the political arena; in this he was like the medieval prelates. Perhaps his finest hour was during the American capture of York, when he defied the American commander and his officers and demanded humane treatment of civilians and protection of private property. William had been in the battle too, so he and Dr. Strachan had respect for each other; both had courage and each recognized this fact in the other.

Socially William and Strachan would meet on fairly equal terms. Strachan stood higher with the Governor and the Family Compact, being a member of the Executive Council. But William too was accepted because he was a medical doctor with a degree from Edinburgh, a Senior Bencher with a good and growing law practice, and the owner of extensive land holdings. Dr. Strachan was blossoming out socially, and in a letter to St.

George in August 1817 William writes: "Dr. S. is building a great brick house which it is said is to surpass yours." But it was in politics that William and John Strachan crossed swords and they were, and continued to be, opponents and sometimes enemies.

Gradually William became less active as a medical practitioner (although he remained "the Doctor" to all and sundry) and the law occupied most of his time, for he enjoyed a busy practice. With the general increase of his work and the complications of St. George's affairs, his health suffered. "York 7 July, 1817. . . . I have the melancholy news to tell you of my poor father's death. He died on the 24th November last, after a few hours illness. I am myself in very indifferent health indeed, my constitution seems to have undergone a change of a serious nature – to walk from home to your house fatigues me as if I had run a mile. It is the remains of the attack which had nearly carried me off last spring." In August of 1817, in a long letter to his friend, he writes, "My health improves – but yet slowly – and I find the ill effects of much application."

So in June of the following year, 1818, William decided to resign as judge of the Home District Court, "as retaining it longer would be very detrimental to my business . . . and retaining it would compel me to decline a great portion of the business of my profession. The Emolument of the office heretofore has been very insignificant – indeed averaging not more than £10 to £12 per annum." But his resignation does not appear to have been accepted, for many sources list William as judge of the Home District until 1836.

By 1817 William's sister Barbara and her husband Daniel Sullivan were thinking of emigrating to Upper Canada and William was considering property for them "at the head of the lake." Nothing came of this plan and the Sullivans did not reach York until 1819. William's brother Augustus Warren arrived in 1817, however, having served in the Royal Navy since 1794. He had seen action in the Napoleonic War and won a gold medal commemorating the capture of the Russian 74, the *Seavold*, in 1807. Now he was a captain on half pay and he settled in York, where he married Augusta Melissa Jackson, daughter of John Mills Jackson, the early reformer.

* *

11

LETTERS TO QUETTON ST. GEORGE

The growth of York and its recovery after the post-war slump was owing in no small way to the North West Company, which had been a power in the town since the days of Simcoe. York was an important staging depot in its trade to the West, and a shorter route to Lake Huron had been developed up the Don River and Yonge Street to the Holland River and Lake Simcoe. In 1815 the company had contributed twelve thousand pounds for the improvement of Yonge Street, and large quantities of supplies were purchased in the town every year. Now in 1818 there was great excitement in York over the outcome of a trial which was about to take place.

Charges of treason, murder, robbery and conspiracy had been preferred by the Earl of Selkirk against certain members of the North West Company following the Massacre of Seven Oaks in 1816. At that time there had been open conflict between members of the company and Lord Selkirk's settlers on the Red River. Now, two years later, York had been chosen as the venue and the trial took place in the court-house on Richmond Street. Presiding were Chief Justice Powell and Judges Boulton and

Campbell, with William Allan as Associate Justice, while counsels for the accused were Livius P. Sherwood, Samuel Sherwood and William Warren Baldwin, with prosecuting counsels Attorney-General Robinson and Solicitor-General Boulton.

The trial resulted in the acquittal of the accused, but matters did not end there, for the North West Company brought counter charges for damages and loss of trade. In these suits Lord Selkirk was again unsuccessful, for in February 1819 William writes: "Lord Selkirk has been worsted here this last week in several trials between him and the North West Company."

Lord Selkirk had not been able to be present at the first trial, which was one of the most important to be held in York. But in August William's sister Ally wrote to her cousin in Ireland: "He [Lord Selkirk] has been here several times – he at one time spent near a fortnight." During these visits he lived in St. George's house, "as this house is one of the best in town." It was occupied at that time by John and Anna Maria. Ally continues, "The other day he came with Lady Selkirk – they have two children . . . their Mother is a most amiable woman – they were on their way to the falls. They spent a day and a half – her manners, and also his, are so gentle and mild."

In 1817 William had written to St. George in France about the planned partnership between John Spread Baldwin and Jules Quesnel for the taking over of St. George's business: "In consequence of some very extraordinary letters from Mr. Quesnel, John has given him notice of a dissolution of the partnership – indeed I think that John is quite right."* And in the same letter it appears that Mary Warren's husband, John Breakenridge, had managed to get under William's skin, for he reported: "Breakenridge and Mary live at Niagara . . . I do feel myself not well treated by him and though I hope we shall always be civil & kind to each other yet I cannot feel him so much ingrafted into the family as to call him brother – I believe he is doing well at Niagara – & I hope he will always do well."

In the same letter William mentioned two old and well-established York families and the tragic consequence of their falling out. "That family [the Ridouts] are grievously afflicted

* This was patched up, however, because in 1820 a new partnership was formed by "John, Mr. Quesnel & Mr. Holme . . . the new firm to be called St. George & Co."

now by the death of their son in a duel with Saml. Jarvis – Jarvis is in prison; Small, Ridout's friend is gone across the water – & Henry Boulton the second of Jarvis is gone on the circuit as counsel for the Crown – it is a wretched affair altogether – & S Jarvis is not free from censure." This disastrous duel between John Ridout, eighteen, and S. P. Jarvis, twenty-five, was fought in Elmsley's field, now the north-west corner of Yonge and College. In his excitement Ridout had fired before the count of three; his pistol was taken from him and he stood unarmed while Jarvis fired and killed him. Jarvis was charged with manslaughter but was acquitted. The seconds were not charged as accessories at that time, but in 1828 they were so tried and acquitted.

During 1818, the great strides made in the improvement of transportation meant increased prosperity all over Upper Canada.

> There are now three steamboats on Lake Ontario and another is to be built next summer making 4 – one American. There are 3 banks in Lower Canada 2 are in operation in Montreal. We will also have one shortly in Upper Canada, at Kingston. Emigration to the Province from England Ireland and Scotland has been very great this season. The town of York has improved increasingly – in fact everyone seems pleased with the appearance of things throughout the Province for generally I do not think they ever presented so flourishing appearance as within the last few months.

Although transportation had improved and the steamship *Frontenac* was in service on Lake Ontario, William, going on circuit to Niagara, still made the crossing in the small sailing schooner *Caledonia.* It was fortunate that William had "oil in his lamp" for this emergency. Mr. M. F. Whitehead of Port Hope writes, "My first crossing to York was in September 1818 with Dr. Baldwin – a two-and-a-half day's passage. The Doctor had thoughtfully provided a leg of lamb, a loaf of bread and a bottle of port: all our fare for two days and a half."

On the twenty-second of that month, William wrote to his cousin John in Ireland:

> Robert is fourteen – and as forward in point of education

> as our school here advances boys of his age – I shall keep him yet two years more at school with Doctor Strachan – I intend please God to bring him up to the bar – Henry is with his Uncle Morgan at New York – a sweet boy, I mean in disposition and manners – the other two William & St. George are yet very young – Wm. is trying his latin grammar – St. George only in English – I am very busy now hurrying on the plastering of house I have built almost 3 miles from Town where I propose to live – the journey in and out every day though troublesome in many respects conduces much to the health of myself & my boys –.

This was the Doctor's first effort in building for himself. The next year the family were spending a considerable part of their time at their new country home. William writes with satisfaction to St. George in July 1819:

> I have a very commodious house in the country – I have called the place Spadina – the Indian word for Hill – or Mont – the house consists of two large Parlours Hall & staircase on the first floor – four bedrooms and a small library on the 2d floor – and three excellent bedrooms in Attic story or garret – with several closets on every story – a kitchen dairy, root-cellar wine cellar & mans bedroom under ground. I have cut an avenue through the woods all the way so that we can see the vessels passing up and down the bay – the house is completely furnished with stables etc and a tolerable good garden, the whole has cost about 15,00£ [fifteen hundred pounds] the land you know was the gift of poor Mr. Willcocks – whom I am sure you will never forget.

The "avenue through the woods" became the approach to the Doctor's house and is now Spadina Avenue. Henry Scadding wrote of it in *Toronto of Old:* "From the water's edge to the base of Spadina Hill nearly three miles and guarded on both sides by a double row of full grown chestnut trees"; and again, "Spadina Avenue was laid out on a scale that would have satisfied the designers of St. Petersburg or Washington." Later this fine avenue, more than a hundred and twenty feet wide, was given to the city on condition that it should remain unblocked.

But like so many private roadways it fulfilled no useful purpose till it served the public – until, as Professor Anthony Adamson put it, "it went from somewhere to somewhere." It served in the first instance as a leg in the old "Belt Line," the circular streetcar route which Toronto enjoyed into the nineteen-twenties. But it is only just coming into its own today; because of its width, it is to be used as the north-west freeway linking Highway 401 to downtown Toronto, in the same manner as the Don Valley Parkway fulfils this function in the eastern part of the city.

Augustus Baldwin also planned to live in the country. The Doctor reported: "The Captain is building also in our neighbourhood – he lives with us in our present rented tenement while his own is building." Augustus' property, which he bought from Miss Russell, was a two-hundred-acre lot on the hill flanking Spadina. He called it Russell Hill, partly in Miss Russell's honour, no doubt, but also because he happened to have been born while his parents were at Ireland's Russell Hill, the property of their Gilman cousins.

In a long letter to his friend written during the summer of 1819 and apparently in answer to a query, William gave St. George news of people and events in York and of his own business affairs.

> Col. Coffin "status quo" – Major Loring lives at Davenport – a very worthy small man and pleasant neighbour – as to all the rest of the bachelors and spinsters, they are as you left them – nor is marriage ever spoken of – a bad sign in a new colony – His Grace the Duke of Richmond was here a few days ago – the gentry gave him a Dinner at the Hotel de W. D. Forrest* – there were about 50 persons amongst them your humble servant – these were great things for York – His Grace & Sir P Maitland have gone . . . to return by way of Detroit – to see the Country. . . . Mr. Dickson has gained his Township case against Penfield – he has built a capital mill in the new Township – Col. Talbot's settlement flourishes – the new Townships flourish more rapidly than the old – I mean those that are so taken up in Large tracts – Maria Willcocks the same as ever – always occupied – and wrapped up in the

* This refers to the Mansion House on King Street, owned by W. D. Forrest.

little boys – she sold some front Land in Whitby at 4 Dol. part down and interest for the residue – Ally & Ann have sold in Clarke at 4 Dol. on 12 years credit. . . . Now to speak particularly of myself. My business altogether brings in clear I suppose about 600 per annum – it is not possible to know it accurately – for such great disbursements to Sheriff, Clk etc that to discover the net amount of my annual briefs is not possible – I have three Clerks who are pretty well employed. I feel great esteem for Jas. Small – & indeed for Washburn and my nephew Danl Sullivan.

Daniel, the son of William's eldest sister, Barbara Sullivan, had arrived in Upper Canada in 1817 and had been taken into William's law office. In December of that year he had written to his father in Ireland urging him, as business was bad there, to emigrate with the rest of the family to Upper Canada and to set up in business. As a result:

> In 1819 Mr. Daniel Sullivan entered Canada at the Port of Quebec thence he and his family pursued the usual route from Quebec to Montreal by steamer and on up the St. Lawrence by bateau. During the journey he landed at a place between the rapids and Kingston and entered a farm house owned by a Mrs. Strange. They got into conversation and hearing he was on his way to York she cautioned him to beware of Lawyers in that town that there was but one honest lawyer in it and that was Dr. Baldwin.

We can imagine "with what zest Mr. Sullivan enjoyed being thus advised by a stranger in a strange land of this characteristic feature of his own brother-in-law."

Daniel Sullivan Sr. had been a brilliant student at Trinity College Dublin, where as well as being an outstanding scholar in the classics, which included Latin, he had won the special prize in Greek. He was to have entered the church but was unable to accept some of the thirty-nine articles and so went into business instead. The arrival of the Sullivans gave William and Phoebe another group of congenial friends and relations, and renewed their ties with Ireland and their friends who were still there. As the two eldest children, Barbara and William had been very close and a great bond of affection existed between them, so it is little wonder that the children of the two families became very friendly. Among the Sullivan children was a younger son, Robert Baldwin Sullivan, aged seventeen, and Augusta Elizabeth, a most attractive and engaging girl of ten.

Again writing to St. George, William gives news of his sons:

> Robert is a fine fellow – he is fond of letters. He has made several translations from the Greek & Latin extremely pretty – William & your namesake are also going on well – . . . Robert is now 15 years old. – I wish not to take him from school yet – this next year will strengthen him in his education much – indeed I hope yet one day please God to be able to send him to England if even for one year – he is liked by all the boys – by Doctor Strachan and Mr. Stoughton the tutor, a very worthy young man.

This letter was written before the public examinations held at the school in August 1819, at which, as head boy, Robert recited a prologue in Latin.

> In the prologue pronounced by Robert Baldwin (in verse) the administration of Hastings in India is eulogized, Sir William Jones is apostrophized in connection with his Asiastic researches, the Marquis of Wellesley and the college founded by him at Calcutta suggests the necessity of a similar institution in Canada, and Sir Peregrine Maitland who was probably present, is told that he could immortalize himself by establishing such an institution. [This last obviously a pet project of Dr. Strachan.]

Two events in 1819 saddened William. He had been aware that St. George was contemplating marriage with one of his own countrywomen, and he received a marriage contract in French dated May 23, 1819, making this marriage official. The lady was Adele de Barbeyrea, and the happy couple were to live on St. George's restored estates at Montpellier in the south of France. William rejoiced in the happiness of his friend, but grieved that he was not returning to Canada, and that he might not see him again. The second event occured towards the end of that year with the marked deterioration in the health of Alice, always the delicate sister. She had suffered a mental breakdown and William writes: "My poor sister Ally who is still in the General Hospital at Quebec under the care of the nuns there who are very kind to her – the poor girl is quite deranged in her mind."

In 1820, at the age of forty-five, William, who was an extremely active man, was expanding his interests. His health had improved, his law practice was prospering and he had three good men in his office, Small, Washburn, and young Daniel Sullivan. And Robert was to join them: "In a short time I am to be a student at law, and am therefore making the best of my time as in April I shall have to attend the office."

William had become increasingly interested and involved in the political affairs of Upper Canada, and now determined to enter politics in earnest. Robert, writing to William Augustus, who was staying with the Morgans in New York, comments: "I shall send you enclosed a copy of my Father's address to the Freeholders, for I suppose you know by this time that he has offered himself a candidate for the ensuing elections. He seems confident of his being returned."

Just as his father had been in Ireland, William became increasingly interested in political reform in Upper Canada. The principal abuses had to do with the alien question, the clergy reserves, education, and the manner in which public money was controlled. There were probably others; but on all these questions a large body of public opinion in the province disagreed violently with the Governor and the Family Compact.

Briefly, the alien problem concerned the granting and selling of land to families immigrating to Canada from the United States. After the war the Governor and most of the Loyalists wished to exclude all settlers from the United States on the grounds that they held republican ideas and might not be loyal to the Crown. On the other hand the province needed settlers and it needed money; and these Americans had money and were willing to pay good prices for land, whereas new settlers from the British Isles were less numerous and for the most part had very little money.

The Government was faced with a dilemma. It tried to stop the flow of settlers from the United States by denying land grants to all those who had not sworn allegiance, and the local magistrates were instructed not to administer the oath to Americans. The Government tried the positive approach of bringing in Scottish settlers, as for example the Scottish settlement around Perth; these were ostensibly for the protection of the Rideau Canal route to Kingston. But settlement schemes proved slow, cumbersome and expensive; and when outstanding Loyalists such as Colonel Nichol, member for Norfolk, hotly opposed the exclusion of American settlers and some magistrates even refused to withhold the oath of allegiance, some answer had to be found.

The clergy reserves were also a thorny question. Under the terms of the Constitutional Act, 1791, land to the value of one-seventh of that granted in each township was to be set aside "for the Support and Maintenance of a Protestant clergy." Other clauses in the Act made it clear that it was the Anglican clergy that was meant. It never occurred to those who in 1791 made what they thought were wise provisions, how an influx of other Protestant denominations would feel about these reserves. But they were also of great concern to many others, in fact to nearly all rural settlers. These pioneers were in dire need of better roads, but they were often bedevilled, blocked and delayed by large sections of undeveloped Crown and clergy reserves, and by tracts owned by speculators and absentee owners. How bad this problem was can be gauged from figures available for 1824. At that time eight million acres had been granted to individuals, but only about three million of these were occupied, and of that a mere half a million were cultivated. This left five million or so acres for speculation.

The clergy reserves became a very hot issue. On one side was the militant and intransigent Dr. Strachan, who was on the Executive Council and was the Governor's chief adviser in these matters. On the other was the equally militant and vocal Egerton Ryerson, campaigning for the Methodists and therefore the champion of the disestablished religious groups. Dr. Strachan's wish to put higher education also under the wing of the Established Church added fuel to the fire.

This then was the political background and these were the issues which William knew he would encounter on entering politics. Contrary to general opinion and to the opinions of Governors Gore and Maitland, which in some of their despatches they conveyed to England, William Warren was no trouble raiser. But when he saw abuses, and measures for improvement were blocked, he had the courage to get up and say so. To the Governor and Council, such criticism was a sin to be punished wherever possible.

William's confidence in the result of the election was justified. He wrote to St. George on August 2, 1820: "I will close by telling you I have been returned as Member of Provincial Parliament for the county of York & Simcoe – My election has given great public satisfaction to the independent part of the community & mortification to others – the populace did me the honour of a chairing."

* *

12

DR. BALDWIN, THE REFORMER

But if 1820 was a year of success, it was also a year of sorrow and loss. In June William wrote to St. George:

> But now my dear friend I have to tell of the death of our beloved little Henry – the amiable boy died the 12 May at New York with his Uncle. – they grieve after him as if he had been their own child, his manly understanding, his sweet disposition, his amiable manner & a rigid regard to truth endeared him closely to Mr. & Mrs. Morgan. It is a sad shock to his poor Mother & myself. We are reconciled because such has been the will of God – he was just 13 years of age. Death affects Robert much, it was only last night that I observed him relax into a smile.

In the same letter William thanks St. George for "the wine and Portrait"* and continues, "let me congratulate you on hav-

* The wine was the product of St. George's own estate at Montpellier and the portrait of him is now in the possession of R. E. Y. Baldwin of Niagara Falls.

ing a son and Heir." This was Henri Charles Joseph St. George, who later was to come out to Canada.

The next year Quetton St. George died suddenly at the age of fifty. He was greatly mourned by William and his family and by the many friends this tall, enterprising and able Frenchman still retained in Upper Canada. So extensive and complicated were his holdings that in order to co-ordinate his affairs in France and in Upper Canada, and to administer the estate, William as his agent and executor was given special authority by the Upper Canada Legislature, which passed, on March 25, 1828, "An Act for enabling William Warren Baldwin Esq. to carry into effect the Will of the late Laurent Quetton St. George and for other purposes relating to the real and personal estates which were of the said Laurent Quetton St. George."

In 1820, when Robert started in his father's office at the age of sixteen, he would have been the youngest clerk there. The others were James Small, who was called to the bar in 1821; Simon Washburn, who married Margaret FitzGibbon that year; and Robert's cousin, young Daniel Sullivan, a clever but delicate lad who died in 1821. The following year the family sustained another loss when Barbara's husband also died. Since his arrival in York he had joined a Mr. Oates, also from Ireland, who ran a successful chandling business with Thomas Stotesbury.

Miss Elizabeth Russell also died in 1822 in her sixty-eighth year, leaving her considerable property to her nearest relatives, Phoebe Baldwin and her sister, Maria Willcocks. Her death left a gap in the lives of both William and Phoebe, for she had been part of the York scene since their arrival. She had been greatly loved, and would have been "Aunt" to Robert and his brothers. Perhaps those who would have missed her most were William's sisters, who had spent so much time with her at Russell Abbey. William and Phoebe's financial state improved very considerably as a result of Miss Russell's bequest, but it was not responsible for Spadina which had been built with William's hard-earned money on the land left him by William Willcocks.

For Robert and his brothers there would have been no lack of congenial companionship, both young and old, at Spadina, which was a meeting-place for cousins and friends. William had made a path through the woods to the creek at the bottom of the ravine for Maria Willcocks, who, since her stay at Millbrook, was fond of poultry; "and to gratify her," as the report runs in Robertson's *Landmarks of Toronto,* "Dr. Baldwin had this path cut through the woods . . . and every day in pleasant weather Miss Willcocks would drive her ducks and geese down to the stream." Later this goose walk was "dignified by the name of Glen Walk" and half-way down it the Doctor built "a little cottage of logs, heavily thatched" where those who come to admire "one of the most charming bits of natural scenery about Toronto" might pause to rest and to sign the book kept in the cottage; "visitors of poetic inclination were invited to write verses in it" and Augustus Baldwin did so on behalf of the geese:

Must we tamely submit, must we give up our rights
Without trying to break up this faction?
Can't we threaten a flight, turn rebels outright,
Or consult Dr. B. 'bout an action?

Robert, who enjoyed versifying, answered for them:

Come all you brave messmates and list to my song
While wonder and joy you are so rapt in
I will tell you good news
Which will pleasure infuse
We have got for our ally the Captain.*

Among the names in the little book are those of Baldwin and Sullivan relatives from as far away as New York, as well as that of Colonel George Wells, a friend and neighbour, and of Stephen Gwynn, an old servant and a favourite of the family, who wrote a "metrical account" of the wreck of the American ship *Patriot* in 1806 of which he was a survivor.

Although William had been elected to the Assembly in 1820, the first session of the eighth Parliament of Upper Canada, in which he was to sit did not begin until January 31, 1821, so he continued to appear in court and on October 26 of that year his brother John described to St. George another encounter between William and Dr. Strachan:

In the suit between Mr. Small and the Attorney General

* This verse is taken from a notebook in the possession of the authors; the book kept in the cottage still survives, in the possession of R. E. Y. Baldwin.

> [John Beverley Robinson] Dr. Strachan swore such and such was the case in favour of Mr. Robinson, and next came Dr. Baldwin who swore almost directly contrary to the parson Strachan – the jury retired and you may suppose how much it flattered me to find them all in favour of Dr. B's evidence and almost set the parson at defiance. So brought in a verdict in favour of Mr. Small with £300 damages against the Attorney General. The latter having dismissed one of his sons without cause.

Dr. Baldwin took his seat in the Assembly as one of the two members for the large riding of York Simcoe; the other member was Peter Robinson. The opening day of this first session was taken up with administering the oath to the thirty-seven members and choosing a Speaker. William proposed, and Mr. Hagerman seconded, Allan MacLean, member for Frontenac, but this was defeated and Livius P. Sherwood (Leeds) was chosen instead. But during the session William either sponsored or took a prominent part in a number of worthwhile pieces of legislation and served on or headed committees.

On February 5, William moved that a committee be formed to take into consideration the internal resources of the province in agriculture and exports and the practicability and means of enlarging the same. This was carried and a committee formed. On February 7 he proposed a Bill, seconded by Mr. Baby, for the more effectual improvement of the highways and roads throughout the province.

After the second readings of the Physic and Surgery Bill on February 12, the House resolved itself into a committee; Dr. Baldwin was chosen as chairman and, after making his report, obtained leave to sit again the following Wednesday.

The Legislative Council showed very little inclination to be co-operative or to implement these items of useful legislation. So on February 15 William introduced an Independence Bill to secure the independence of the Commons House of Assembly. After receiving third reading on February 17, which was passed by a majority of fourteen, William and Mr. Nichol were appointed a committee to take the Independence Bill to the Legislative Council. It obviously came back with a number of amendments for on March 8 Mr. Nichol moved that William and Mr. Kerr be a select committee to carry the resolution of the House requesting a conference on the amendments of the Legislative Council to the Bill, "An Act for Better Securing of the Independence of the Commons House of Assembly."

On March 13 Mr. Nichol decided on another course of action; since the Assembly voted the money for carrying on the Government, they would have an accounting. So he moved the appointment of a committee, which included William, to examine into and state the annual income and expenditure of the province from January 1793 to December 1820. Its terms of reference were: "To investigate and enquire into the emoluments annexed to the several offices of the Provincial Government all paid from the Provincial funds. The committee shall have power to send for persons and papers."

Behind this move was the fact that two or three years previously the Assembly had been asked to contribute support to the civil government. From the accounts it became apparent that back in 1816-17 some of this money had been used for pensions paid to certain retired officials without the approval or knowledge of the Assembly. When these grievances were addressed to the Prince Regent the Assembly was immediately prorogued without voting supply, the Governor and Council having other funds on which they could depend.

With regard to the control of public money, under the Constitutional Act of 1791 funds such as the revenues from Crown Lands and, after 1826, the sales and leases through the Canada Company, were at the disposal of the Executive Council, and out of reach of the Assembly. This meant that in a pinch the Executive and Legislative Councils could manage, even if the Assembly decided to withhold supply. This would of course completely short-circuit the fundamental power of the purse enjoyed by the Commons under the British Constitution. It was obvious that some remedy must be found if the majority of the people were to have a rightful voice in the government of Upper Canada. William, with his legal mind, was probing for such a remedy.

But now in 1822 public attention was dramatically switched when it appeared the province was headed towards bankruptcy, and that the British Government, without consulting either Upper or Lower Canada, was contemplating a union of the two provinces.

With this proposed union the British Government believed it had found a brilliant solution to a number of the problems. By this step it hoped to balance the so-called republican element in Upper Canada against the ultraconservative French majority in Lower Canada, and at the same time to rescue the English minority there and let them combine with the Loyalist group in Upper Canada. When the news leaked out, the union was strongly attacked by the majorities in both provinces, and by the Opposition in Great Britain.

Among those who vigorously opposed this union was William Warren Baldwin. A copy of the petition which he drafted, called "The Freeholders of York" and dated October 1822, is among his papers. It was forwarded to the Governor, Sir Peregrine Maitland, and in it was this resolution, which might be called the first step in the birth of a concept:

> Resolved that the projected union of the two Provinces and the newly modelled enactments proposed and probably now passed for regulating the trade and revenus of the Canadas as reported . . . contain innovations not only against the letter of the Statute but against our birthrights as British Subjects, innovations alarming and distasteful to us in the highest degree . . . among these most painfully obvious are the transformation of our House of Assembly . . . and all innovations enlarging the means of influence in the Executive and greatly minishing the defence of the People's liberties.

This significant resolution recalls vividly the editorial on the front page of the *Volunteer Journal* of December 1783, published (and possibly written) by William's father, Robert Baldwin, and addressed "To the People of Ireland," which included this statement: "The first thing to be considered is to settle the form of representation on such a footing as to preclude for ever from the executive power, all means of procuring a corrupt majority in the House of Commons." In Canada this corruption of power was centered in the Executive (the Governor and Council) which in its turn was able to short-circuit the wishes of the people.

If, therefore, those in Canada who favoured reform wished to accomplish anything, they would have to strive after three objectives: to weld those of similar views into one united group or party, to get a leader into the Assembly, and to put forward a platform that these reformers could support.

The opportunity came in 1821-22 when the alien question again came to a head with the election and expulsion from the Assembly of Barnabas Bidwell, an American immigrant of some ability. On January 2, 1822 the Assembly voted that certain allegations against Bidwell, even if true, were not legal disqualifications; yet two days later he was expelled by a vote of one on the grounds that he was an American and had sat in the legislature of the United States. The Canadian electors then put forward his son, Marshall Spring Bidwell, who had been born in the United States but had come to Upper Canada with his father in 1798. In Upper Canada he had studied law and had been admitted to the Law Society after taking the oath. However, on the grounds that he too was an alien, the returning officer refused to recognize his nomination in the election. When this was brought to the notice of the Assembly, it reversed the decision and censured the returning officer.

Finally, Marshall Spring Bidwell was elected and in subsequent Parliaments served twice with distinction as Speaker and led the Reform Party in the Assembly. It soon became clear that the other Reform leaders were Dr. Baldwin, his son Robert, and a Dr. John Rolph who referred to the four of them as "the Cabinet." Now, in 1824, for the first time the Reformers had a definite majority, although the Doctor was not elected,* and were led by Bidwell. They drew popular support from all over the province on such grievances as roads, the granting of land, the clergy reserves, education, and the control of the revenue. And they were determined to break the stranglehold of the Family Compact.

* Some authorities state that he sat in the ninth Parliament, but the *Journals* of the Assembly do not bear this out.

* *

13

W. W. BALDWIN & SON

In 1823 the nephew who had come out from Ireland with his parents in 1819 replaced his late brother Daniel in William's Law office. The chandling business had not suited Robert Baldwin Sullivan, who was witty and extremely clever; so, having passed the necessary examinations, he became articled to William's firm for five years. During this time a warm friendship grew up between the two Roberts, as we can see from this letter from R.B.S. written in August 1825: "Methinks I see you put on one of your grave looks with a half smile behind it . . . Methinks I hear your pronounce emphatically, 'What stuff to torment a professional gentleman with on circuit.' " He goes on to point out that it was Robert's own fault for not writing, "why did you not write to me instead of leaving me as melancholy as a lonesome schoolboy in the Holidays?"

Robert Baldwin by this time was over twenty and had fallen deeply in love, although a year or two previously he had written to his brother William Augustus: "Mr. Morgan seems apprehensive that I spend my time signing love notes to some black-eyed Susan. Pray tell him therefore that neither black nor blue eyes have any effect on me." Now the object of his affection was his first cousin, the young sister of R.B.S., Augusta Elizabeth Sullivan. This romance had started before 1825 because at that time, if they were not already engaged, there was certainly a strong understanding between them. Unfortunately we have only one letter from Robert to Augusta Elizabeth and none from Elizabeth to Robert of the many that we know passed between them. But the one we have is of considerable interest. For one thing it was written from Russell Abbey, so for a time at least the Baldwins must have been living there after Miss Russell's death; for another it was written at four in the morning, which shows that Robert's habit of writing at such unusual hours was one he acquired as a young man. Here is an extract from his letter to Augusta Elizabeth, who was then seventeen years old.

Russell Abbey.
27th June 1825
4 o'clock A.M.

My dear Elisa

Your Mother read your letter to me, "Robert Baldwin is so ceremonious that you suppose he wishes you to be so to him, therefore you did not write to him by the same opportunity." Had not my Elisa sufficient confidence in her Robert to believe that there must have been some reason for her not hearing from him . . . but was it absolutely necessary to account for it by attributing it to *ceremony?* To your Mother it must have appeared as if I had been unkind to you – if I have my dearest Elisa, it was inadvertently. . . . If I have in any other instance *appeared* less kind, less affectionate than heretofore do, my dear girl, point it out to me and I am sure I will be able to explain it perfectly to your satisfaction. For be assured every day increases my affection. Every account which we hear either of you or from you makes me more proud of the *choice* of my heart. . . . When you write do tell me always how your health is, particularly your cough, – how often you cough in the course of the day if at all. You do not know how anxious it makes me – by being particularly careful for a few years at this period of your life it will render it less necessary hereafter, but if you neglect yourself now your constitution may acquire a habit which will make you be obliged to be careful all your life – therefore, for your *own,* for *my* sake do take care of yourself. Give my love to Aunt Anne and make interest with her for me. I know you have influence for she says of you "to me she is a dear and amiable friend" – be ever so for she has been so to me.

Adieu, and never distrust,
your Robert.

In this same year, Robert came of age and was called to the bar. His father took him into the firm as a partner, changing the name to W. W. Baldwin & Son. As a young lawyer he became well liked and respected, taking part with his father in the legal and social life of York. His old habit of being a poor correspondent is shown in the letter from his brother William Augustus, written in August 1826: "I would advise you to give Eliza and myself satisfactory reasons for not writing to us. Eliza says that I must write and tell you how angry she is with you. I am afraid to see her unless I have a letter, I suppose we shall not hear from you now, as you will soon be returning."

Eliza could not have remained angry very long for the account of her wedding the following spring, on the anniversary of Robert's parents' marriage, is entered in the family Bible in her husband's own hand:

> On Thursday the thirty-first day of May in the year of Our Lord one thousand eight hundred and twenty-seven, at the Protestant Episcopal Church of St. James in the Town of York in Upper Canada, by the Reverend Thomas Phillips D.D., was married Robert Baldwin, eldest son of William Warren Baldwin of Spadina in the County of York, to Augusta Elizabeth Sullivan, second daughter of Daniel Sullivan formerly of Bandon in the County of Cork in Ireland and late of the said Town of York, deceased; in the presence of James Hunter Samson of Belleville in the County of Hastings, groomsman, and Anna Maria Baldwin and Anne Burns of Niagara in the County of Lincoln, bridesmaids.

Among those who attended the wedding were: "William Warren Baldwin of Spadina, William Augustus Baldwin, Quetton Saint George Baldwin, Augustus Baldwin Sullivan, Thomas Gibbs Ridout, Anna Maria Louisa Ridout, Barbara Sullivan,

Augustus Warren Baldwin, John Spread Baldwin, Anne Baldwin [Mrs. John Spread], Mary Breakenridge, the Honourable Thomas Ridout, and Laurence Heyden."

This was to be a wonderfully happy, but tragically short, marriage. Apparently Robert and Eliza joined the Doctor's large household and lived at Spadina until it burned down in 1835. William then built a spacious town house at the corner of Bay and Front Streets and replaced the house at Spadina with a small country house.

The eleven years from 1824 to 1835, which took the Doctor from forty-nine to sixty, were his most active in planning and building. During the War of 1812 some houses were destroyed and little new construction took place for some years; now, with increased prosperity and a growing population, York was badly in need of a new jail and court-house. William, being a lawyer and a district court judge, was understandably interested. So it is not surprising to find that when the jail and court-house were erected in 1824, the plans had been drawn up by William Warren Baldwin and John Ewart, a leading contractor in York. Again quoting from Professor Arthur in *Toronto, No Mean City*: "Sufficient credit has not been given to the planner who so arranged these buildings between Toronto and Church Streets that they formed a public space which for many years was called Court House Square. It was one of the earliest attempts, in Toronto, at civic design."

In 1826 William entered the competition for the proposed new provincial Parliament Buildings; his plans are in the Metropolitan Toronto Central Library. Although his design was not successful, his efforts in building from 1829 to 1832, following three busy years in politics, were most successful. During one of his terms as secretary-treasurer of the Law Society of Upper Canada he again combined with John Ewart and, possibly with some advice from J. G. Chewitt, they drew up the plans and erected the original building, now the east wing, of Osgoode Hall. This was and still is a fine building architecturally, from both the exterior and interior points of view. James Lesslie, a contemporary, recorded in his diary: "Feb. 10, 1832. Conducted by R. [Rolph] through all the Rooms of Osgoode Hall and admired the workmanship much – the Convocation Room particularly elegant."

In 1830 the Bank of Upper Canada built on the north-east corner of Duke and George Streets, and Dr. Baldwin is credited with having a hand in designing this building, which still stands. This is possible, though by no means certain, for he and Robert were among the original directors of the bank.

Another architectural venture of the Doctor's was a housing scheme on land he had acquired in Port Hope. Here the ground plan shows his definite ideas on town and municipal planning. In some of the legal documents dealing with these houses he stipulates not only the width of the road, but also the building line which was to be well back from the road, thus lending a gracious and dignified air to the project. These were points on which Peter Russell had been most insistent some years earlier, and his influence can be clearly seen here. A number of the compact little houses still stand on the site; at the junction of Church and Baldwin Streets stands the church, which now, with its steeple dismantled, has been converted into a twin dwelling.

In 1831 William collaborated with J. G. Chewitt, and the resulting building was the second market at York. It occupied the site of the present St. Lawrence Market and was a not unpleasant functional structure built around a large courtyard for the market and farm waggons. A gate-house surmounted the main entrance, while there were arched entrances on the other three sides. The large upper room over the gate-house was used by the City Council for their meetings from 1833 to 1844. So this was in a sense the birthplace of the City of Toronto.

In the Michaelmas term of 1828 William's nephew, Robert Baldwin Sullivan, was called to the bar, having completed his apprenticeship in the office of W. W. Baldwin & Son. He decided to join Dr. John Rolph in his law practice at Vittoria, south of Brantford. Dr. Rolph was an Englishman whose career paralleled in some respects that of Dr. Baldwin, for he too practised both the profession of law and that of medicine. Rolph was born in Gloucestershire in 1793 and first came to Canada in 1812. Soon after, he returned to England and trained as a doctor and as a lawyer; according to Henry Scadding, "On arriving [back] in Canada he transferred himself to the Bar." This was in 1821. He was eighteen years younger than William, so it was with Robert that he worked occasionally, as when they conducted the defence of Francis Collins, editor of the *Canadian Freeman*.

In February 1828 Collins was brought up for libelling the Administration in his paper. The trial was conducted before Judge Willis but ended in uproar when Collins made countercharges against Attorney-General Robinson, accusing him of failure in his duty by not having preferred charges against H. J. Boulton and J. E. Small; they had been seconds in the duel in which Samuel P. Jarvis had killed John Ridout in 1817. On pressure by Judge Willis, both Boulton and Small were committed for trial, with Robert Baldwin as prosecutor; but as Jarvis had been acquitted in 1817 it was logical that both Small and Boulton would now also be cleared.

Then in July 1828, Judge Willis, puisne judge of the Court of King's Bench, was summarily dismissed by Sir Peregrine Maitland. The Governor was within his rights but this dismissal was reminiscent of the treatment of Judge Thorpe in 1807 and the popular outcry which followed gave Dr. Baldwin and the other Reformers the opportunity of expressing their grievances to the Imperial Parliament and of suggesting remedies. This was done by means of a formidable petition drafted by William Warren. It contained in the eighth clause of grievances and the sixth clause of suggested remedies, William's earliest public formulation of the principle of responsible government.

But the matter did not rest here and the Administration, smarting under the stings of its opponents, determined to go after Mr. Collins again. "On Saturday last, the Editor of the *Canadian Freeman* was put on his trial for a libel upon the Administration of justice, a libel against Judge Hagerman, a libel against the Attorney General, and a libel against the Solicitor General," reported the *Canadian Freeman* on October 30.

The case was tried by Judge Hagerman, and after deliberating five hours the jury found Collins guilty. "Messrs. Rolph and Baldwin were Counsel for the defendant, and managed his cause with great ability." This case had obvious political overtones; it enhanced Robert's reputation as a young liberal-minded lawyer, but it did not endear him to the Administration.

Law and politics were interwoven in York, as we have seen, as far back as the time of Weekes and Thorpe; and the expulsion of Willis and Robert's defence of Collins only confirm this. It was to be expected that Robert would follow his father into politics for, as he said, he had "imbibed" reform principles from him and they worked together in complete accord for the political reform which was summed up for them in the phrase "responsible government." Indeed it was during these ten years, 1828 to 1838, that the Doctor transferred the torch of responsible government to his son, who was to carry it with even greater zeal and determination.

Now in 1828 Robert decided to seek election in the County of York riding. There were four candidates for the two seats in this riding, one of whom was William Lyon Mackenzie. Although Mackenzie and Robert were both in opposition to the Administration, Mackenzie was extremely hostile to the Baldwins for no apparent reason, and certainly none as far as Robert was concerned, as Mackenzie himself admitted. The following extract from Collins' *Canadian Freeman* of July 17, 1828 shows this very clearly:

> We proposed Mr. Baldwin to the nominating committee in which we had a voice. "No," said Mackenzie, "his father is a candidate for the country – so am I, and I will oppose the whole Baldwin family – they are a poor set." "Do you know anything about young Mr Baldwin?" said we. – "No," said M'Kenzie, "I know nothing about him – but I will oppose him because I do not like the family."

Robert, who undoubtedly had a lot to learn in the art of campaigning, was "low man on the totem pole" and Mackenzie and Jesse Ketchum were elected.

William, on the other hand, who ran in the election of 1828 as a candidate for Norfolk County, was elected. Evidently he threw himself into the campaign with great vigour, so much so that, according to his opponents, "Baldwin has become a regular stump orator going about from place to place – the man is certainly mad and will soon require shaving and blistering."

R. B. Sullivan, who was working with Rolph in Vittoria, helped his Uncle William in this election. He was extremely critical of Robert's campaigning, as shown in a letter to him that is unfortunately undated, but from internal evidence appears to have been written in 1828:

> The pleasure which our victories have afforded me was very little damped by hearing of your failure in York, for I cannot call it a disappointment. You were entirely too late for your County – and your reserved manner almost the opposite to your favourite Mr. Foxe's way with the people caused you to be comparatively little acquainted with them personally . . . That familiar acquaintance which the people of this Country so familiarly require – I ought not to lecture you on this head again – as I remember your once taking my advice on it – How do you do Mr. Simpson! Poor Simpson was very much delighted with your condescension that day – Your enquiries after his family and his health – for the Blackguard was cheating you out of six dollars all the time! Now I have no doubt of your having public favour and confidence at your command – but it requires time with you, as it will be from real value and worth you will be prized.

Robert's decision to contest the election had been taken during his defence of Collins, and R.B.S. continues:

> I dare say Collins – & my brother Henry & some other of my brethren of the sod [Irishmen] had a good deal of influence in persuading you to set up. But the fact is they know nothing about the people – Irishmen always believe whatever they will – they are perhaps the most sanguine people in the world. And although I must say that they display ten times the political knowledge and political consistency of your Countrymen – Yet I never would ask or take their opinions as to the state of the Public pulse in Canada –

He goes on to paint an interesting picture of William's election and to comment on his defeat in 1824. "You remember – how little your father's political character availed him – at the former election – contemptible as the persons were by whom he was opposed –" Then, as to the 1828 election in Norfolk:

> A friend is really better in this part of the Country than the best Political character . . . I believe we never should have succeeded but for the mistaken zeal of McCalls Brother who I understand exclaimed to a party of your voters from Towns-

> end "Here are the radicals "here come the Democrats – the men who had with difficulty been persuaded to leave their harvest took offence came and voted – and instead of returning home rode day & night and set others riding until there was not a man in the two townships that did not feel his honour concerned in getting your father in. Accordingly we got on gallantly towards the end of the election – it was a great enjoyment to me you may be sure – after hearing the hurrah! in his [Mr. Walsh's, the opposing candidate] favour in Mon. Tues. Wed. to see his countenance change on Thursday as we began to gain possession of the grounds – the wagons from the South and west began to come in empty much to the joy of the unfortunate horses – while those from the North generally contained three or four voters – and as many friends – who shouted louder because it was their only way of expressing their approbation – I took advantage of the change in the Poll – & when we were gaining issued tickets thus Baldwin – or Baldwin for ever . . . Hurrah for Baldwin upon which the people shouted – The Poll was seven times even in one day – so that this excitement kept up very strong all the time.

In 1829 R. B. Sullivan was asked to act as counsel for Dr. Thomas Morrison before the Legislature. Again the case had political overtones and Sullivan acquitted himself so well that his friends insisted that he must leave Vittoria and return to York. So Robert acquired his brother-in-law as a partner and the firm became Baldwin and Sullivan. The Doctor continued to have his Surrogate Court office nearby.

Undeterred by his failure in 1828, Robert decided to try again in 1829 and contested the seat for the town of York left vacant by the elevation of John Beverley Robinson to the Chief Justiceship. This time Robert was successful and beat Mr. Small, only to have the election declared void as the writ had been issued by the Governor and not by the Speaker of the Assembly.

Finally, in November 1829, Robert made a third attempt to enter the Assembly, running this time against Sheriff Jarvis for the Town of York riding. The *Journal* of the Upper Canada Provincial Assembly for the second session of the tenth Parliament, page 33, contains these entries:

Saturday January 30th 1830

The Speaker also stated that he had, this morning, been informed by the Clerk of the Crown in Chancery that he had received a return Writ of Election for the Town of York and that Robert Baldwin Esqr had been duly elected to represent the said Town.

The Speaker also mentioned that Mr. Baldwin had taken the oath required by law in his presence this morning.

And on the same page:

Legislative Council Chamber January 29th 1830

Mr. Baldwin, the member representing the Town of York, was introduced by Dr. Baldwin and Mr. Ketchum and conducted to his seat.

But even now Robert's triumph was to be short lived. On June 26, 1830 George IV died, Parliament was dissolved, and another election was called.

* *

14

BOND HEAD AND THE BALDWINS

In the election which followed the death of George IV in 1830, both Dr. Baldwin and his son Robert lost their seats. This was a bitter pill for both; they felt they had been defeated by their friends, since the Reformers were again in the majority in the Assembly, with Marshall Spring Bidwell as Speaker. Both father and son now retired from politics.

But if William was inactive in politics he was far from inactive in other fields. His law practice and his duties as Master in Chancery and in the Surrogate Court kept him very busy. Another interest was the foundation of the Mechanics' Institute in 1830; here it was as an architect that the Doctor became involved. Building at this time in Upper Canada was almost entirely in the classical tradition; and no matter by whom the plans were drawn, or who supervised construction, the actual work of building was done by craftsmen who were guided in cutting mouldings, framing windows, and designing doors by a few cherished "source-books" which were the craftsmen's bibles.

So one very important function of a Mechanics' Institute, of vital interest to William, was to see that these craftsmen were made aware of any change in basic design by new and up-to-date source books. Also there were lectures and talks in what amounted to an early attempt at adult education. One such illustrated lecture was given by John Fenton on the manufacture of steel. The institute attracted a number of others besides craftsmen.

According to Dr. Scadding, the first meeting of the York Mechanics' Institute was held on the second floor (reached by an outside staircase) of the Masonic Hall, which was on King Street opposite the court-house and "situated off Market Lane." The meeting was organized, as Scadding recalls, under the auspices of Moses Fish, a builder, in 1830. A footnote in *The Town of York, 1815-1834,* edited by Edith G. Firth, gives the date of this founding meeting as December 24, 1830, and states that Joseph Dunn was chosen patron and John Ewart elected president. However, William Canniff, in *The Medical Profession in Upper Canada,* gives Dr. Burnside as the promoter of the Institute and mentions that Dr. William Warren Baldwin was its president in 1831.

William was also interested in encouraging the local cabinetmakers. Perhaps he inherited this appreciation of well-made furniture from his uncle John Baldwin in Cork, who used to make some of his own furniture and build sailboats for his own enjoyment. In regard to Canadian furniture, among the family possessions are a fine walnut sideboard and six Trafalgar-backed dining-room chairs, handed down from father to son, and believed to be some of the first pieces of furniture made at York for the Doctor (the dining-room table was destroyed by fire). There is also a walnut secretary which was made for Robert's use at Spadina, as well as his travelling desk, with his name engraved on the brass lock and with some of his cards as Attorney-General and a pair of rhinestone buckles for his court shoes still therein.

In the summer of 1832 there was an outbreak of cholera at York of epidemic proportions. This involved the Doctor in arduous duties, for in June he had been appointed president of the Board of Health which had been formed earlier that year. This memorandum to his Excellency the Governor, dated July 16, 1832, is self-explanatory:

> I regret exceedingly that there should have happened any interruption to the daily communication to his Excellency

of the Report of the Board of Health. This is now the 8th day since I have been confined, most of the time to my bed [and then the following crossed through] with either the drain of cholera or something very like it.

W. W. Baldwin, Pres of Board

William was also concerned with the York Dispensary, which opened on August 22 of that year and was administered by Drs. Baldwin, Tims and Morrison. In April of 1833, after it had given free medicine and clinical care to some 746 patients and spent over £118, its funds were exhausted; but, from what Francis Hincks said in his obituary of William, it would seem that the Doctor continued this clinic or one like it for some years at his own expense.

Francis Hincks was the brilliant young Irishman who had come with his bride to live next door to the Baldwin office on Yonge Street in 1832. Like the Baldwins, and most Irishmen, he took an intense interest in politics. Hincks had been well educated, was very intelligent and had gone into commerce at an early age. At first he carried on an import-export business in York, but soon found that he had a great flair for banking and finance. He also found that he was in entire agreement with William and Robert in their political views.

The first step in their collaboration came with the founding of a new bank. William had always realized what a tower of strength William Allan's banking and financial experience had been to the Family Compact. So, when the time was ripe to open a bank in the interests of the Reform Party in 1835, Francis Hincks, who had been a director of the Farmers' Joint Stock Banking Company, was obviously the man to call on and he became first cashier, then secretary, then manager of the People's Bank; William was one of the directors.

The Baldwins continued to visit their farm at Millbrook where John Large, the Irishman from Cork who had arrived before the war, lived with his family and operated the mill for William. In the *Conservation Report* of the Department of Planning and Development published in 1956, the ownership of the mill on Lot 14, Concession 3, Markham Township, is traced and a note states that Dr. William Warren Baldwin, a leading Reformer, had inherited this property from his father-in-law William Willcocks, who bought it from Francis Schmedt in 1804. Captain John Large is given as the occupant in 1817 and is shown as living there in 1837.

The letters which passed between the Doctor and John Large from 1834 to 1837 give the same sort of insight into William's family affairs and career as did his correspondence with Quetton St. George. In September 1834 he commented shrewdly about being out of Parliament: "So I find that withdrawing oneself from politics withdraws us from the notice and recollection of the world – the good people of Markham seem to forget the name of Willcocks and Baldwin – I never see any of them."

In the same letter he tells of the forthcoming wedding of his son William Augustus, ancestor of Lawrence Baldwin of Masquoteh:* "Dear William is to be married to Miss Isabella Buchanan on the 25th inst – then sets off for Philadelphia on October 1 is to sail for London and from thence to Dublin and Belfast."

Eliza, Robert's wife, was in very poor health, but by September of the following year she had recovered somewhat: "We are all, thanks be to God in good health children and all. Eliza of course yet delicate, but greatly improved – Mrs Baldwin [his wife Phoebe] is in Belleville – I think I told you she went down with Mrs Murney. She writes back to say she arrived there quite well and safe and all astonished and happy to see her there – I am sure they would be – for she has the happy art of spreading happiness around her wherever she is." What a nice tribute from a husband of sixty! Then in the same letter, "The big house [the one William was building on the corner of Bay and Front Street] is almost finished and the carpenter gone – they promise to leave us this Wednesday. I am just setting off to see what is doing at Spadina."

Although William and Robert Baldwin had both failed to gain seats in the Assembly dominated by the Reformers, they remained the arch-exponents of responsible government as the answer to Canadian political problems. The mechanics of colonial government hinged on this vital question of responsibility. If the Executive Council was to be responsible to the

* Indian name of the large house on Avenue Road, near Heath Street, in Toronto where a hitching-ring remained embedded in an ancient tree on the front lawn until house and tree were razed to make room for an apartment building.

Governor, then the Council was a mere cipher; if it was to be responsible to the majority in the Assembly, then the Executive Council would be a Cabinet, its leader the Prime Minister, and the people of Canada would have a real voice in their own affairs. As William and Robert pointed out, this momentous step required no changes in the Constitution. To the achievement of this great principle both men dedicated their lives.

Even in the early eighteen-thirties, the words "responsible government," as Professor A.R.M. Lower points out in *Colony to Nation,* "had not become popular currency and there were possibly only two men in the province who really understood what they involved, Dr. William Baldwin and his more famous son, Robert." This is not surprising when it is recalled that this idea of parliamentary reform and this concept of responsibility were familiar to, indeed traditional in, this family since the days when the Baldwins published the *Volunteer Journal* in Cork and had reported so fully the debate in the British House of Commons of March 7, 1783, in which one of the earliest and clearest definitions of responsible government was given: "Why did it [the Crown] not keep a Minister in office, in spite of the voice of Parliament? It was impossible for such influence to interfere, for it did not exist; while he enjoyed the confidence of Parliament he continued in office; when he lost that confidence, he was obliged to cease to be a Minister; the breath of Parliament made him, the breath of Parliament unmade him . . ."

Although it was not until the British Parliament passed the Reform Bill of 1832 that final constitutional acceptance of the principle of responsible government became concrete, there were a number of instances before that date when ministers of the Crown acted on it. Why had it not become established before? For one thing, Britain has had no written constitution and these were, and are, matters of precedent; for another, the Tory Party in Britain dominated politics from 1783 to 1831, except for a brief period 1806 and 1807, and thus there were few opportunities to test this concept. Finally, the King still exercised great powers in Parliament and even the skilled parliamentarian William Pitt knew this well.

The document embodying William's, and later Robert's, ideas on this constitutional concept was written by William himself;

it contains his comments and indicates on what occasions and under what circumstances he advanced these ideas. It also shows when and how Robert entered into the deliberations, a point on which there has been much discussion. It is in the form of a memorandum, dated 1841, and is headed "Responsible Government." It is identified by a notation by Lawrence Heyden, Robert's brother-in-law,* and is attached to William's own copy of Charles Buller's booklet entitled *Responsible Government for the Colonies,* which was printed in London in 1840; both these documents are among the Baldwin Papers in the Metropolitan Toronto Central Library.

William's memorandum reviews, in effect, his ideas on the concept of responsible government and how they developed over the period 1822 to 1841. The date 1822 is given with the first item; this is the petition of the people against the union of the two provinces attempted by the Imperial Parliament in Britain. William writes that this item does not deal specifically with the point of responsible government, yet its last sentence plainly shows the dissatisfaction with the persons in the executive office in Canada, and by including it as the first item in this memorandum, specifically entitled "Responsible Government", William clearly shows that he considers it the first step in emphasizing the concept.

The second item is a "Report of the proceedings of a public meeting held at York (now Toronto) on the 15th August 1828, with the petition of the people grounded thereupon to the Imperial Parliament – see, especially the 8th Clause of Grievances and the 6th Clause of remedies." William was the chairman and drafted this petition, in which there were twenty-one resolutions, eleven clauses of grievances and at least seven clauses of suggested remedies. His drawing attention to the two particular clauses emphasizes their succinct statement of the principle involved. In form, the petition is addressed "To the King's most Excellent Majesty" and the grievance described in the eighth clause is "the want of carrying into effect that rational and constitutional control over public functionaries, especially the advisers of your Majesty's Representative, which our fellow subjects in England enjoy in that happy country." The remedy

* Lawrence Heyden came from Ireland in 1820; he married Barbara Sullivan, younger sister of Eliza Baldwin and Robert Baldwin Sullivan.

proposed in the sixth clause is "that a Legislative Act be made in the Provincial Parliament to facilitate the mode in which the present constitutional responsibility of the advisers of the local Government may be carried practically into effect; not only by the removal of these advisers from office when they lose the confidence of the people, but also by impeachment for the heavier offenses chargeable against them."

It is extraordinary that William does not list under the second item his letter to the Duke of Wellington, who had recently become Prime Minister. This letter, dated at "York, 3rd January 1829," accompanied the petition, and its omission from the memorandum is baffling as it contains an even more specific, albeit lengthier, definition of responsible government.

The third item is "Letters addressed to Lord Goderich & the Honle Mr. Stanley." These were written early in 1830 and William attached great importance to them. He goes on to explain that they were never published, but are preserved in his letter book, and he continues, "they contain the development of the nature of the responsibility required and the means of effecting it after the example of the British Constitution." And then he adds this significant sentence: "The suggestion in its distinct shape was made by Robert Baldwin, the present Solicitor General [1841] in a conversation with me on the occasion of penning these letters." Thus we know that it was at this point that Robert took a hand in the framing and development of this great principle. And this seems to prove beyond all reasonable doubt that it was William's concept up to this time.

The struggle for the adoption of Cabinet responsibility to the majority in the Assembly now took a new turn. It became a definite constitutional issue and, as such, a confrontation between the Governor and the exponents of the idea. Primarily these exponents were William and Robert Baldwin, Francis Hincks, and Dr. John Rolph. From this time the Family Compact took less and less part in the confrontation except to back the Governor. Certainly in earlier periods this role of opposition to the Reformers had been reversed, with the Governor in the background.

The roles were also being reversed between William and Robert. Up to this time William had been predominant in these matters. He was still the senior partner but now they were to work in concert for a while with Robert taking over the major political assignments, such as accepting political office. Both were to confront the irascible Governor Francis Bond Head but, twelve days before his arrival in Upper Canada in January 1836, Robert sustained a personal loss that overshadowed the rest of his private life.

This was the death of his wife Eliza, who had borne him four children during the less than nine years of their happy marriage – Phoebe Maria in 1828, William Willcocks in 1830, Augusta Elizabeth (Eliza) in 1831, and Robert in 1834. The account of her death in the family Bible is entered in her husband's own hand:

> On Monday, the eleventh day of January in the year of our Lord one thousand eight hundred and thirty six, at six o'clock in the forenoon, at the family residence in Front Street in the City of Toronto, died my beloved wife Augusta Elizabeth Baldwin . . . of an Attack of water on the brain, in which the general derangement of the system consequent on the extensive hemorrhage Attendant on her last confinement (to me at least most unexpectedly) terminated – During our short married life we were blessed with the most perfect and unbounded mutal confidence and affection – She was all a husbands love could wish her. The loss to her family and friends in general all who knew her can estimate – the loss – the sad-sad loss to me and her poor children none can know but myself – I am left to pursue the remainder of my pilgrimage alone – and in the waste that lies before me I can expect to find joy only in the reflected happiness of our darling children, and in looking forward, in humble hope, to that blessed hour which by Gods permission shall for ever reunite me to my Eliza in the world of Spirits – May the Lord God Almighty look down upon me with mercy, and of his infinite Goodness, vouch-safe unto me wisdom to bring up those dear pledges of my Eliza's affection in the ways of his truth and after the words of his commandments; that both I and they in this life, steadfastly relying upon and looking up to him as the giver of all our blessings and the kindest soother of all our afflictions, may in the life to come meet her whose loss we now deplore, and enjoy with her everlasting Glory and

Felicity – through our only Saviour and Redeemer – Jesus Christ our Lord –

Robert appeared to rally from this blow as far as his public life was concerned and his mother took over the care of his four young children.

Francis Bond Head seems to have been as surprised as everyone else by his appointment to succeed Sir John Colborne but, as the change of governors had been made because of the stir created by the seventh report of the Committee of Grievances, Head came out to Upper Canada as a self-styled "political physician" and he came armed with William Lyon Mackenzie's report.

On arrival he found that it was necessary to add new members to his Executive Council, and to this end he consulted the Chief Justice, Mr. Bidwell the Speaker of the Assembly, and the three existing members of the Executive Council. "After making every inquiry in my power, I became of the opinion that Mr. Robert Baldwin, advocate, a gentleman already recommended to your Lordship by Sir John Colbourne for a seat in the Legislative Council, was the first individual I should select, being highly respected for his moral character, being moderate in his politics, and possessing the esteem and confidence of all parties."

But Robert was reluctant to return to politics, even though this might mean a seat on the Executive Council; and he was certainly unwilling to co-operate with Bond Head unless he was prepared to put into effect Cabinet responsibility as a means towards responsible government. But Bond Head's subsequent actions proved that he was hostile to "the smooth and insidious doctrine." At this time neither Bond Head nor the Baldwins were fully aware of the political intentions of the other. All Bond Head wanted was to add three new moderate men to his council. This struggle between Bond Head, his Executive Council and the Reform majority in the elected Assembly over the question of ministerial responsibility was round one in the struggle for responsible government which was to last for more than ten years.

The Governor's offer of a seat on the Executive Council was considered very seriously by Robert, and he consulted, not only his father from whom he had "imbibed the idea," but also Dr.

Rolph, as a leader of the Reformers. He then refused, explaining to the Governor that he would accept only if the present three members of the Council, in whom he had no confidence, resigned. Only in this way, he argued, could he and a new Council enjoy the support of the Assembly. The Governor refused to consider any such far-reaching suggestion, and he offered the seat in turn to Dr. Baldwin, and then to Dr. Rolph; both refused.

At this point the Baldwins and Rolph went into further consultation, having received word of some concessions by the Governor, and it was decided that as Bond Head was willing to meet them part way and appoint men of their choice, even though he would not dismiss the existing Council, "It would not be performing our duty to His Excellency or to the country were we after his having gone thus far to meet our views – peremptorily to refuse all concession on our part." So, with considerable misgivings, Robert Baldwin, Dr. John Rolph, and J. H. Dunn, the Receiver General, entered the Executive Council in February 1836.

This Council now considered itself as a Cabinet, and so much unanimity had been instilled among its members that on March 4 they acted in concert and wrote to the Governor: "They have been undeservedly subjected to the heaviest reproach throughout the country from a prevalent belief that they have been called upon to fulfil the duty imposed upon them by the constitution as advisers upon public affairs." In other words, they were being blamed by the people for all the acts of the Governor, although "the policy and measures which have led to the present condition seldom passed under the review of the Executive Council." They demanded that the Governor should abide by the constitution and consult them in all matters, although he was not bound to take their advice. This "representation" is the fourth item of William's memorandum.

The Governor was quick to reply that the Council must choose between his confidence and their principles. Baldwin and Dr. Rolph refused to submit to the Governor, but the other four councillors offered to retract. This was too good an opportunity for the Governor, who said he must have a unanimous decision by the Council, and he would not accept the retraction by only four. So the Executive Council resigned.

This stung the Assembly into action and William's fifth item is its address to the Governor asking for an explanation and stating that it has no confidence in the newly appointed Council. At the same time, the Reform leader in the Assembly, Peter Perry, was appointed chairman of a select committee to inquire into the matter.

The battle was joined. Robert Baldwin wrote promptly to Peter Perry to explain to him and to the Assembly exactly what had taken place at his first confrontation with Governor Head:

> I would not [Robert had said] be performing my duty to my Sovereign or the country, if I did not, with his Excellency's permission, explain fully to his Excellency my views of the constitution of the province, and the change necessary in the practical administration of it; particularly as I considered the delay in adopting this change as the great and all absorbing grievance, before which all others, in my mind, sunk into insignificance; and the remedy of which would most effectually lead, and that in a constitutional way, to the redress of every other real grievance, and the finally putting an end to all clamour about imaginary ones; and that these desirable objects would thus be accomplished without in the least entrenching upon the just and necessary prerogatives of the Crown, which I considered, when administered by the Lieutenant-Governor through the medium of a provincial ministry, responsible to the provincial Parliament, to be an essential part of the constitution of the province. [To objections put forward by the Governor, Robert had replied] . . . that as far as regarded the internal affairs of the province, the Lieutenant-Governor was, in point of fact, as far as this province and its parliament were concerned, as completely irresponsible as the King himself, as there certainly neither existed, nor, in my opinion, ought to exist, any legal or constitutional means of calling him to account in this country for any act of his government. That his responsibility was to the King and Parliament of the Empire, and was perfectly proper and necessary for the preservation of the paramount authority of the mother country, and the protection of her interests in matters properly and constitutionally belonging to the exercise of that authority. But that what the constitution required was, that there should be persons within this country itself who could

be made responsible to the provincial parliament here for the administration of the internal affairs of the province. . . . To another objection of his Excellency, that the adoption of my views would deprive the Lieutenant-Governor of all power, and convert him into a cipher, . . . [I answered that] he had always the same constitutional right to accept or reject the advice of any of his executive councillors, and that, as in England, the only alternative for them was to resign, when they and the Lieutenant-Governor differed on any point which they conceived of sufficient importance to call for such a step; in which event the Lieutenant-Governor was perfectly free to call to his council whom he pleased. . . .

His Excellency very candidly declared his entire dissent from such views and opinions; he nevertheless, with the most gracious expression of satisfaction at the very full and candid manner in which I had opened them to him, renewed his solicitation for my acceptance of a seat in the Executive Council, suggesting, as an inducement for such acceptance, the increased facilities which, by my place in the Executive Council, would be afforded towards the more efficiently representing and urging my views; . . . his Excellency at the same time remarking, that he had no objection to the council, each continuing to entertain and urge his individual opinions, as the opinions of one would be neutralised by those of another. . . . After some further consultation upon the subject with Mr. Dunn, his Excellency was finally informed, that Mr. Dunn, Dr. Rolph and myself had, though reluctantly, consented, in compliance with his Excellency's wishes, and as a mere experiment, and one which we feared would fail, to accept seats in his Excellency's Executive Council, without the retirement of the three gentlemen who were already members of it.

That experiment had failed; and now, if the Governor was hoping that in its findings the select committee would support him, he was sadly mistaken. It declared that Dunn, Baldwin, and Rolph had given general satisfaction, and that "The House and the Country were not then aware that the Executive Council had been used as a mere screen for the acts of the Lieutenant-Governor; on the contrary it was generally understood that they were consulted on the affairs of the province . . . Your committee are forced to believe that the appointment of new councillors was a deceitful manoeuvre to gain credit with the country for liberal feelings."

The report of the select committee was adopted by the House, and to add weight to its disapproval of the Governor's action, a motion was introduced withholding supply. This was the traditional parliamentary weapon and, in fact, the only way the House of Assembly could assert its authority.

The Governor was incensed and Glenelg, the Colonial Secretary, cried foul; he considered, he wrote to Bond Head, that the Assembly had no right to use this weapon "to enforce changes in the system of government itself." This opinion is entirely at variance with that in Lord Stanley's letter to Dr. Baldwin of April 24, 1829, which clearly stated: "– and a constitutional mode is open to the people, of addressing for a removal of advisers of the Crown and refusing supplies if necessary to enforce their wishes."

In the meantime Bond Head had an ace up his sleeve and countered the move of the Assembly in withholding supply by refusing his consent to all their money bills. This was a far more serious handicap in those days as the money bills financed such essentials as roads and schools and entailed more than £800,000, whereas the voting of supply totalled some £84,000. After leaving matters to stew for a time, the Governor prorogued the House on April 20, 1836, and dissolved it on May 28, determinded to throw the country into an election on the fallacious grounds that the British connection was in grave danger.

* *

15

MODERATE VS. RADICAL REFORMERS

During the political strife with Bond Head, Robert had had no time to brood; but now, in this period of forced inactivity and frustration of his hopes for responsible government, the great loss of his wife hit him with redoubled force. He decided not to run in the election, and there is little doubt that his father and mother persuaded him to visit England and to leave his children with them. His mother saw in this trip a wonderful opportunity to distract him from his sorrow with new thoughts and new faces, particularly as an extension of his trip had been suggested to include a pilgrimage to Ireland. His father not only looked on the journey from the medical side as being beneficial to his son, but he also hoped that great good might come of it if Robert's visit to England was politically successful, for the plan was for him to see, among others, Lord Glenelg to try to convince him of the precarious situation in Upper Canada.

The beginning of Robert's journey retraced the route taken by his grandfather in 1799 and his brief account of his trip to New York marks the tremendous advances made in transportation during the intervening thirty-seven years:

I left Toronto* for Europe on Saturday, 30 April, 1836, at about 11 p.m. proceeding by steamer to Oswego; thence through Utica, Schenectady and Albany to New York by stage, railroad and steamer. I took my passage for Liverpool on board the Roscoe Packet ship, "Captain Delario" for Liverpool. I had as fellow passengers among others, Mr. and Mrs. Gapper, Mr. and Mrs. Barwick and children and Mr. and Mrs. Caley, all from Toronto or its neighbourhood . . . and a Mr. Jones, an infirm, old gentleman from one of the southern states. This latter occupied the lower berth of the same little state room with myself. We sailed on Monday, 9th May, at 3 p.m. and reached Liverpool, Sunday, 5th June.

The details of his journey to London show the different forms of transport, one of which, the railway between Liverpool and Manchester, was one of the first built in England:

I went with many of my fellow passengers to the Adelphi Hotel and left the next day for Manchester by railroad . . . proceeding on by stage through Conventry to London. Arrived in the city at 7 o'clock a.m. on Wednesday, 8th June. After breakfasting at the Ship Inn, in the neighbourhood of where the coaches put me down I proceeded to the Salopian Coffee House, near Charing Cross [where he remained until June 16] . . . Mr. George Rolph, who wished to have come to Europe in company with me, having missed the Roscoe, had taken his passage in a private merchantman . . .[and] had been inquiring for me but without success when we met by accident in Parliament St. . . . we both shortly after took up our quarters at Mr. Barwell's [No. 4 Trinity Court]. The entrance to this little court is immediately opposite to the statue of King Charles in Charing Cross and one side of the court is formed by the wall of Northumberland House.

Robert was to stay in London until August 24, and during this time his prime object was to secure an interview with Lord Glenelg, the Colonial Secretary. But this was the last thing that Sir Francis Bond Head wished to happen, for he realized

* York had reverted to its "fine old Indian name" when it was incorporated as a city in 1834.

The young lawyer who became the Honourable Robert Baldwin in the struggle for responsible government.

Elizabeth Augusta Baldwin, the Honourable Robert's wife, who was "all a husband's love could wish her."

full well that Robert was the kind of person whose integrity might have convinced the Colonial Secretary of the urgency of the situation in Canada and of the danger. Indeed the Governor had written to Glenelg two days before Robert left Toronto, saying: "I therefore hope that, should he directly or indirectly, communicate with the Colonial Office, your Lordship will give him that style of answer . . . which . . . would at once put an end to that sort of left-handed attacks upon the constitution." Robert did try to see Lord Glenelg but the Colonial Secretary scrupulously followed the Governor's request and Robert was rebuffed.

However this did not prevent his addressing three letters to the Colonial Office, and the one he wrote on July 13, 1836 has become a historic document. Of the following two passages, the first shows clearly the great importance that the Baldwins attached to the continuing connection with the British Crown:

> Educated in the warmest attachment to the monarchial form of Government, believing it to be best adapted to secure the happiness of the people, and fully sensible that it can be maintained in Upper Canada only by means of the connexion with the Mother Country, I have always been most earnestly anxious for the continuation of that Connexion: I believe it to be now endangered.

In the second he shows his conviction that responsible government is the only path to colonial tranquility:

> . . . to put the Executive Council permanently upon the footing of a local Provincial Cabinet, holding the same relative position with reference to the representative of the King and the Provincial Parliament, as that on which the King's Imperial Cabinet stands with respect to the King and the Parliament of the Empire, and applying to such provincial Cabinet both with respect to their appointment to, and continuation in, office; the same principles as those which are acted upon by His Majesty with respect to the Imperial Cabinet in this Country.

While waiting for a reply from Lord Glenelg, Robert was far

from inactive; he had come armed with letters of introduction, and he also received great courtesy from his cousin Dr. Herbert Baldwin, member for Cork, who "kindly got me on the Speaker's Supplemental list," as he wrote to his father. And he continues in his memorandum:

> I dined with Mr. Hume several times and met there Mr. Leslie of Montreal, Mr. McGregor, Mr. Roebuck, Mr. Burnie from the West Indies, Mr. Hume's brother-in-law, and others. I dined also with Mr. Henry Chapman, with Mr. Wilkinson to whom I had a letter from Mr. Bidwell at whose table I met Mr. Harrison, the author of the "Digest", who himself, had some intention of coming out to settle in Canada, and at Mr. John Ridout's, cousin of Mr. Thomas Ridout of Toronto. At the Ridout's, I met several gentlemen, one of whom seemed to take more interest in Canadian affairs than I found usual with those I met thus casually. Most of whom seemed rarely to have had the fact of the existence of such a country present to their minds . . . At Mr. Hume's, of course, there was more acquaintance with colonial affairs. At all events they seemed all of them, to know that there was such a place as Canada and that it was not in the Southern Hemisphere.

In some of these gentlemen Robert was to find the influence of Mackenzie's ideas:

> Mr. Roebuck seems to think that the making the Legislative Council elective ought to be the great object of Canadian Politicians. An absurdity – if I may be allowed to say so with the respect to the opinions of one so long conversant with the politics of my native country and himself a Canadian. But I was never more satisfied of any thing than that this is merely grasping at the shadow and losing the substance.

Of Mr. Hume Robert writes: "Mr. Hume is an entirely different man, sees things in a different light and affords us, I am sure, a cordial and conscientious support. Mr. McGregor, also, whom I met at Mr. Hume's seemed to take up the question of Responsible Government in its true light and to deem it worthy of deliberate commendation." And Robert "Dined also at Mr. Richard King's, one of Mrs. Wells's brothers, who was particularly attentive and kind to me. Mr. Wells, also, the Colonel's brother, was polite in having me to the Clubs, etc."

Robert was a great sentimentalist, and during his time in London he made a pilgrimage: "I visited the vault in St. Anne's Church, Blackfriar's in which my poor classfellow, Horace Ridout, is buried. I got the sexton to open the Vault for me and succeeded in identifying the coffin in which repose his mortal remains, and thus paid a last tribute to his memory. Poor fellow, we were in the same class from Dr. Strachan's first removal from Cornwall to York, till we left school." And he also, as a matter of course, visited "Windsor, Richmond, Hampton Court and the neighbouring suburban villages, or most of them."

Robert had seen John Morgan on his way through New York and he was much pleased by receiving, in a letter from his father, the following commendation of his mission by his uncle:

> I have all along thought that the ground you & Robert took, is the true, British constitutional ground. – What ministry in England would not resign, if they were not consulted by the King, or if being consulted, their advice was rejected. . . . So in Canada, the executive council is created, to advise the Governor, in respect to every measure bearing upon the interests of the Country, and they are alike unfaithful to him, and to the people, if they do not do so, or if they suffer any important measure to go forth as if with their sanction, when they have either not been consulted about it, or disapprove of it.

Robert replied to his father from Cork:

> From what you say Mr. Morgan did not visit you this summer. His opinion of our view of the political question is very gratifying because it is that of a man peculiarly qualified to form a correct judgment and peculiarly free from the influence of all extraneous circumstances at all likely to mislead him – When you write to him remember me most affectionately to him and my dear Aunt Eliza remember me also to General Dix, Catherine and the Children –

General Dix, a distinguished soldier-diplomat, had married Catherine, a niece and the adopted daughter of John Morgan.

Robert's political mission to England was not altogether in vain, for he did have an interview with Lord John Russell, a future Colonial Secretary and Prime Minister, and he was able to write to Lord Glenelg on August 12, before he left: "I feel, however, that I have now discharged my duty, and your Lordship will, I am sure, be my witness that I have omitted nothing which was in my power, that could tend to impress His Majesty's government with the importance which I attach to the principle." But if Robert was satisfied that he had done all he could, William was not, and he wrote on August 27, 1836, "I really wish you had an interview with the Minister in the presence of a friend – Mr. Hume or Baldwin or Mr. O'Connell." But by this time Robert was on his way to Ireland.

The Doctor not only kept Robert informed of the political situation at home but, of course, sent him news of the children:

> My dear and excellent Robert,
>
> Your mother went to see Mrs. Humpherys who has opened a Childs School and returned much pleased with what she observed – Satisfied of Mrs. H's good sense and fitness for her charge of Children she sends Willy to her he has gone the third day and meets three little Truscotts, two Powells, two Munroes, in all six or seven boys . . . Maria goes as usual to Mr. Hincks . . . little Libby [Eliza] quite well and happily occupied with her play. [In another letter in July 1836:] I have just finished yesterday, the turnpiking of the West Cresent Road to the great joy of the people there. . . . , Spadina house is rough cast all over and looks extremely pretty.

Robert was much pleased with the invitation one of his friends in London had procured for him to the British Association for the Advancement of Science, which was holding its annual meeting at Bristol. So he left London on August 24 and found the Association's meeting very interesting: "Tell Robert [Sullivan] I have some specimens for him from Bristol and Clifton." Leaving Bristol, he continues:

> Tell Dr. Rolph that I was not able to go to his Uncle Mr. Lawford's although he gave me a very kind invitation – but I saw his brother Thomas who shewed me every attention at Cirencester & would have insisted on my remaining with him longer in the way you know the Rolphs have – And in fact the stage was at the Door of the White Lion ready to start when I got back to Bristol – So that I was very near losing my passage from his assurances that there was "plenty of time".

Whereas Robert's sojourn in England had primarily concerned politics, his visit to Ireland was a sentimental journey.

> From the moment I set my foot in it I felt at home – The faces seemed more familiar – the Children seemed more like my own – the accent so soft and agreeable – the voice of every one I met sounded like the voice of a friend – I know William will laugh & say I am prejudiced – And I admit it I am prejudiced and hope I always will be in favour of this dear land of my parents and of my own Eliza and if it makes me a worse philosopher I shall be satisfied if it makes me a better Irishman.

From Bristol Robert had taken ship to Dublin, where he "received every attention" from family friends, including Dr. Coles, who had been an undergraduate at Edinburgh with William and who

> was full of his old college stories & among others told of some caper that you and he and Scotto played on Bernard or you & he & Bernard on Scotto I forget which – you will probably remember – though I should from the detail be sceptical as to the accuracy of the recollection of any of the party with respect to what occurred – . . . At Belfast the Hincks's & Stuarts & Moores were particularly attentive – With Dr. Hincks you would be particularly pleased – the plate is a strong likeness of him – more so I think than the picture from which I understood it was taken – of Mrs. Moore I hardly know how to speak she is a most amiable woman – She is very like her Sister [probably Mrs. F. Hincks]

in person and appears to me to be like her in everything – hers seemed to me such a mind as my own dear Eliza would have felt a joy in communing with.

Robert's letter was dated September 24, 1836 and was written at Cork, where he was to spend nearly two months. During this time not only did he visit Lisnegatt and Summer Hill, but he also spent some time arranging for a memorial headstone to be placed on his grandmother's grave in Temple Martin churchyard, the parish church of both Lisnegatt and Mount Pleasant. This memorial to Barbara Spread Baldwin had been commissioned by his father.

Very few of Phoebe Baldwin's letters have survived but this one was evidently treasured by Robert, for it is included in the Robert Baldwin Papers now in the keeping of the Metropolitan Toronto Central Library:

Toronto, 2nd Sept – 1836

Your Father My ever Dear Robert having so constantly occasion to write to you, has prevented my doing so, long since; but I cannot altogether, deny myself the heartfelt gratification of communicating with you, My Dear Dear Child – You do not know the comfort which your few pencil'd lines have been to me since you left us.

How shall I my Dear Robert say all we feel for your dear little ones – they are truly deserving *each* & every *one* of a Father's tenderest feelings; & we bless God, that they have a Father, so capable of directing their every step through life & pray, *earnestly* pray that they may be spared to *you* & *you* to them – We have given them a great deal of bodily & Carriage exercise in the open air; which under providence has I think contributed to their uninterrupted health during a very [bad] summer amongst Children . . . Willy is delighted with his school . . . Maria's fondness for reading increases; she however plays a good deal & joins Willy in flying his Kite; now his favourite amusement – Mr. & Mrs. Hincks are unremitting in their attentions to her – you will find your little Eliza, the same affectionate little creeping plant you left her; she grows every day more like her dear Mother. Robert is a fine manly fellow, & I think must be the counterpart of what

your Grandfather Baldwin was at his age . . .
I must leave a little room for your Father, otherwise know not when I should stop –

ever Dr Robert yr affecte Mother. P. Baldwin

William's addition to this letter is practically indecipherable!

In November Robert journeyed up to Dublin and wrote to his father on November 27, saying that he had hoped to cross to Liverpool the previous day but had been delayed. His journal of the trip concludes:

> I took my passage to New York in the Packet ship, "United States," Captain Harvey. We sailed on Tuesday, the 20th of December, with a whole fleet of vessels for all parts of the world, which with us, had been waiting the clearing up of the weather.
>
> We reached New York, Friday, 27th January, 1837, after having encountered a tremendous storm, the same in which the "Mexico" was lost, attended with so great a loss of life. As we approached the shores of America, we saw several pieces of wreck and one which seemed the remains of the hull of a large vessel.
>
> I remained in New York till Tuesday, the first of February when I left in the stage for Albany, which I reached in the evening of the next day. I first went to the "Eagle" and afterwards to Mrs. Lockwood's Boarding House, where Mr. Dix and his family had their quarters, and remaining the third, fourth, and fifth I left for Utica on the 6th, reached the "Eagle" at Rochester at night on the 7th, Lewiston at night on the 8th and on the morning of Thursday, 9th of February was again in Upper Canada, my own, my native land. . . .
>
> Having visited General Brock's monument, I left the same day for Toronto, reached Hamilton at night and was in the arms of my dear parents, children and family at 5 o'clocke, Friday, 10 February, 1837.

At the time of Robert's and then William's refusal to accept seats on the Executive Council, the Doctor had been thoroughly irked by the fact that both his brother, Augustus Baldwin, and his nephew, R. B. Sullivan, had accepted similar appointments with alacrity. Robert, writing from Cork in September 1836, tried with some success to pour oil on the troubled waters. Speaking of family: "Let us cling to it as the most valued inheritance with which the Almighty has blessed us. Above all things let us not let political differences interfere with the cultivation of it – but on the contrary, where such unhappily exist, always forget the politician in the relation." He sent his love to his cousin and added, "If it [his appointment] was unconnected with political difficulties, I should indeed rejoice although it will deprive me of my partner."

During the year that Robert Baldwin had been away, Governor Head having dissolved Parliament on May 28, 1836, an election was called for the following July. To promote the idea of responsible government, the Constitutional Reform Society was formed with Dr. Baldwin as president and Francis Hincks as secretary. Bond Head threw all his influence on the side of the Tories and against the moderate Reformers, claiming that responsible government would sever the British connection.

It was Mackenzie and the radical Reformers whom he should have combated, for the concept of responsible government did not entail one change in the British constitution, and so long as the moderate Reformers had a chance of success Mackenzie and his followers had no reason to act. One of the deciding factors at this time was the change in attitude of Egerton Ryerson, who also was in England before and during this election but whose letter supporting Bond Head was published in the *Christian Guardian;* it switched the allegiance of his Methodist followers from the Reform Party to the Governor. In consequence the Reformers were defeated.

This convinced Mackenzie and the radicals that it was futile to try to obtain changes in government by constitutional means. Moreover these men had never been sold on the principle of responsible government, and they began in the summer and fall of 1837 secretly to train and arm their followers. These actions were hidden from a large majority of the moderate Reformers, partly because Mackenzie knew that he could expect little support from them in such radical actions, and partly because he and the other radical leaders wished to maintain security.

Sir Francis Bond Head, having won the election, was filled with unbounded confidence. He was certain that he had saved Upper Canada from radicalism, whereas, by defeating the moderate Reformers, he had pushed Mackenzie and his followers to the use of force. Inklings of their secret preparations reached Head, for he reported to Lord Glenelg: ". . . as a last dying struggle, they have, I understand, been assembling at Toronto night after night, for the purpose of appealing for assistance to his Majesty's Government!"

So little did Head fear revolt that he sent a large contingent to Lower Canada as, in his opinion, the trouble being fomented there by Papineau was far more dangerous. This was possibly true, but when, in November of 1837, Papineau asked Mackenzie for assistance, a joint action in both Upper and Lower Canada was decided on by the two rebel leaders.

The date set finally for the revolt in Upper Canada was Thursday, December 7, but word reached Samuel Lount on the Sunday before that the rebel plan was known and Lount's forces moved down Yonge Street, well in advance of the date set. When Mackenzie learned of this, he tried to stop all movement until the Thursday, but things had by now gone too far and Lount's column was approaching Montgomery's tavern, a few miles from Toronto, on Monday night. The first skirmish occurred that night. Captain Anthony Anderson, one of the few able military leaders of the revolt, was killed, and the Governor was finally persuaded that the rebels were at his doorstep.

Whereas before he had been over-confident, he was now in a panic, but determined to play for time, if this were possible, and to parley with the rebels. With this in mind, the Governor would have sent Sheriff Jarvis, but he was a marked man, having already been shot at. James Hervey Price was then approached and refused. Finally, pressure was put on Robert Baldwin, since he was respected by both sides. He reluctantly consented on condition that another reliable person accompany him, and suggested Bidwell. Bidwell refused, and Dr. Rolph was finally persuaded to accompany Robert. Rolph must have been most unhappy about being selected for, although no one suspected it at the time, least of all Robert, John Rolph was deeply implicated with Mackenzie.

It was about two in the afternoon of Tuesday, December 5,

when the small rebel force reached the crest of Gallows Hill (about the corner of Yonge Street and Rosehill Avenue). Now they could look down on Toronto, a few miles away, and Mackenzie and Lount decided to split their forces into two columns and march on the city. A guard's cry warned them of the approach of three horsemen under a flag of truce. As these came nearer one was identified as Robert Baldwin and another, to their amazement, was John Rolph, one of their secret leaders. The third member of the party carried the flag.

The message from the Governor was a promise of full amnesty if the rebels would disperse immediately. But Mackenzie and Lount sent the mission back for a written guarantee to that effect. In the meantime the rebels agreed to march only as far as the Red Lion Inn by the Bloor Street toll-gate, which was only a mile and a quarter from the outskirts of the city.

By the time Robert's truce party reached the Governor, word of reinforcements had come, so the party returned to inform the rebels that the offer of truce was withdrawn. It was apparently at this time that Rolph managed a brief aside to Mackenzie and urged him to attack without delay as the town was still weakly defended.

After this second abortive journey Robert returned home in disgust, and for the rest of his life he bitterly resented having been used in this manner by Sir Francis Bond Head, who never bothered to make an official explanation of Robert's mission or to vindicate him.

After the Rebellion of 1837 had been suppressed, conditions in Lower Canada were far from encouraging. Elective government had been suspended and the Administration was exclusively in the hands of the Governor and his Council. The mood of the French was sullen and bitterly resentful, while the prisons were full of political prisoners awaiting trial.

In Upper Canada Governor Head, who had been weak and vacillating at the time of the rebellion, was now engaged in rounding up political suspects. Backed by the Family Compact, he and his successor, Sir George Arthur, the last Governor of Upper Canada, encouraged the law to take its course, in spite of the fact that Lord Glenelg had counselled moderation, and in the British House of Commons, on January 17, 1838, Lord John Russell had said: "The Government had not interposed, nor would they interpose with respect to the cases of any individuals upon whom judgment had been pronounced in Canada. All they had done was to give an opinion as to the expediency of clemency."

Samuel Lount and Peter Matthews, Mackenzie's lieutenants, were hanged, but Mackenzie himself escaped to Navy Island on the American side of the Niagara River, and later to the United States. The trials continued well into 1838, with Chief Justice Robinson presiding. The chief prosecutor, nicknamed "the hungry tiger," was Attorney-General Hagerman, while Robert Baldwin was chief counsel for the defence in a number of the cases, including those of Montgomery and Morrison.

Internally the rebellion had been suppressed, but for many months incidents in support of Mackenzie were to occur on the Canada-United States border from Prescott to Detroit.

Part III

"THIS GREATEST OF PEACEFUL REVOLUTIONS"

A. R. M. Lower in *Colony to Nation*

1838 - 1858

THE BALDWINS OF YORK AND TORONTO

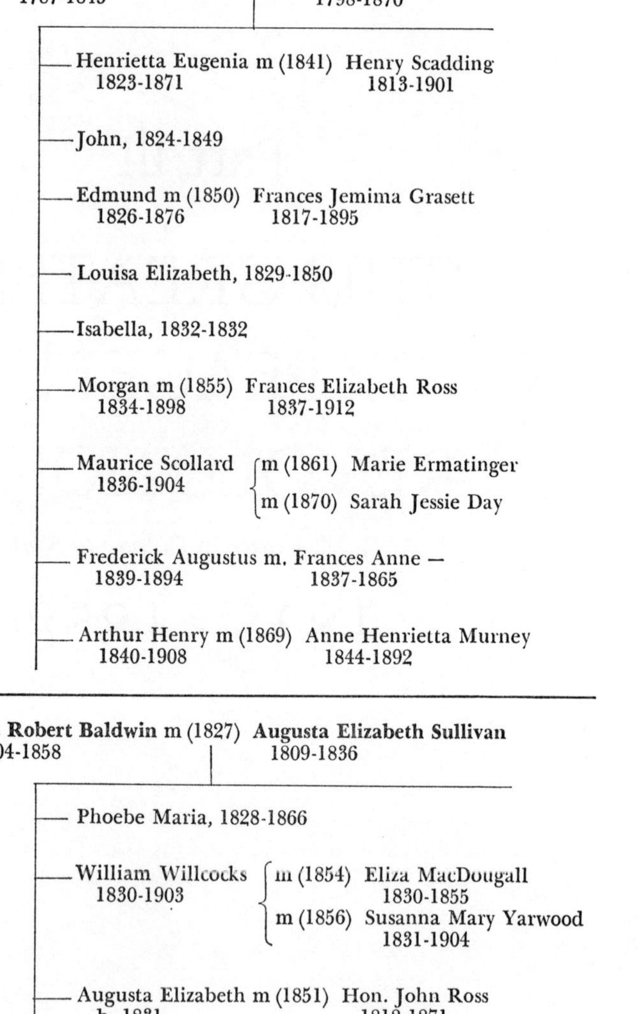

John Spread Baldwin m (1822) **Anne Scott Shaw**
1787-1843 — 1798-1870

- Henrietta Eugenia m (1841) Henry Scadding
  1823-1871 — 1813-1901
- John, 1824-1849
- Edmund m (1850) Frances Jemima Grasett
  1826-1876 — 1817-1895
- Louisa Elizabeth, 1829-1850
- Isabella, 1832-1832
- Morgan m (1855) Frances Elizabeth Ross
  1834-1898 — 1837-1912
- Maurice Scollard, 1836-1904
  - m (1861) Marie Ermatinger
  - m (1870) Sarah Jessie Day
- Frederick Augustus m. Frances Anne —
  1839-1894 — 1837-1865
- Arthur Henry m (1869) Anne Henrietta Murney
  1840-1908 — 1844-1892

Hon. Robert Baldwin m (1827) **Augusta Elizabeth Sullivan**
1804-1858 — 1809-1836

- Phoebe Maria, 1828-1866
- William Willcocks, 1830-1903
  - m (1854) Eliza MacDougall, 1830-1855
  - m (1856) Susanna Mary Yarwood, 1831-1904
- Augusta Elizabeth m (1851) Hon. John Ross
  b. 1831 — 1818-1871
- Robert, 1834-1885
  - m (1859) Jemima MacDougall (sister of Eliza), d. 1873
  - m (1877) Elizabeth Mary Walker, 1844-1903

* *

16

LORD DURHAM AND THE BALDWINS

If the rebellions had done nothing else they had rung the political alarm bells in London, where there was keen awareness that mistakes in British colonial policy and administration prior to 1775 had resulted in the rebellion and loss of Britain's other North American possessions. The Government realized that history might well repeat itself unless every effort was made to get to the bottom of the trouble in Upper and Lower Canada and to eradicate the causes.

Thus the Imperial Government did its best to select the man most able and best fitted to deal with the many problems which would confront him in the Canadas. And what was more, it was prepared to grant him extraordinary powers to enable him to carry out his mission. The choice was John George Lambton, Earl of Durham, who was sent out to North America as a special High Commissioner and Governor-General with wide powers. He arrived at Quebec with a large retinue on May 29, 1838, and among his advisers were Charles Buller, his able secretary and a member of the British House of Commons, and Gibbon Wakefield. The former not only took a very active part in drafting Lord Durham's Report but on his return to England wrote the booklet on "Responsible Government for the Colonies" to which William attached his own memorandum on the development of responsible government in Upper Canada.

Gibbon Wakefield also took an active part in assisting with the Report; but later when he returned to Canada again he did not endear himself to the Reformers, as he first backed their program and then switched his allegiance to Sir Charles Metcalfe.

Lord Durham had many qualities which fitted him for the part he was about to play. He was himself a former Minister in the Cabinet of Lord Grey, having held the office of Lord Privy Seal. He had been one of the leading supporters of the British Reform Bill and thus was a man of liberal and advanced ideas. Finally he was a man of great energy, impulsive, and prepared to use his almost dictatorial powers as widely as possible in order to achieve success in his mission.

His wisdom is shown by one of his first acts on assuming office. This was to grant a general amnesty to all political prisoners in Lower Canada, with the exception of eight of the ringleaders. But his impulsive action of banishing, on his own authority, certain leaders of the insurrection to Bermuda (which was not in his jurisdiction) exposed him to severe attack and eventually brought about his recall.

From the moment of arrival he was determined to get to the root of the troubles in the Canadas, and he set up special commissions of inquiry. These included inquiries into municipal government, education, Crown lands, and immigration, as well as the fiscal arrangements in the two provinces.

In the short space of five months, most of it spent in Lower Canada, Lord Durham accomplished more than most governors in their whole term of office. As a state paper on colonial affairs, his Report will always stand as one of the greatest. In his masterly analysis of the causes of trouble and discontent he placed first the bitter animosity which had grown up between the French in Lower Canada and the English minority in that province; and he put the blame squarely on the arrogance of the latter. He found, he said, "two nations warring in the bosom of a single state." In Upper Canada he found "the absence of that system of responsible government which could alone confer upon the people of Canada the political liberty to which they were entitled."

During his brief stay in Canada Lord Durham had found time

to visit the upper province and while there had summoned both Dr. Baldwin and Robert to an interview. He had encouraged them to put forward their ideas and at the conclusion of their meeting he asked them to submit these to him in writing.

William was the first to submit his ideas to Lord Durham, in a rather long and somewhat involved document. This listed approximately twenty-one grievances followed by certain recommendations, among which one was for the adoption of responsible government. Thus William saw many grievances; Robert on the other hand, submitted a much shorter report some three weeks later in which he recognized that most of the ills in Upper Canada could be remedied by the adoption of the one principle of responsible government. Together with his letter to Lord Durham he enclosed a copy of his letter to Lord Glenelg, submitted by him while in London in 1836. Lord Durham had not seen this document, probably the clearest enunciation of the great principle ever made by either of the Baldwins. Undoubtedly it exercised a great influence on his Lordship and his Report in regard to this principle. Durham wrote:

> I now come to the consideration of the fourth remedy, which consists of nothing more than having the provincial Government as far as regards the internal affairs of the Province, conducted by the Lieutenant Governor (as Representative of the paramount Authority of the Mother Country) with the advice and assistance of the Executive Council acting as a Provincial Cabinet, and composed of Men possessed of the public confidence, whose opinions and policy would be in harmony with the opinions and policy of the Representatives of the People. This, as I have before said, I look upon not only as an efficient remedy, but as the only efficient one that can be applied to the evils under which the Province is at present suffering.

From Robert's letter to Lord Durham it is quite clear that until his interview with the Baldwins his Lordship was contemplating a scheme of uniting all the British North American colonies under one legislative body. This early confederation idea would be doomed to failure, as Robert was quick to point out, unless it envisaged responsible government within the federated units:

> The short interview with which I was honoured . . . added much to my alarm for the result; because I thought I discerned if not a final opinion at least a strong bias in favour of a measure which in my own mind I am convinced can end in nothing but disappointment. The establishment of a general Legislative body for all the Colonies, unless as a preparatory step to making them independent, would in my humble opinion be worse than useless: And would unquestionably tend rapidly to bring about a separation from the Mother Country.

How Lord Durham was influenced by Robert's ideas on responsible government can be seen in the following comparisons. Here is an extract from Baldwin's letter to Lord Glenelg:

> The Concession of the principle therefore calls for no legislative interference; – It involves no sacrifice of any constitutional principle, – It involves no sacrifice of any branch of the Royal prerogative, – It involves no diminution of the paramount Authority, of the Mother Country; . . . From being an English Principle, it would strengthen the Attachment of the People to the connexion with the Mother Country; and would place the Provincial Government at the head of Public opinion, instead of occupying its present invidious position of being always in direct opposition to it.

The following shows how Lord Durham used almost the same phraseology in his Report:

> It needs no change in the principles of government, no invention of a new constitutional theory, to supply the remedy which would, in my opinion, completely remove the existing political disorders. It needs but to follow out consistently the principles of the British constitution, and introduce into the Government of these great Colonies those wise provisions, by which alone the working of the representative system can in any country be rendered harmonious and efficient.

It was probably at this point that Robert became the leader of the Reformers in pressing this great principle both in and out of Parliament and against all opposition to it in London. It was most fortunate for the Baldwins and for the moderate reform movement that a great and powerful personage had been sent out to the Canadas and that he backed the cause of responsible government; otherwise the moderate Reformers, seeking this constitutional solution, could never have risen like a phoenix from the ashes.

However, the forces ranged against them were still formidable: the Tory Party in Upper Canada, many of the Methodists and followers of Egerton Ryerson, the Imperial Government until 1847, and at least two hostile Governors, Lord Sydenham and Sir Charles Metcalfe, who did all in their power to prevent the achievement of responsible government in the colony.

The moderate Reform Party was badly in need of favourable press coverage, and Francis Hincks, in his *Reminiscences of His Public Life,* describes how this was supplied: "In the summer [1838] I visited in company with a political friend [presumably Robert Baldwin] the settlements north of Toronto and on our return we had a good deal of conversation on the position of the Reform Party and on the importance of having our views regarding Responsible Government advocated through the press. There not being a single paper in Upper Canada to defend the great principle." Hincks set about remedying this and obtained the services of Michael Reynolds, who had been with the *Correspondent,* to take charge of the mechanical side of the production. He sent Reynolds to Buffalo to purchase press and types suitable for a weekly paper.

Hincks brought out the first copy of his paper the *Examiner* at Toronto on July 3, 1838 with the motto, "Responsible Government." Then in the course of two months he added the subtitle, "The Voluntary Principle," very much as John and Robert Baldwin had done with the *Volunteer Journal* in Cork in 1782 when they added the subtitle "The Independent Gazeteer."

For many months Hincks devoted the front page of the *Examiner* to "Three extracts which were intended to explain the principles it was intended to advocate." The lead article in the first number was written in support of Lord Durham, and urged the reformers to have confidence in him. (This was before the Durham Report had appeared but after Lord Durham had seen the Baldwins and asked them to submit their ideas.)

The *Examiner* was a success from the start. Mackenzie's

Colonial Advocate had been a radical paper and nearly all the other papers in Upper Canada were Tory; the *Examiner* was moderate and it was very well written and edited. Sir Charles Bagot, who was certainly a judge in such matters and had no reason to praise the paper, wrote to Lord Stanley, February 2, 1842, regarding Hincks, "the editor of the *Examiner,* by far the best-written paper in the country."

But there were other subtle links being forged to bind the Reformers together, even stronger than the outward and visible signs, and these were the bonds of shared political dangers, disappointments and failures, as well as triumphs, which united men like the Baldwins, Hincks, and later, LaFontaine. In 1839 the Reformers held what were called "Durham meetings" in various parts of the province, and as William was on his way to one held on Yonge Street, Nicholas Flood Davin, an eyewitness, reports in *An Irishman in Canada*: "The old doctor was pulled off the waggon and they told him it was only his grey hairs saved him. Hincks was there too and had to run for his life." About the same time, Hincks wrote to William:

Dear Doctor,

I have just got home Geo Ridout & I came thro' Scarboro – I narrowly escaped with my life, a drawn dagger having been lunged at me by Platt – Ridout and I were anxious about you & I am truly glad to find you escaped so well; our motto was necessarily "Sauve qui peut" We tried to convey a message to you but could not do it. I think we have done our duty & what is more I think good will come of the proceedings of this day.

Believe me always
Yours
F. Hincks

The final link in the chain remained to be forged, and this was perhaps the most vital of them all. It was begun in April 1839 when Hincks wrote to LaFontaine regarding Lord Durham's Report, and this correspondence continued, and culminated in the introduction of the two leaders, Robert Baldwin and Louis LaFontaine. It was probably Hincks who first realized that, if there was to be a union of the two provinces as suggested by Lord Durham, then the Reformers in Upper Canada must make common cause with the solid block of the French followers of LaFontaine in Lower Canada. In this way they would command a common majority and achieve their objectives. Thus the friendship and unbounded confidence which grew between Baldwin and LaFontaine was the cornerstone on which rested the French-Canadian co-operation with the Reformers in Upper Canada.

* *

17

CEMENTING THE PARTNERSHIP

The Governor-General sent out to succeed Lord Durham was Charles Poulett Thomson, later created Baron Sydenham. In contrast to Durham, who was a statesman, Sydenham was a politician with all that that implies. He was sent out by the British Government to carry out some of the recommendations made by Lord Durham, the most important being to bring about the union of Upper and Lower Canada. On the issue of responsible government the Imperial Parliament had serious reservations, so that when the new Governor-General arrived in Canada in October 1839, everyone was in the dark as to the prospect for responsible government.

Sydenham was determined to administer the affairs of Canada in his own way, and to him this end justified any means necessary to accomplish it. How far he was prepared to go in this regard can be seen by the following extract from a confidential letter from his successor, Sir Charles Bagot, to Lord Stanley on September 26, 1842: "It was only by dint of the greatest energy and I might add the unscrupulous personal interference of Lord Sydenham, combined with practices which I could not use and your Lordship would not recommend, that Lord Sydenham managed to get through the session."

But in Sydenham's defence it should be stressed that he was a highly skilled administrator as well as a very able and adroit politician, and he organized and trained the departments of government in Canada as few other men could have done.

He had three main political objectives in Canada. The first, and part of his mandate, was to unite the provinces of Upper and Lower Canada; with this recommendation of Lord Durham's he was in full sympathy. Secondly, he was determined to call the political tune himself, to be his own Prime Minister, and not to hand over the direction of affairs to his ministers. Thus he was opposed to Lord Durham's recommendation for responsible government, although he was too adroit to say so. Finally he was determined to pick his councillors from all parties; in this way he hoped to divide and rule.

On first sight it would seem that Sydenham faced almost insurmountable difficulties in trying to force union on both Upper and Lower Canada. Certainly in Lower Canada the French population was bitterly opposed to a union which they saw as aimed at absorbing them into the British way of life and crushing their nationalism. But, fortunately for Sydenham, the constitution had been suspended in Lower Canada after the rebellion and had not been reinstated. Thus control of that province was still vested in the hands of the Governor and Council. So in spite of the feeling of the great bulk of the French the Act of Union was passed without much difficulty.

In Upper Canada, the Tories were strongly opposed to being coupled with the French. Sydenham at this time had a poor opinion of the Tories and Francis Hincks in his *Reminiscences* quoted him as saying:

> The Assembly is such a house split into half a dozen parties, the Government having none, and no one to depend on . . . I do not wonder at the cry for Responsible Government, when I see how things have been managed. Think of a House in which half the members hold places yet in which the Government does not command a single vote, in which the [Tory] placemen generally vote against the executive; and where there is no one to defend the Government when attacked, or to state the opinions of the Governor.

No wonder then that the Reformers were misled into thinking that the Governor favoured responsible government, and had it not been for their unexpected backing, Sydenham might have had to resort to forcing union on the Canadas by imperial decree. This unexpected backing of the Reformers was occasioned by the strategy, probably propounded by Hincks, that if the Reformers of Upper Canada could make common cause with the large block of the French in Lower Canada, they could command a solid majority in a united Assembly to their mutual advantage; for the first time, there seemed to be sound common sense in backing the Act of Union.

Sydenham may have seen the dangers of accepting aid from this quarter but evidently he felt that the advantages outweighed them; he wrote: "It is impossible to describe to you the difficulties I have had to contend with to get this matter settled as it has been in the Assembly. I owe my success altogether to the confidence which the Reform party have reposed in me personally, and to the generous manner in which they have acted by me."

This attitude is borne out by the letter which Robert Baldwin wrote to Louis LaFontaine on November 26, 1840:

> I sincerely regret the position of parties which an untoward series of events, seems to have brought about in Lower Canada and am therefore, more than ever anxious for the proclamation of the Union as the first step towards changing it and mitigating the evils which appear to me to have grown up under it. There is and *must be no question of races.* It were madness on one side and guilt, deep guilt, on both, to make such a question. But, my dear Sir, while the Reformers of Upper Canada are ready to make every allowance for this unfortunate state of things and are resolved, as I believe them to be, to unite with their L.C. Brethren cordially as friends, and to afford them every assistance in obtaining Justice *upon precisely the same footing* in *every* particular as *ourselves,* it is to be assured not by the adoption of a course of proceeding leading necessarily to collision and tending to stop unavoidably, the whole machinery of the Constitution that they look for the accomplishment of this just and necessary object but on the contrary to the harmonious working of the Constitution itself, by means of the new principle which since recent events in Nova Scotia, no one can doubt is to be applied to its practical administration coupled with that forbearance, mod-

eration and firmness on the part of the people which, so long as it compromises no great principle, affords the best assurance of the possession of fitness for the exercise of political power.

At this time Robert Baldwin was at the peak of his political career. Sydenham had appointed him Solicitor-General in 1840 and a few days after the proclamation of the Act of Union, that is, after February 10, 1841, he appointed him an Executive Councillor in the United Parliament. He was the undisputed leader of the Reform Party (although Hincks might have shown reluctance in bending the knee). For the elections in the first United Parliament, the Reformers in no less than five constituencies in Upper Canada, now Canada West, proposed to elect him, while the Reform candidates in four other constituencies voiced their willingness to retire in his favour.

In January 1841 Robert had given up his idea of running for the Toronto riding when an unsavoury clique was successful in the municipal elections. Hincks approved of this decision, and in writing to LaFontaine in February 1841 he says that had Robert been elected in Toronto it would have been "by the votes of men who supported him not for his principles, but as Solicitor-General."

However this may have been, Robert was determined to seek election in two ridings, but the question was which two. He considered his father's former constituency of Norfolk County, but Mr. Powell, the sitting member, objected. This lack of co-operation on the part of Mr. Powell resulted in a rebuke from Robert, printed in the *Examiner* March 3, 1841. Writing to Mr. Crouse, he says: "but while I continue to occupy it [the leadership], the party, if they do not rally to support me, will be guilty of a sort of political suicide, – and confirm the doctrine of Sir Francis Head and his friends, that the system of responsible government is not adapted to the state of the colony."

Finally Robert decided to contest the riding of Hastings and the Fourth Riding of York.* He was successful in both, but

* In 1833 an "Act to repeal part of an Act" had divided the County of York into four ridings, the Fourth Riding being the northern end from Whitchurch and Uxbridge up to Lake Simcoe. For years afterwards, however, this was referred to as the North Riding, just as Upper and Lower Canada were used to designate English and French Canada long after the Act of Union had changed these to Canada West and East.

not without a stiff fight in Hastings against Edmund Murney, who went so far as to be ready to offer "proof" that Robert had been implicated in the rebellion in Upper Canada, although he knew very well he would be perjuring himself. Murney had married Robert's cousin Maria Breakenridge, daughter of Mary Warren and John Breakenridge, the brother-in-law by whom William had felt himself "not well treated" in 1817, and now there was no love lost between Robert Baldwin and Edmund Murney.

The political situation in the Canadas during the period from February to early June 1841 was extremely delicate, with both sides feeling their way very carefully. Once Sydenham had succeeded with the Union Bill, he turned to the important matter of elections, particularly in Canada East where they were to be held in March and April. Louis-Joseph Papineau was still in exile and the French rallied to Louis Hippolyte LaFontaine, who had been imprisoned briefly but was released without trial. Sydenham wanted to get LaFontaine into his Council and offered him the post of Solicitor-General for Canada East. But LaFontaine and his large block of followers were not to be won, and the offer was refused.

As Sydenham could not get the co-operation of the French, he was quick to handle the problem in another way. He determined to exclude them, and particularly their leaders, by every means in his power. To this end a great deal of gerrymandering went on in the redrawing of many of the constituencies in Canada East. As the Governor had power, under the Act of Union, to change electoral boundaries, he used it in the Montreal and Quebec areas to ensure the return of at least four English-speaking members who would support him.

In some constituencies, notably Terrebonne where LaFontaine was assured of a majority, a mob of toughs from Montreal, approximately a thousand strong, held off LaFontaine and his supporters. This resulted in the defeat of the French leader, who was anxious to avoid bloodshed so that Sydenham might have no grounds for claiming that the French resorted to force. The defeat made LaFontaine and his followers even more bitter against the Union. Originally the basis for their opposition to it had been threefold: Canada East was given the same number of members (forty-two) as Canada West, although its population was approximately one-third greater; French was not to be recognized as an official language; and the United Parliament was to assume the public debt incurred by Upper Canada. To this were added irritants such as a civil list and the selection of Kingston as the new seat of government.

In Canada West, the Reformers wanted Robert to stay in the Executive Council, at least until after the elections, when the relative strength of the various parties could be more accurately known. On the other hand it was also essential that Robert's acceptance of a place on the Executive Council should not be misinterpreted, either by the French as a surrender to the "enemy," or by the Reformers in Canada West as implying that Robert was convinced that responsible government had been conceded by the Governor.

The first of these objectives was attained through a spirited correspondence, first between Hincks and A. N. Morin,* who stood in the same relation to LaFontaine as Hincks to Baldwin, and later between Baldwin and LaFontaine themselves. The other objective, that of keeping the Reformers in Canada West informed, was gained by articles and letters printed in the *Examiner,* as well as reports of Robert's speeches. As editor, Hincks did a fine job of liason and he and Robert co-operated very well at this time. Robert was willing to accept Lord Sydenham's protestations that he would consult his ministers, as long as both the Governor and the Reformers knew where he stood. An open quarrel with the Governor would destroy any advantage they had gained, and force Lord Sydenham into the arms of the Tories. Fortunately Hincks took Robert's advice and toned down his articles, although he and all the Reformers were most incensed by the arbitrary and questionable treatment meted out to the French by his Excellency.

The first Parliament of the United Assembly was to meet in Kingston on June 14, 1841. Preparations had been made in a commodious stone building about a mile west of the town. The good taste and elegance of the appointments impressed even Sydenham and were in contrast to the stark simplicity of the benches at Westminster: "These fellows in their colonies have been spoilt by all sorts of luxuries, – large arm-chairs, desks, with stationary before each man, and heaven knows what –"

* Morin was the fluently bilingual editor of *La Minerve.*

But with the gathering of the elected members at Kingston at the beginning of June, Robert's first action was to call a meeting of the Reform members. It was essential for him to get their opinions and to find out what backing he could count on in the House. This meeting showed clearly that men like Morin, D. B. Viger and T. C. Aylwin, leaders of the French in the absence of LaFontaine, were willing to support the Reformers of Canada West.

The strength of the parties in the new House appeared to be: moderate Reformers from Canada West, 20; French support from Canada East, 20; radical Reformers, 5; moderate Tories and supporters of the Governor, 24; plus the old Compact party under McNab, 7. This left 8 doubtfuls. Thus the Reformers could count on a clear majority in the House with the French support.

Now the chips were down and Robert and his party had to know where Lord Sydenham stood in regard to responsible Government. Robert was determined that the French should be represented on the Executive Council, and equally determined not to desert them. On June 12, two days before the session opened, he wrote to Lord Sydenham, pointing out that there was no French representation on the Council and requesting that the Tory members should be replaced by French. The result of this and of further correspondence between the Governor and Robert was the Governor's refusal to act on this advice, and Robert resigned his seat on the Executive Council. His resignation was proffered on June 14, and had not been formally accepted when Parliament met on that day.

As the House came into session, strategy and tactics were of the greatest importance. The Reformers, who commanded a majority, wished to bring about a confrontation as soon as possible. Sydenham, on the other hand, was determined to avoid this as long as he could. He was ably assisted in his aim by his leader in the House, Attorney-General William Draper, a clever and able debater and parliamentary leader, whose manner and form of speech had earned him the name of Sweet William.

The post of Speaker of the House was an important one and the Reformers set out to capture it if possible. They had decided to nominate Augustin Culvillier, a man of ability, respected by all parties, and completely bilingual.

The Reformers expected his nomination would be opposed and that in consequence they would be on firm ground. Government forces countered by accepting the nomination; but Hincks, determined to make an issue over this point, declared in the House that he had given his support because of Cullvillier's statement that he had no confidence in the Administration. At this the Government took up the fight and Allan MacNab's name was proposed. After a heated debate, MacNab, the member for Hamilton, had his name withdrawn and Cullvillier was elected.

It was now Sydenham's turn to show his skill. His Speech from the Throne outlined a most tempting program of public works to be undertaken by the Government, and in addition a loan of £1,500,000 sterling to be guaranteed by the Imperial Parliament to finance this program. Nothing could have been better calculated to appeal to all parties, for if anything was desperately needed it was the improvement of roads, canals, and schools in both provinces.

During the debate following the Speech from the Throne Robert was able to give the House the reasons for his resignation. There followed a long-drawn-out debate on the issue of responsible government, during which Draper made at least seven speeches, purposely involving the issue as much as possible, but finally admitting that under certain specific circumstances he would resign. But no conclusive assurance as to Cabinet responsibility was forthcoming.

John Neilson, member for Quebec County and owner of the bilingual *Quebec Gazette,* had brought in an amendment that "there are features in the Act now constituting the government of Canada which are inconsistent with justice and the common rights of British subjects." This was voted down, but Robert, Hincks, and a few others from Canada West voted in favour, showing their support for the French and their belief that the French had not received proper treatment in certain aspects of the union.

Lord Sydenham and his Administration (he was virtually his own Prime Minister at this time) were now in a position to proceed with their legislative program. To organize the various departments of government a new executive position was created; the title was President of the Council, but the post was rather general manager of heads of departments, and not President of the Executive Council. R. B. Sullivan was appointed. (At this time Sullivan was not a supporter of the Reform Party.)

Sydenham's program, financed by the imperial loan, embraced the purchase of the Welland Canal and its improvement, canals at Lachine and Cornwall to improve the navigation of the St. Lawrence, and the deepening of the channel in Lake St. Peter to facilitate the passage of vessels to Montreal. New roads were constructed in the Eastern Townships and the Baie des Chaleurs, and also in a number of areas in Canada West.

As a result of this program party lines were very often broken. Hincks, Robert's chief lieutenant, who was entirely in sympathy with these practical measures, was at times seduced into voting with the Government. So serious was this split that on one occasion Hincks received a note from Robert, sent across the floor of the House, asking him to state with which party he wished to identify. Although Hincks came back into the fold at a later date, the relationship between him and Robert was never again so cordial, and he continued to be extremely sensitive and touchy regarding his loyalty to the party and to Robert Baldwin.

Apart from the public works program, the Government brought in a number of other practical measures, some of which were again to divide the Reform Party. One of the most controversial was the Municipal Bill. It was controversial because it concerned Canada West only and sought to give a measure of municipal government to that part of the United Provinces. (In Canada East Sydenham had by ordinance set up municipal bodies of government appointees.) Naturally the French voted against the Municipal Bill, as did Robert and his party, on the grounds that it did not go far enough and that officers in all municipalities in both the Canadas should be elected.

Hincks broke openly with Robert on this issue, declaring that "half a loaf was better than no bread." This spirit of compromise was a most dangerous one to party unity and the quarrel between Robert and Hincks deepened as a result.

The least controversial piece of legislation was the Act to establish a system of common schools. This had almost universal support, as up to that time the Government had only helped in the establishment of grammar schools, and given assistance to private schools. Now it was estimated that only about one in eighteen children attended the elementary schools that had sprung up, and the number attending in French Canada was even less. It is interesting to note that so many petitions were received requesting the teaching of the Bible in elementary schools, that finally a clause was added to the Act for the setting up of separate schools in areas differing in faith from the majority.

During this session Robert was awaiting an opportunity to pin down the Administration on the vital question of responsible government, and it was the Lower Canada Election Bill that enabled him to set in motion the most brilliant manoeuvre of his political career.

Following the elections in Canada East, petitions had been received from a number of constituencies where corrupt practices and government interference were alleged to have taken place. These petitions were rejected on a technicality. A large number of the members of the House felt that the interests of justice were not being served by this offhand dismissal of real grievances. Allan MacNab introduced a Bill which would permit the presentation of these petitions and authorize investigation of the corrupt practices.

Sydenham was most anxious that this Bill should not become law, as it would have forced inquiries into such elections as that in Terrebonne, where LaFontaine had been defeated. The Bill was passed in the Assembly with a substantial majority, the Reformers voting wholeheartedly behind MacNab; but rather than see it become law, Sydenham had it rejected by the Legislative Council.

This was in August 1841. On September 3, toward the close of the session, Robert saw his chance to act. He presented a series of resolutions which embodied the principles of responsible government.

The Government party was clearly in a quandary; if it opposed the resolutions it declared itself against responsible government. This the Governor wished to avoid at all costs, as it would have lead to the defeat of the Government. So, by introducing an amendment in the form of four resolutions, almost identical to those of Robert Baldwin, the Government put the shoe on the other foot. The Reformers were now on the spot, and after consultation Robert and his followers accepted the amended resolutions as presented by Secretary Harrison. It is almost certain that these were drafted by Lord Sydenham and William Draper in an adroit move which saved the situation and the political face of the Governor.

However, the resolutions as now constituted gave the Reformers a powerful weapon for the future. For whether they liked it or not, the Governor and his party had framed and adopted resolutions which embodied the principles of Cabinet responsibility. As such their importance cannot be overestimated. Robert's first resolution:

> That the most important, as well as most undoubted, of the political rights of the people of the province is that of having a provincial parliament for the protection of their liberties, for the exercise of a constitutional influence over the executive departments of their government, and for legislation upon all matters which do not, on the grounds of absolute necessity, constitutionally belong to the jurisdiction of the imperial parliament as the paramount authority of the legislature.

The resolution as amended and presented by Harrison:

> That the most important, as well as most undoubted, of the political rights of the people of the province is that of having a provincial parliament for the protection of their liberties, for the exercise of a constitutional influence over the executive departments of their government, and for legislation upon all matters of internal government.

Baldwin's second resolution:

> That the head of the executive government of the province being, within the limits of his government, the representative of the sovereign, is not constitutionally responsible to any other than the authorities of the empire.

Harrison's amended version:

> That the head of the executive government of the province

Robert Baldwin Sullivan at the time when he was his brother-in-law's partner in Baldwin & Sullivan.

Louis Hippolyte LaFontaine, who led Lower Canada's Reform Party in the fight for responsible government.

Phoebe Baldwin, wife of Dr. Baldwin,
with her granddaughter Phoebe Maria, eldest child of Robert and Eliza Baldwin.

being, within the limits of his government, the representative of the sovereign, is responsible to the imperial authority alone; but that, nevertheless, the management of our local affairs can only be conducted by him, by and with the assistance, counsel and information of subordinate officers of the province.

Baldwin's third resolution:

That in order to preserve that harmony between the different branches of the provincial parliament which is essential to the happy conduct of public affairs, the principal of such subordinate officers, advisers of the representative of the sovereign, and constituting as such the provincial administration under him, as the head of the provincial government, ought always to be men possessed of the public confidence, whose opinions and policy harmonizing with those of the representatives of the people, which our gracious sovereign has declared shall be the rule of the provincial government, will at all times be faithfully represented to the head of that government and through him to the sovereign and imperial parliament.

Harrison's amended resolution:

That in order to preserve between the different branches of the provincial parliament that harmony which is essential to the peace, welfare and good government of the province, the chief advisers of the representative of the sovereign, constituting a provincial administration under him, ought to be men possessed of the confidence of the representatives of the people, thus affording a guarantee that the well-understood wishes and interests of the people, which our gracious sovereign had declared shall be the rule of the provincial government, will, on all occasions, be faithfully represented and advocated.

Robert's fourth and last resolution:

That as it is practically always optional with such advisers to continue in or retire from office, at pleasure, this House

> has the constitutional right of holding such advisers politically responsible for every act of the provincial government of a local character, sanctioned by such government while such advisers continue in office.

Resolution four as amended:

> That the people of this province, have, moreover, a right to expect from such provincial administration the exertion of their best endeavours that the imperial authority, within its constitutional limits, shall be exercised in the manner most consistent with their wishes and interests.

The first session of the United Parliament ended on a note of tragedy, for on September 4, the day after the adoption of the amended resolutions, the Governor-General, Lord Sydenham, was thrown while out riding, and received serious injuries. He had already asked to be recalled, and had received permission to take six months' holiday, and then resign. To this end he had written: "I long for September, beyond which I will not stay if they were to make me Duke of Canada and Prince of Regiopolis." Still attending to matters of state, he lingered on in great pain for two weeks and died on the nineteenth of September the day after the first session of the United Parliament had ended.

Whatever may be said against Lord Sydenham, he was a brilliant and able man, and he taught Canadians, including the Reformers, a great deal about practical politics. He may have been hated by the French, but if he had not brought about the union of the Canadas, responsible government might not have been achieved.

Robert's next skilful manoeuvre hinged on the fact of his having been elected in two ridings. He had decided to represent Hastings and had asked his father if he would accept the nomination of the committee for the Fourth Riding of York. Although Phoebe was loath to see her husband re-enter politics because she feared for his health, the Doctor had been persuaded to accept the nomination.

However before matters went any further the Lower Canada Election Bill was rejected. This put an end to the hope of reinstating LaFontaine at Terrebonne. Robert, foreseeing the defeat of the Bill, wrote to his father on August 10, 1841:

> I think it would be very desirable that you should, even though you may have already accepted the nomination for North York, suggest to them the expediency of accepting your retirement and of returning Mr. LaFontaine if he will accept the nomination instead of you. I am satisfied that nothing that could be done at this juncture would have a better effect upon the state of the parties in the House than his return just now from North York. . . . It will greatly cement the union between Upper and Lower Canadian Reformers.

Quickly grasping the significance of this plan, the Doctor lost no time in implementing it. On August 13 he wrote to Robert:

> Your proposal and my letter to the North Riding have had the desired effect. My messenger has just returned with the answer, which I send by the same post with this. So as soon as you can communicate with M. LaFontaine, the better. He cannot avoid coming up, and I will go out with him to introduce him to our friends, and do what I can for the great object in view.

The proposed visit of LaFontaine caused quite a domestic flutter in the Baldwin household, as Robert wished his mother and father to entertain him. Phoebe was worried that she would not be able to make him comfortable, and because she did not speak French. After clever staff work by William and Robert, the invitation was sent and Phoebe found that she need have had no anxiety; Louis LaFontaine, at thirty-four, proved not only to be charming and courtly but to have an extensive command of English.

The Doctor and LaFontaine together canvassed the riding, and on September 11 William wrote to Robert:

> Mr. LaFontaine, William [Robert's brother] and myself all returned last night about 8 o'clock after a most agreeable circuit of North York – politically speaking, we were most

> favourably received at all the meetings. Mr. LaFontaine addressed them generally after I had so done – the proceedings and resolutions at each I have this minute left with Mr. Reynolds for publication in the *Examiner* on Wednesday – not a word of opposition was uttered anywhere –

William had gone out to the riding prior to LaFontaine's visit and laid the proposal before the Reform Committee: "At first the strangeness of this proposal made them hesitate but after twenty minutes deliberation they were unanimous for LaFontaine."

As a result of William's kindly efforts and the good impression made by LaFontaine, the latter was returned by the Fourth Riding of York with a majority of 210 votes in a special election on September 21, 1841, much to the delight of the Reformers. In the next election he was nominated and returned by the same riding.

* *

18

BALDWIN AND LAFONTAINE

In May of 1841 LaFontaine had written to Robert: "I seize this opportunity to send Miss Maria the plans of education adopted in the Convent of the Congregation at Montreal, and also one *Télémaque* in French, with engravings – I hope she will accept of it, as the expression of my desire she should speak French, when she comes to Montreal." No doubt Robert had discussed with his colleague the advantages of bilingualism and wanted his children to enjoy them, for, although he did not send Maria, his eldest, to Montreal to school, she was to study in Quebec City on the advice of John Neilson, the editor of the bilingual *Quebec Gazette*.

In 1843, her grandfather, William Warren, wrote to Robert, expressing his somewhat conservative views on female education; this is one of the few times father and son appear to have differed:

> I hope in my hurried postscript to you on the subject of the course of instruction mentioned in Mr. Neilson's letter . . . I have not appeared to you at all to dictate to you, who alone

> have not only the right, but the lawful judgment in the matter. In general my opinion as to female education of the present day, . . . (my view being extremely narrow) I think the most important of all objects (that of preparing young ladies to make good wives) is too much neglected . . . as I say, I fear the habit and taste for domestic duties is not adequately attended to in any of the very big seminaries, . . . Do not suppose I made my thoughts a subject of discourse with Maria. . . . On receiving your letter to her yesterday, Maria exclaimed to her Grandmama with a smile, "Why Papa has answered all my letter that I wrote him yesterday." I asked Maria, "Did I say anything to you on the subject of Mr. Neilson's Letter?" "No," says she, "you did not, but I wrote to Papa." She seems however, much pleased with your letter.

But, in spite of her grandfather's objections, Maria went in 1843 to attend the Ursuline Convent in Quebec City.

By that time, the political climate had changed with the arrival of Sir Charles Bagot in January 1842 to replace the late Lord Sydenham, and the appointment by the new Tory Prime Minister, Sir Robert Peel, of Lord Stanley in place of Lord John Russell as Colonial Secretary. The new Governor-General was, of course, a Tory; he was a man of considerable experience in diplomacy and he spoke impeccable French. Lord Stanley had made clear to him that the Imperial Government was unwilling to concede responsible government or majority rule, and this is confirmed by Peel's reply to a confidential memorandum from Lord Stanley regarding this policy:

> I would not voluntarily throw myself into the hands of the French Party, through fear of being in a minority. My hope certainly has been that acting as a Mediator, & keeping the various Parties in mutal check, Bagot might be able to detach Individuals from both extremes; and this is the policy which I still think it wd. be desirable to attempt.

One of Bagot's first moves was to appoint Judge Vallière as Chief Justice of Canada East and Dr. Meilleurs as Superintendent of Public Instruction; both were men of sound character and outstanding ability, bilingual, and moderate in their views.

Sir Robert Peel's note of approval reiterates the policy of divide and rule:

> Sir C. Bagot says that he has derived great advantage & has created an impression favourable to his Gov't. by making appointments to office of men of high character – not on the dictation of Party, but on the score of civil desert & personal qualification for official Trust. I would persevere in this system.

The new Governor-General found the necessary appointments to his Executive Council more complicated. If he was to choose from all parties, a Reformer, a member of the Family Compact party, and a senior Frenchman would seem the desirable combination. In an attempt to arrive at this, Bagot suggested to the Colonial Secretary in February Dr. W. W. Baldwin, as one of the senior Reformers of Canada West; Denis Benjamin Viger, as a prominent member of the French community; and John Neilson, as a bilingual moderate Reformer from Quebec.

Lord Stanley was shaken by these ideas. Viger, who had been implicated in the rebellion in Lower Canada, he rejected out of hand, and he wrote to Bagot expressing stern reservations regarding the appointments of Dr. Baldwin and Neilson.

After this rebuff Bagot realized that the policies suggested by the Imperial Government were going to be even more difficult than he had anticipated. Since February he had been toying with the idea of appointing Hincks to the post of Inspector-General, a position approximating that of Minister of Finance. Now the fact that Hincks had quarrelled during the previous session with Robert Baldwin made his appointment even more desirable; and this was to be balanced by the selection of a Family Compact man of character and ability in the person of J. S. Cartwright from Kingston. But Mr. Cartwright refused. Bagot was almost in despair until he found Henry Sherwood, another Compact man, willing to accept the post.

In the meantime the leaders of the various parties and groups were jockeying for position. William Draper, leader of the Tories in power, was in constant consultation with the Governor. Sir Allan MacNab, leader of the old Family Compact party, was in London vigorously pressing his party's claims and his own, and writing to Lord Stanley:

> I seized the first opportunity after the accession to office of the present administration, to come to London. . . . I fully expected that the deep injury, public degradation & injustice I had received at the hands of Lord Sydenham would at once be compensated for by your lordship, . . . in favour of my application to Her Majesty's Government for the honor of a Baronetcy on my return to Canada. [He had been made a knight bachelor in 1838.]

Sir Charles was well aware of MacNab's ambitions, for Lord Stanley wrote of the baronetcy, "I have told him that at present this is out of the question – but this is the object, which dangled before him, will be more likely than anything to keep him quiet." Nor was the Governor's opinion of MacNab very flattering, for he scorned, he said, to buy someone "whom he would have to re-purchase every Monday morning."

The two men who held the key to the political situation were Robert Baldwin and Louis LaFontaine. Both were now members of the Assembly and leaders of the solid majority in the House but neither was a member of the Executive Council. Their strategy at this time was to continue to consolidate their majority and to cement more closely the French and the moderate Reformers of Upper Canada. Robert's policy was to hold the members of the Executive responsible, rather than place any blame on the Governor, and to assume that responsible government was in operation, even if not conceded. He and his followers adopted a wait-and-see policy. Time was in their favour; they held the trump cards.

In July Provincial Secretary Harrison wrote confidentially to the Governor urging him to admit the French and Mr. Baldwin to the Executive Council, as he would find it impossible to get the one without the other. Draper gave Sir Charles the same advice, but stated that he could not serve as a member of the Council with Baldwin.

The new session had been summoned for September 8, 1842, and time was running out. But Bagot was determined to meet the impending crisis in his own way and on his own terms. He had already approached some French leaders but none would accept office, as they would immediately face the epithet of *le vendu* (the one who has been bought). Rather than approach Robert Baldwin, Bagot contacted LaFontaine, whom he was very desirous of getting into his executive. LaFontaine made it clear that he would not accept office without Baldwin and the resignation of certain members of the Council in whom he had no confidence.

On September 9, the day after the session opened, Bagot summoned LaFontaine to Government House and a frank discussion ensued. LaFontaine and the Governor met for further consultations on September 10 and 11 and each time LaFontaine consulted Robert. Finally the Governor proposed to give LaFontaine the post of Attorney-General for Canada East, and this was coupled with the offer of the Solicitor-Generalship for the French colleague of his choice. Draper had tendered his resignation and Bagot expressed his willingness to accept Robert Baldwin as Attorney-General for Canada West in his place. Still LaFontaine hesitated. There were two points on which he and Baldwin insisted: first the resignation of Henry Sherwood, who did not have the confidence of the majority in the House; secondly the question of pensions for C. H. Ogden and John Davidson, who were being retired to give place to LaFontaine and his colleague.

Bagot's offers were contained in a letter to LaFontaine dated September 13, not marked confidential. While LaFontaine hesitated, Bagot arranged that Draper should read to the House this letter, which also contained Draper's resignation. The French were astounded that LaFontaine should consider refusing what to them seemed a most generous offer.

After hurried consultation Baldwin and LaFontaine accepted office and Bagot agreed to drop Sherwood; the question of pensions was held over.

Thus was born what has been known as the first Baldwin-LaFontaine Ministry, though as Hincks rather waspishly declared afterwards, LaFontaine and Baldwin were not the senior members of the Executive Council; these were R. B. Sullivan and Francis Hincks. But whatever Hincks might say, LaFontaine and Baldwin were, and remained, the acknowledged leaders.

But the very fact that Sullivan and Hincks were allowed to remain on in the Executive unchallenged would seem a contradiction after the forced resignation of Henry Sherwood. The answer to this riddle is to be found in Robert's intimate knowledge of both men. R. B. Sullivan, President of the Council, he could scarcely have known better as first cousin, brother-in-law, and former law partner; R. B. S. was brilliant, flamboyant, and had been an inner and outer in politics. By corralling him at this time Robert won a staunch supporter, a gain which was to pay off in 1843 and 1844.

The case of Hincks is harder to understand, except for the fact that none knew better than Robert how completely committed Hincks was on the fundamental issue of responsible government. As far as Robert was concerned, this was the touchstone. And incredible as it may seem, Robert and Francis Hincks remained firm personal friends; at the height of their political differences, Robert Baldwin defended Francis Hincks in a lawsuit.

What was the effect of bringing in the Baldwin-LaFontaine Ministry? In the Canadian Parliament there was, for the most part, content and tranquility. In French Canada there was satisfaction but in the Tory press in English Canada there was anger and abuse, and Sir Charles Bagot was the subject of the most vitriolic attacks in the English press. The Imperial Government was far from happy but, apart from a stormy outburst from the Duke of Wellington about rolling his country in the mire, it stood behind Sir Charles. In December 1842 Lord Stanley wrote to Bagot, "You have commenced a great experiment. It is for your honour that you shall, if possible, remain to work it out."

In the meantime the session came to an end on October 12 as it was necessary for both Baldwin and LaFontaine to seek re-election on their appointment to government office.

LaFontaine was returned successfully, again for the Fourth Riding of York, but Robert was defeated in Hastings after one of the stormiest and most unruly contests, during which the military had to be called out. Robert wrote to LaFontaine during the election, predicting his possible defeat by his cousin Edmund Murney and all the forces that the Tories could muster. The final result was that after his defeat M. Bonne of Rimouski stood down and Robert was elected for that French Canada riding by acclamation, although he spoke no French. Thus was the debt of LaFontaines' election for the Fourth Riding of York repaid with honour.

From the point of view of the Baldwin-LaFontaine party, it was a disaster that Sir Charles Bagot was not destined to carry on the experiment of responsible government. The British Government had been willing to allow him to go along with this new principle in colonial administration but they were not enthusiastic, and his mortal illness (he died in March 1843) gave them the opportunity to reverse the trend.

The appointment of Sir Charles Metcalfe, a distinguished civil servant and career diplomat, was an unfortunate one. His experiences as Governor-General of India and Governor of Jamaica unfitted him for the rough-and-tumble of North American politics where assemblies had fought hard to achieve a fair amount of autonomy. To one who was accustomed to very wide powers and scrupulous deference, the attitude of the Council was presumptuous and lacking in respect. Their hard-won claim to responsible government savoured to him of radicalism and seemed to threaten imperial supremacy. He sensed quickly the vastly different political atmosphere in North America; as he wrote later to Lord Stanley, "The violence of party spirit forces itself on one's notice immediately on arrival in the colony." The new Governor was determined to "resist all encroachments by his Council" and the Council was equally determined to assert its right to be consulted.

The struggle which ensued was the toughest and nastiest yet, but it was not so far-reaching or important as the Sydenham fight had been. It was slow in developing as both sides were cautious. But once the battle lines were drawn it became a bitter contest, primarily between Baldwin and Sir Charles Metcalfe, with LaFontaine and his party sturdily backing up and supporting Baldwin and his smaller group in English Canada.

It was also, of course, a contest between the Reform majority in the Union Parliament and the Tory minority backed by the Governor and the influence of the Crown. The Governor believed, as the Tory press assured him, that the British connection was at stake. On the contrary, the fact that responsible government and the right of self-government in colonial internal affairs did not mean separation from the mother country became abundantly clear six years later, when it was the Tories themselves who advocated secession.

When the Assembly met again on September 28, 1843 after

a number of prorogations, there were four or five pieces of legislation which were to prove contentious. The first of these was the removal of the seat of government from Kingston, a location which had never been popular with any party. To Canadians, Toronto and Montreal were natural alternatives. The decision, of a kind usually taken by the Imperial Parliament, was left to the Canadian Government, with the stipulation that the choice was to be either Kingston or Montreal (Toronto and Quebec City were considered too far from the centre of the United Provinces). Thus Montreal was chosen but not without a good deal of opposition.

Another very contentious piece of legislation was Baldwin's University Bill, which proposed the secularization of higher education in the province and the amalgamation of all the secular colleges, such as King's College in Toronto, into one university, but with the sectarian colleges retaining much of their autonomy. This upset many of the Tories and the militant Protestants, particularly Bishop Strachan of Toronto, who had pointed out to Robert, himself a devout Anglican: "In destroying King's College by enactment, you have placed yourself in open defiance to God and his revealed word and turned an Institution in which the Saviour was worshipped into a nursery of infidelity and delivered, so far as you are able, the lands of Christ's flock into the hands of his enemy, the Prince of this world." Ryerson, on the other hand, considered the University Bill a wise piece of legislation. It would have passed, but because of the resignation of the Government it did not become law during this Parliament.

The Bill which was to have the most serious effect on the relationship between the Governor and his Executive Council was one for the discouragement of secret societies. It was aimed particularly at the Orange Society and other semi-political organizations whose members were intimidating voters and trying to influence the course of elections. Baldwin and LaFontaine sought and obtained the permission of the Governor to introduce the Bill, which passed the House by the large majority of fifty-five to thirteen.

In the Orange lodges feelings ran high, as this letter to Robert from his youngest child Eliza, then twelve, describes. After saying, "Grandfather received your letter by Mr. Small telling us that the Orange Bill has passed," she recounts the excitement of the night of November 8. The children had just gone to bed,

> when all at once we heard great screaming. I jumped out of bed and ran into the nursery as fast as I could and looking out of the window I saw a great crowd and they had a large paper lantern. There was written on it, "Behold the traitors Baldwin and Hincks" and there was something about Uncle Robert Sullivan on the other side but we could not make out what it was. One [effigy] they had for you and the other for Mr. Hincks. They had them both placed in a barrel of tar, then they put the barrel right in front of the hall door, they set the tar on fire and were knocking it about. Mr. Hincks burnt up very quickly but they could not get you to burn at all. At last they succeeded and then they gave a groan for you when you were burned up. They said that "they might go down amongst the Yellow Frenchmen." Willy [Robert's eldest son] heard from someone who was there, that they were going down to burn Mr. Small to-night.

In Kingston, another stronghold of the Orange Society, the mob set the Government at defiance, and in one ugly incident a man was killed and several were wounded.

In spite of the fact that the Secret Societies Bill was passed in the Legislature by a large majority, the Governor, on his own authority, reserved the Bill. This naturally enhanced him in the eyes of the Orangemen, but Baldwin and LaFontaine had every reason to think that Sir Charles's action in sanctioning the introduction of the Bill and then withholding his consent, was a breach of both political integrity and confidence in his Ministers.

This lack of confidence between the Governor and his Council is shown by a number of actions taken by Sir Charles Metcalfe which were guaranteed to annoy and frustrate the Executive Council, notably his appointment to the Speakership of the Upper House, without consulting them, of someone opposed to the views of the Executive Council. In fact, over the whole question of appointments the Governor and his Council were deeply at odds. It was obvious in late September 1843 that matters were rapidly coming to a head, and that Robert and LaFontaine had reached a point of exasperation. When, therefore, they heard that the Governor was about to make a certain appointment to a post in Canada East, Mr. Higginson, the Governor's Private Secretary, and LaFontaine had a discussion. Higginson expressed the view that in the practice of responsible government a minister was responsible only for the actions of his department, and was perfectly free to vote as he pleased on other matters. LaFontaine replied that if this was the view of responsible government held by his Excellency, then the sooner his Council was informed the better.

There the matter rested for a while. The Governor was determined to make the issue one of appointments, which he contended were the prerogative of the Crown. On the other hand Robert and LaFontaine saw in the lack of consultation, and in the independent actions of the Governor, a direct threat to responsible government itself as embodied in the Resolutions of 1841 and their practical application under Sir Charles Bagot.

On November 24 Robert and LaFontaine went to the Governor-General and stated their views; the next day the whole Council was brought into the discussion. On November 26 all resigned save Mr. Daly, the Provincial Secretary, and Metcalfe wrote to Lord Stanley that he had accepted their resignations.

So ended this brief session, which had lasted from September 28 to December 9, 1843. Besides its more general historic importance, it had afforded Robert the opportunity to state in Parliament, and for the record, the facts behind his actions during the rebellion. Following the Speech from the Throne, the Opposition had brought into debate a series of personal attacks, the most violent of which was made by Allan MacNab accusing Robert Baldwin of disloyalty, the implication being that he had gone out to join the rebels on that December afternoon in 1837. The *Examiner* of October 11, 1843 reported Robert as saying, in impassioned rebuttal, that:

> He was a Canadian by birth, education and by feeling and he felt proud in the avowal. Canada contained all he possessed in the world. – It held all that was dear to him. In its prosperity he had a large stake and far from wishing to add to the spirit of dissention he could only desire to see any measure calculated to advance the interests of his native country. It was a matter not of choice with him but in a manner forced upon him. He had, indeed, as the Hon and Gallant member

had affirmed, gone out with a flag of truce to the armed men who had approached Toronto but at whose insistence? . . . It was at the personal desire and upon the urgent solicitation of the panic stricken Government of Upper Canada which came to him in the person of the High Sheriff to request his interference to stop the deluded men who were approaching the city. He complied and went with a flag of truce – He was sent back for some evidence from the head of the Government that he really came in the character and with the authority he pretended to have and what was the return he received from the very man who sent him out? Sir F Head, through the same functionary [Jarvis] refused to give him a single line to show that he had really gone out under his sanction.

By 1843 William's health was giving way but at the same time honours and recognition were being accorded him. In August he wrote to Robert:

I yesterday received your letter of the 7th informing me of the interest through which I was honoured by being placed amongst the magistrates in the District. I, however, was favoured with a letter from Mr. Higginson dated the 5th, saying that he had it in command from the Governor General to inform me that His Excellency would have great pleasure in summoning me to the Legislative Council if I was so disposed to render my services to the Legislature in that Chamber. I replied to Mr. Higginson, requesting him to inform His Excellency that I was very sensible of the honour intended me, but that my declining health forbade my acceptance, and at the same time to inform His Excellency from me that ill health alone prevented me.

I am sure you will approve of my refusal, which was made with perfect deference to His Excellency – who, I have no doubt, in offering the honour meant it sincerely. I am, however, within this last week better than heretofore. My breathing continues short and I cannot speak without labour – my appetite is quite sufficient.

Apparently the Governor did not accept this refusal, because the patent for the Doctor's appointment to the Legislative Council is signed and "Recorded 22nd August 1843." But by the beginning of 1844 the deterioration in William's health had become more serious, as R. B. Sullivan's letter of January 2 to Robert makes quite clear:

> Your father's state of health gives us much alarm. I feel for you all very much but more for your mother than any. It is a fearful thing for the survivors when a generation, to which they belonged is fading away, but He who sends affliction and bereavement upon earth can also send consolation. My smattering of medical knowledge almost forbids me hope for a prolongation of your father's life, at a season of the year so unfavourable, and I have not the heart to express to you a hope which I cannot feel. I feel quite satisfied that my dear Uncle has lived to see us fully together in the cause of the country for which he had done so much, a cause to which he adhered through good and evil report and to which want of success always seemed to attach him the more firmly.

Robert had known LaFontaine for only three and a half years when the Doctor died on January 8, 1844, yet it was to him rather then any other that he wrote of his grief for the loss of his father:

> My dear Friend:
>
> You have long ere this heard the fatal termination of my poor father's malady and have, I am sure, attributed to that my having not written to you. When I first arrived from Kingston I found him looking much better than I had expected and he continued to do so for a week or ten days after my return. On Christmas Eve I observed his appetite seemed to fail him and though he appeared cheerful on Christmas morning, he ate little and seemed to linger with us in the evening, remaining a full hour beyond his usual time of retiring, as if he had a presentiment of its being the last he was to spend with us here. He had to be carried upstairs to his room that night and never left it after. He, however, occasionally rallied after this and particularly so the day before and the day of the public dinner [for the ex-ministers] and again for a couple of days in the following week, but evidently

lost strength with each bad turn and finally breathed his last between 12 and 1.00 o'clock in the morning of the 8th. While he was with us it seemed to me as if I grudged every moment that I was obliged to pass out of his room, and when he was gone, when he who had been the protector of my childhood, the guide of my youth and the counsellor of my manhood, was no more and I felt in all its weight the truth that I was indeed for the first time without a father, I was more overwhelmed than I had expected. I had seen his gradual decay and the certain termination was daily before my eyes but my mind had been occupied by the attentions which I was yet able to pay him, but when this was over and all I had to dwell on was the past – that past which brings him back to my memory as one of the kindest of parents and best of men, it seems as if I could scarcely realize it to myself that all was indeed past. And you, my dear friend will not, I am sure, be surprised at my feeling little able to return at once to other subjects and least of all to that of politics from which, if I could with honour, I would fly forever.

LaFontaine replied on January 25. He had been received as a member of the family by the Baldwins and it is evident that he reciprocated that affection in his regard for the Doctor.

My dear Friend,

I have received your letter of the 20th and a few days before, I had also received Mr. Heyden's. If you were conversant with my native language, or if I could express myself in your own as well as I can do in French, I would not fail, I am sure, in conveying to you the true expression of the deep and and painful feelings which were produced on my mind when first by Mr. Heyden's letter and afterwards by yours, I heard of your good and venerable father's death. I liked him as if he had been one of my *parents*. For a long time his state of health had, no doubt, prepared you and your family for such a painful event. Esteemed and respected as he was, the citizens of Toronto did but their duty to pay to his remains the last tribute which he could receive in this world. Yet it did them honour, and at the same time it must have been gratifying to you and your family.

It is to Francis Hincks, friend and neighbour of the Baldwin family, and the obituary in his paper the *Examiner* for Wednesday, January 10, 1844 that we owe some of those intimate sidelights on William's character that are so revealing.

"The obituary notice of the late Hon. W. W. Baldwin will undoubtedly attract the attention, engage the feelings and touch the sympathies of United Canada. Our country has lost a friend . . . [whose] life was all spent in the public service." Hincks recalls that in private life, the Doctor was always cheerful, yet always dignified. And then he records little-known facts about William's consideration and tenderness towards the destitute. "For years he appropriated a portion of his income as a fund upon which to issue a sort of bank accomodation to small mechanics and labourers who became pressed." He also tells us of "the establishment – many years since – of a public dispensary for the relief of the indigent sick."

William had put both his medical talent and part of his wealth to work for the public good, and in particular for the benefit of those who most needed help. And so his funeral, which was a large one, was attended not only by the great but by many of the sick and the poor who had known the genial and kindly Doctor as a friend.

* *

19

THE BRITISH CONNECTION

After the resignation of the Executive Council in November 1843, Metcalfe's tactics were first to prorogue Parliament, and this he did seven times, then to avoid dissolution and an election as long as possible so as to gain the time to win over as many members of the majority as he could, in the hope of gaining support for a new Executive Council.

In his first efforts to form a Council he was able to obtain the services of William Draper and of D. B. Viger, who had defended the Governor and had consequently become *Le Vendu* in the eyes of the French. These two became members of the Executive Council but did not hold government office, although the Governor-General had ordered Robert, who had resigned as Attorney-General, to hand over all official papers to Draper. Had they taken office, the practice of that time would have required them to seek re-election; but as it was, they continued to hold their seats in Parliament.

It was obvious that a great crisis was building up and both sides girded their political loins. The Governor and his Tory supporters had the powerful weapon of propaganda. LaFontaine was well served by such papers as *La Minerve,* the *Quebec Gazette* and *Le Canadien,* but the English-speaking Reformers needed coverage in Toronto since Hincks had moved to Montreal where, after briefly editing the *Times,* he founded his own paper, *The Pilot,* in March 1844. Fortunately for Robert, George Brown, a recent immigrant and a clever journalist, started a bi-weekly newspaper in Toronto early in 1844, the now famous *Globe.* For the Reformers, this excellent paper replaced the *Examiner,* for it was inevitable that George Brown with his liberal views should make common cause with the Reformers. "I am rather prepossessed in favour of the man as far as manner goes," wrote Baldwin to LaFontaine on January 20, 1844; and George Brown was to serve the interests of the Reform Party energetically and well until 1850.

The issues of religion and of race were allowed to muddy and distort the main issue, as was that of loyalty to the Crown (which was not at stake although Sir Charles insisted that it was). The real question was whether the Imperial Parliament was willing to abide by the Resolutions of 1841 and grant responsible government in fact.

In regard to religion the fact that the University Bill had been proposed was used to try and prove that Baldwin and his Reformers were against the established Church of England. The fact that Montreal was now to be the seat of government was cited as an indication that Canada West was being sacrificed and the French being favoured, even though it was the Imperial Parliament that had narrowed the choice to Kingston or Montreal (that fact was conveniently forgotten). Finally, Lord Metcalfe claimed that *he* supported true responsible government, and that the brand sponsored by Baldwin, LaFontaine, and their followers was one which was sure to lead to separation from the mother country.

In both Canada East and Canada West the political situation was in ferment. Invective, abuse and violence all had their place, and as in the Bond Head crisis, Ryerson, like Don Quixote, came riding into the fray again, this time in support of Sir Charles Metcalfe in what the Governor believed to be the defence of the British connection. Baldwin had all through his life been a staunch supporter of the British constitution and connection; now he was supported by LaFontaine:

> What reasons has he [Sir Charles Metcalfe] to charge us and the majority of the People of Canada, with disaffection and aiming at separation? I blame Mr. Viger for allowing Sir Charles to cast upon us such imputations – Far from thinking of separation, I quite agree with you, and I do not hesitate in stating that I sincerely believe it to be the mutual interest both of England and Canada that the connection should subsist as long as possible – and a good Government, based upon our managing ourselves, our local affairs, will secure the connection.

In fairness to the Governor, it is certain that he had convinced himself that it was a question of adherence to the Crown that now confronted Canadians. The inexplicable fact was that he had convinced not only Lord Stanley and the Tories under Sir Robert Peel, but also Lord John Russell and the Opposition, including Charles Buller, himself a strong advocate of responsible government.

There is no doubt that Baldwin, supported by LaFontaine and the Administration, had made a political error in standing pat on the question of a fairly minor appointment, and choosing this for a showdown with the Governor-General. It certainly alienated a number of Reformers in Canada West, although the French as a block supported the decision. But most of all, it gave some creditability to the claim of the Governor-General and his supporters that the issue was one of patronage and not of responsible government, whereas as far as Robert, LaFontaine and the majority in the House were concerned it was a question of their right to be consulted on all decisions and to resign if the Governor did not accept their advice. These principles had clearly been accepted, both by Lord Sydenham in the Resolutions of 1841, and by the Imperial Government in sanctioning Sydenham's actions. Thus there followed in Canada many months of bitter controversy. Canadians were split into two opposing camps and the Governor-General, just as Sir Francis Bond Head and Lord Sydenham had done, personally entered politics with all that that implied.

In May there was a by-election held in Montreal. "I am glad," wrote Robert to Louis LaFontaine, "that the *Pilot* has assumed a higher tone since the election. I did not altogether like all his [Hincks's] papers during the contest, but, of course, we must make allowances for the fiery oven into which he was cast. How perfectly savage the Tory papers were upon him."

R. B. Sullivan was now back in the fold and solidly supporting Robert and the Reformers:

> I sent you a copy of an address and hope you will approve of it. Sullivan drew it up. He has, as you have already learned, taken the temperance pledge and it is most gratifying to see the change it has wrought in himself and it has had a powerful effect also in restoring him in the estimation of his former friends throughout the country. I mean his political friends.

Political pamphlets were the order of the day. Egerton Ryerson's *Sir Charles Metcalfe defended against the attacks of his late Councillors* was answered by a series of very witty and mordant articles in pamphlet form. These were entitled *Letters on Responsible Government by "Legion"*, and were written by R. B. Sullivan. "Never in Canada had more scathing letters on a political subject been written by any man," writes Judge David Read in his *Lives of the Judges of Upper Canada and Ontario.*

Finally, by September 1844, the Governor-General had been able to muster sufficient strength in his Council, which contained Draper, now officially Attorney-General for Canada West; Daly, continuing as Provincial Secretary; Viger as President of the Council; and Smith from Montreal as Attorney-General for Canada East. W. Morris and D. B. Papineau (brother of Louis-Joseph, the rebel) were also on the Executive. So on September 24 Metcalfe dissolved Parliament, and an election was called for November. There followed one of the bitterest elections in Canada.

In spite of his many absences during this tense election of 1844, Robert found time to arrange for the three younger children (who were living at home with their grandmother Phoebe and himself) to start learning French in earnest. The boys – Willy, aged fourteen and Bob, ten – were sent to the seminary in Quebec City and Eliza joined her sister Maria at the Ursuline convent there. On October 10, 1844, Maria wrote to her father:

My dear Papa,

. . . Uncle William has doubtless arrived at home before this and has told you all about the journey down. All at the convent were surprised to see me, particularly when they found that I had Eliza with me.

The boys came to see us last Saturday and though from what they said it appears they are a little lonesome, yet I hope that will soon pass off . . . Willie said that he had already begun to speak French a little with some of the masters who do not understand English . . . As for Eliza, though she was also lonesome at first yet she is now pretty well reconciled and will soon, I hope be able to make a beginning in speaking French . . .

The boys desire me to give their best love to you all particularly to their dear Grandmama, Papa and Aunt Anne in which Eliza and I heartily join, and now dear Papa do try and let us hear from you more often and believe me your ever affectionate and dutiful daughter, Maria.

That Robert was very keen to have his children make progress in French is evident in this letter to Bob:

The interruption which removing you to Quebec has necessarily occasioned in your classical studies will I am satisfied be more than compensated by the advantage you will derive from a thorough knowledge of the French language. I have in my letter to Willcocks [Willy] mentioned the embarrassment that I feel at not understanding it and which occurs almost every day. And I hope that you will make it a point to acquire such a thorough knowledge of that language as will enable you to speak as fluently whether in public or in private conversation in the one language as in the other – Nothing short of this ought to satisfy yourselves –

Maria was to have a number of opportunities to put her French to good use, and the following year Robert writes to the boys of one such occasion when she was staying with General and Mrs. Dix in Washington: "Maria in her last letter to me says that she had gone with Mrs. Dix to call on the Belgian Ambassador and that as he and his lady did not speak English her French had been called into requisition." Robert was extremely pleased and adds, "Maria has asked me to send her a paper so I have to get another *Minerve* to send to Washington – You see I am determined to make you read our politics in French."

Before starting his campaigning Robert visited Rimouski where he received a public ovation and would have been elected again by acclamation, had he so wished; but since LaFontaine was now seeking election in his old riding of Terrebonne, Robert felt it would be more fitting to be returned for a riding in Canada West. He was approached by the electors of Middlesex, which he took as a great compliment, but felt that he had no reason to desert his faithful followers in the Fourth Riding of York, and he was returned for that riding.

LaFontaine's letter to Robert of November 12, 1844, following the election, shows the affection and accord which existed between the two men:

> I see your party completely routed in Upper Canada, and you who have done so much for them, you seem to be once more abandoned by them – Then I may ask, what are the materials you have to deal with? How different they are from ours – We have a people, and you have not – Religious dissensions exercise their baneful influence in Upper Canada – A. will not vote for B. because B. is a Methodist, B. will not vote for A. because A. is an Espicopalian – C. will not vote for D. because D. is I do not know what – but nearly all will agree not to vote for a Catholic – To this cause I ascribe the reason of the defeat of our friend and your cousin Col. Baldwin in 1841 & 1844 – Our French Canadian population are all Catholics to a man – Still, you will never see any of them ask a candidate, to what religion do you belong? What are your politics is the only question they put to him – You have an example of it in your own case – In the County which I may call yours, the County of Rimouski, I speak the truth when I say that no one, nor Morin, nor myself, nor even Papineau himself, could be returned in opposition to you – And yet you are a Protestant, and perhaps that very fact would induce them, approving as they do your politic principles, to choose you in preference to anyone of their own, though a Catholic –

The Reformers, with the loss of support from Egerton Ryerson and a number of his Methodists, were defeated by a small majority. LaFontaine's letter continues:

> I see our friends are quite discouraged – The Government organs have already trumpeted that the Opposition is reduced to the French constituencies – and you know for what effect they say so – It is with the view to excite feelings of hostility against us in England – We feel it, and I feel it – . . . I wish you had come down – I hope to see you soon – I wish to have your advice. . . . If we have any chance to carry the [Speaker's] chair, it is by putting Morin forward – I think Papineau will not dare to vote against him; and then the Administration is paralyzed – For us it would be a victory to have one of the Ex-Ministers in the chair – . . .

Metcalfe and his Government Party had won the election, but it soon became apparent to disillusioned Canadians that the election was not a question of loyalty at all. Instead of rebellion, which had followed in 1837, constitutional government proceeded as usual. As this point was brought home to the Canadian people, the ultimate winning of responsible government became certain. However the members of the British Government were among the last to realize this. They were delighted that Metcalfe had conducted himself as they felt Bagot should have done in 1842. As a result Sir Charles Metcalfe was created Baron Metcalfe of Fern Hill.

A new member who took his seat after the elections of 1844 was a tall, craggy-faced young lawyer from Kingston. His name was John A. Macdonald and he was elected for that city in support of William Draper and his party.

Parliament now met in Montreal, with Draper and the Government Party possessing a slim majority. This second Parliament of the United Canadas was to last until July 1847, and during the intervening period there were three sessions: November 1844 to March 29, 1845; March 20 to June 9, 1846; and June 2 to July 28, 1847.

With such a slim majority the moves made by both the Government and the Opposition took on an added significance, although on the face of it the three sessions were relatively unimportant and unproductive. Sir Allan MacNab was elected Speaker by a majority of only three, and in order to compensate for the lack of leadership in the Assembly, and to introduce a worthy spokesman in debate against such formidable opponents as LaFontaine, Morin and Baldwin, Draper resigned his seat in the Upper House and was re-elected to the Assembly.

While Draper was seeking re-election, "The business of the House goes on very slowly," Robert wrote to his son Bob in February 1845, "and it is quite uncertain when we shall be prorogued – Mr. Draper is to come to our House as Member for London and if they are to wait for his return to bring forward their measures we may be here until the opening of the navigation –"

During the first session the adroit Draper introduced a University Bill, hoping thereby to steal a march on Baldwin and the Reformers. But the move back-fired, as Baldwin and many of his supporters voted against it, feeling that the Bill was not liberal enough, and that the finances merely subsidized the sectarian colleges. In consequence, although it passed the second reading, the Government did not risk the final stage.

Draper's second effort was much more successful and this time he really stole the Opposition's thunder. He anticipated their move to introduce a resolution to amend that part of the Act of Union which had proscribed the official use of the French language. So Draper had Papineau introduce a Bill giving both languages equal official status. The significance of this Bill was the fact that Metcalfe, by consenting to its introduction, went directly against his instructions from the Colonial Secretary. The result was as might have been expected – the Bill was welcomed on all sides and passed without opposition.

Between the first and second sessions, March 29, 1845 to March 20, 1846, Robert had to attend to family affairs. In January 1845 he had written to his brother William Augustus, on whom had fallen the burden of winding up their father's estate: "I do I assure you regret sincerely the trouble and difficulty that our land affairs intail upon you and if I could would be right glad to get home to assist you. When I return I must devote myself wholly to the business with you till it is got through."

Letters from Robert's uncle John Morgan were always read with pleasure, but this one, written in September 1845, was particularly welcome:

> It was with much pleasure that, by your letter of the 20th instant, I learned that Maria was to pass the coming winter at Washington with Catherine. I had not heard before of the invitation – that and its acceptance are very gratifying to your Aunt and myself. I think the winter society of Washington very agreeable. . . . An universal courtesy prevails – . . . they all mingle most thoroughly with the outmost good humour and on the footing of the most perfect equality.

In the same letter Robert received high praise from his uncle for his and his father's efforts to achieve responsible government. This, at a time when Robert's spirits must have been at a low ebb and from one who had no political axe to grind, must have been particularly gratifying. "Your father and yourself are entitled to the credit of having given to Canada the practical benefits of the constitution of England, and that influence which, when the people choose to use it, will put all things to rights."

In 1845 John J. Morgan was seventy-five years of age. He had retired from the New York Assembly in 1840 but still took a lively interest in politics and was very well informed on current affairs.

Robert had been overworking and overtaxing his strength, and early in 1846 suffered a bad attack of measles. In February John Morgan wrote again: "Your recovery from the measles, you may well think, has given us much relief; . . . I consider it, at all ages, a trying disorder, and generally more so according as the subjects are older." And then, knowing Robert, Morgan adds: "The convalescent should be careful until the health is perfectly re-established."

Robert's illness showed only too well that his health was slowly being undermined by the demands of both his political and his private life. Parliament might be in recess, but he and LaFontaine and their followers were in constant touch.

In this interim period (1845 to 1846) it became quite apparent that Draper and his Government must do all in their power to enlist French members and French support; and there began a strange and somewhat devious correspondence between Draper and René Edouard Caron, the Speaker of the Legislative Council, in which Draper tried to ascertain what terms, in seats in the Council and appointments, the French would demand to secure their support. Draper was quite cold-blooded in his willingness to sacrifice both Papineau and Viger, who had not been able to command the support of the French party. He was also quite candid about the fact that while Metcalfe was Governor, no direct approach could be made to LaFontaine. All this was relayed to LaFontaine, who in turn consulted with Baldwin, feeling that Caron looked perhaps too favourably on Draper's offer. After some hesitation LaFontaine expressed the view to Caron that either the French came in as of right, or not at all. This was the birth of that fateful political theory of the double majority which was to bedevil Canadian politics for more than two decades.

The basic idea was that for every appointment made in Canada West, a corresponding appointment should be made in Canada East, and in fact there should be virtually two Cabinets. LaFontaine was a keen supporter of this idea, and he wrote to Caron that he would ask for nothing more, but that he would be willing to settle for nothing less.

On the other hand Robert Baldwin saw its dangers and its racial implications, and from the first strongly opposed the idea of the double majority. He wrote to LaFontaine on October 16, 1845: "The principle itself is one that I conceive to be inadmissible and indeed wholly impracticable."

But Francis Hincks, although he opposed the idea, thought it might be tried for tactical reasons. "It would drive the Tories mad, effect a breach between them and their allies in Upper Canada, reunite the Liberal party and give a lesson to the Lower Canadian loose fish [party deviates] that would not be forgotten," he had written to Robert on September 23. But there the matter rested for a time because, during the months prior to the second session, Lord Metcalfe's ill health forced him to resign and he returned to England in November 1845 a dying man. Cancer of the cheek had spread to the eye; he had carried on with great fortitude. He died in England the next year.

* *

20

PEACE AND GOOD GOVERNMENT

Lord Metcalfe's successor was Earl Cathcart, a military man, whose appointment was occasioned by the inflammatory situation that had grown up between Great Britain and the United States over the Oregon boundary dispute. At the National Democratic Convention in the United States in 1844 the slogan adopted had been "Fifty-four forty or fight," referring to the American claim to the territory up to this parallel. The question was settled by the Oregon Treaty of June 1846, which established the United States boundary on the 49th parallel.

During this time Robert Baldwin received two interesting letters, one from his uncle, that admirable American John Morgan, and the other from his daughter Maria. John Morgan wrote from New York in February 1846:

> Maria seems to be much pleased with Washington, and goes much into company. She is considered very amiable, very intelligent and very discreet, and has no small claim to the character in society of a very agreeable and a fashionable young lady. . . . We think there will be no war. The notice in respect

to the occupation is to be given no doubt but it will be given in such a manner as will take from it everything like ill-temper.

The general feeling of the country is far better, and we do not doubt that the same feeling exists in England. It would be terrible after a peace of thirty years to bring upon the world the horrors of war. Certainly apprehension of war has very much passed away within a week or two and I really think war will not take place. Tell your Aunt Anna Maria not to distress herself about it – there will be no war.

In March 1846 Maria herself wrote from Washington: "Mr. Dix said that he would have the Congressional Globe sent to you today and he has also promised to send you one of his speeches." Mr. Dix was John Morgan's son-in-law, and at this time was a United States senator from New York; later he became Secretary of the Treasury and finally U.S. Ambassador to France. Maria continues:

Your alarm about war is, I trust, entirely unfounded. Mr. Dix desires me to assure you most seriously, that the United States has not the slightest idea of annexing Canada and that if they want to enlarge their territory it is rather to the South than to the North. I am sure that if you were here, you would agree with me in thinking that there is no probability of war. Indeed in the city I have spoken to but very few who have believed in it. Mrs. Polk, the President's lady said to Catharine [Mrs. Dix] and myself in the course of a morning visit that she had never thought nor does she think, we are to have war. . . . I must, as you say, feel, as a true Canadian, indignant at the idea of an enemy's entering "our Country", yet I feel almost certain that all will be settled amicably between the two countries. This is not merely my opinion, as I said before, but that of many and most of the Government here. . . . You say you cannot help smiling at the long yarn you have spun on politics to a young lady of eighteen, but do you think I have lived all my life among politicians for nothing. No indeed! Politics are with me as though they were a second nature and although I do not think ladies should allow such differences to interfere with their social intercourses, still I do think they should take an interest in the politics of their country. It is always an interesting subject to me and therefore, you need never be afraid of saying too much at least for fear of fatiguing me.

With the departure of Lord Metcalfe, the official attitude towards LaFontaine changed, and when the second session began it was enlivened considerably by his reading to the House the Caron-Draper correspondence. No group could feel more annoyed or hoodwinked than the Tories, particularly those of Canada East, and the attempt on the part of the Government to obtain French support collapsed for a time.

Another attempt to introduce the University Bill failed, and a motion was passed saying that this was not the time for such legislation. This demonstrated again the weakness and ineptitude of the Government in power.

Hincks and George Brown were already talking in terms of a new election. Robert's cautious approach had the fiery and impetuous Hincks on political pins and needles, so in characteristic manner he took Robert to task:

> I think it is time to let Lord Cathcart see that we are not going to be quiescent under another pro constitution [a pseudo-constitution]. Mr. Brown thought that we ought to prepare for the next election. There can be no doubt that such preparation is very necessary and I think something should be done this Fall. . . . It appears to me that you ought to visit if possible, the constituents in London and their districts to have arrangements for public dinners. . . . Had this been done in the last election all would have gone well.
>
> You do not *lead* enough. You seem rather to follow their lead.

Hincks in Montreal was short of funds for the *Pilot,* and he continues in this letter: "I wrote you a letter by John Rolf [Rolph] a few days ago which I fear did not reach you. I am terribly worried at the moment about money matters for it is really impossible to obtain assistance from the group." Hincks claimed that he had been promised support by the Reform Party and by March 1847 was threatening to sell the *Pilot.*

Brown, on the other hand, claimed that Hincks did receive assistance and that this enabled him to undersell the *Globe.*

These were among the many headaches Robert had to contend with; but, more important, the Reformers and the French were again confronted with a major problem. There is no doubt that the French knew that they were being wooed by the Government Party. Negotiations began again, after the second session, between Draper and Caron; and the French, particularly in Quebec City, were hungry for power. There was real danger at this time that Draper would succeed in splitting the French of Quebec City away from the French of Montreal, who were the ardent supporters of LaFontaine. But an even greater danger was the possibility that the Quebec members might stampede their Montreal confrères into office, thereby breaking the connection between Baldwin and LaFontaine, and splitting the Reform Party along racial lines. Fortunately the leadership and discipline of LaFontaine were very evident at this time. He refused to have anything to do with Caron or to enter into any negotiations.

During August 1846 Robert Baldwin again wrote to Louis LaFontaine vehemently denouncing the idea of the double majority, and the dangers in the Draper-Caron overtures:

> Mr. Draper may be as you say a cunning man but with all his cunning I think he has made and seems still to be making some grand mistakes. . . . I may be mistaken however, but whether I am so or not I should deeply regret, for their own sakes, as well as for that of the Country, if any of our political friends should consent to make shipwreck with him in his present troubles. . . . You already know my opinion of the Double Majority Scheme as respects the interests of the Province at large. . . . The arrangement will be viewed as one based essentially on a natural origin distinction wholly irrespective of political principle . . . British and French will then become in reality what our opponents have so long wished to make them, the essential distinctions of party, and the final result will scarcely admit of doubt.

It was a strange contradiction that during the last years of Lord Metcalfe's administration, and then under Lord Cathcart, Draper exercised much greater executive power than Baldwin and LaFontaine had ever done under Sir Charles Bagot, the kind of power over which Lord Metcalfe and the Imperial Government had raised such a hostile outcry. In fact it had been on this issue, the power of the Cabinet, that the bitterest of all elections up to that time had been fought.

On the question of patronage which had sparked the great quarrel, Lord Elgin wrote to the Colonial Secretary on March 17, 1848: "Mr Draper's last speech in Parliament . . . contained the most arrogant assertions of the rights of ministers in this matter ever propounded in the Canadian House of Commons."

In the matter of ministerial responsibility, too, Draper had virtually a free hand and responsible government was certainly operating under him in default of any effort by the Governor or the Imperial Government to say him nay. But in spite of this, his administration was woefully weak and commanded the slimmest of majorities.

The policy of Baldwin and LaFontaine was to give the Government Party enough rope to hang itself. They were in no hurry, and as Robert suggested to LaFontaine on December 22, 1846, it would be a good thing if the country "had longer experience of the administrative qualities of the present gentry in office."

The third session opened on June 2, 1847 with a drastic reshuffle of the ministry. Denis-Benjamin Papineau was the only French member in the Cabinet. Sherwood, who had been dismissed, was now brought back as Attorney-General of Canada West and a new election was a certainty. Hincks had written to Robert the previous July urging him to start campaigning, and this he had done by making an extensive tour through the western ridings of Canada West.

Meanwhile, during 1846, a political change had taken place in Great Britain. Lord John Russell was now Prime Minister and Lord Grey had become Colonial Secretary. The Whigs were back in power.

With the signing of the Oregon Treaty and Lord Cathcart's departure from Canada, a new Governor-General was appointed. This was Lord Elgin, a Scottish peer, like Metcalfe a former Governor of Jamaica. The fact that he was the son-in-law of Lord Durham was in his favour, but Robert and LaFontaine were distrustful of the Whigs, and they saw no hope of a change in the policy towards Canada. LaFontaine wrote to Robert in

September 1846: "We have a new Governor; he is a young man, since he is younger than you and myself . . . I must confess that I have some apprehensions. I have little confidence in the Whigs, in relation to colonial matters."

Lord Elgin did not arrive in Canada until early in January 1847. His charm, his obvious desire to conduct himself in a constitutional manner, his fluent French, his ability to get on with French Canadians, and his ready grasp of Canadian problems gradually dispelled the fears of the Reformers, and were to make Lord Elgin the most popular Governor-General Canada had had.

But the new Governor was content to make haste slowly. He presided over the dying moments of the third session of the second Parliament, and he watched with interest the elections which followed his dissolution of that Parliament in July 1847.

The election of 1847-1848 was a double triumph for the Reformers. LaFontaine and his party were returned in full force in Canada East, while in Canada West, to the surprise of many including Lord Elgin, the Reformers won by a handsome majority. Parliament met in February 1848.

The defeated Administration chose to meet the new Assembly before resigning, thus sticking to office till the last moment. This pleased both the Reform leaders as it avoided the necessity of naming a new Cabinet prior to taking office. But Baldwin and LaFontaine had been busy in making their selections, and had even devised a secret code to inform Baldwin should the Governor send for LaFontaine.

The session under the Tories lasted less than a month. A. N. Morin was elected Speaker and during the reply to the debate on the Throne Speech Robert moved what was in effect a vote of no confidence, and the Government, after being defeated, resigned. Lord Elgin then called on LaFontaine and Baldwin to form a Ministry.

Both were ready with their Cabinet, which had been whittled down from twenty-one to the following: Attorneys-General, L. H. LaFontaine and R. Baldwin; Solicitor-General, T. C. Aylwin; Inspector-General, F. Hincks; Receiver General, Louis-Michel Viger; Commissioner of Public Works, E. T. Taché, and Assistant Commissioner, Malcolm Cameron; Commissioner of Crown Lands, J. H. Price; President of the Executive Council, James Leslie; Speaker of the Upper House, R. E. Caron; Provincial Secretary, R. B. Sullivan.

So opposed was Robert even to the suggestion of the double majority that although there had always been two Attorneys-General, one for each of the Canadas, still at this time he made it quite clear that he considered LaFontaine the leader of the Reform Party.

Not long after this a change was made in the Ministry; T. C. Aylwin was raised to the Bench and William Hume Blake became Solicitor-General – "your Solicitor-General," as Robert pointed out to LaFontaine.

All but the members of the Upper House had to seek re-election upon taking office, but this was to present no difficulty, it was only time-consuming. In the meantime the House was prorogued and did not sit again for nine months.

Ever since Lord Elgin had arrived in Canada his relations with all parties had been frank, friendly and impartial. Although he had not anticipated the return of the Reformers in the elections of 1847, he was willing to accept and act with the new Ministry. This attitude of his went a long way to allay the bitterness that had generated under Lord Metcalfe. One incident is sufficient to show this new feeling of confidence.

In 1844 LaFontaine had been so angered by continued imputations of disloyalty that he had resigned his appointment as Queen's Counsel in protest; Robert had followed suit, but with strong reservations, as he wrote to LaFontaine, September 10, 1844:

> I did not hesitate in deciding on following the step you and our friend Morin had taken in the matter. . . . I hold it to be due to you individually as Head of the late administration, and the acknowledged leader of the party to which I belong, I, moreover, think that for me to have omitted following your resignation would under all circumstances, be productive of worse consequences than any than can arise out of the contrary course. . . . It is however, due to you as well as to myself, to add that I think the step a mistake . . . I fear it may . . . be made the ground of charges upon us and converting the question into one of a personal character as between us and the Governor General.

But these resignations had not been accepted, and now, with the renewed confidence on both sides, Baldwin had written to Small, who had also resigned, as early as March 9, 1848, that in deference to the Queen's representative they resume at once their positions as Queen's Counsel as "conferred upon us by our patents."

In the larger question of responsible government, the attitude of the Imperial Government had undergone a marked change under Lord Grey, the Colonial Secretary. His avowed policy was that "[it is] neither possible or desirable to carry on the government of any of the British provinces in North America in opposition to the opinion of the inhabitants." In this same famous despatch of November 3, 1846 to Sir John Harvey, Lieutenant-Governor of Nova Scotia, Grey went even further in defining responsible government with the result that, although the fight for responsible government had been initiated and carried on in Upper Canada prior to the struggle in Nova Scotia, conditions in the Maritimes, without the complicating factor of two races and a Metcalfe crisis, had favoured the fruition of party rule there prior to its being formally accepted in the United Provinces.

Thus with the summoning of LaFontaine and Baldwin in 1848, Elgin with quiet dignity set the seal of imperial approval on the principle of responsible government. It was fitting that Lord Durham's son-in-law should be the instrument by which so many of the brilliant recommendations contained in the famous Report should be implemented. It is significant that the great principle for which William and Robert and their Reform colleagues had fought came into being in this quiet and constitutional manner as the Baldwins had always claimed it should, that principle so ably described in Dr. William Warren Baldwin's letter to the Duke of Wellington, then Prime Minister of Great Britain, January 3, 1829:

> I am . . . to invite your Grace's thoughts to that principle of the British Constitution, in the actual use of which the Colonists alone hope for *peace, good government* and *Prosperity* . . . the principle alluded to is this, the presence of a provincial Ministry/ if I may be allowed to use the term/ responsible to the Provincial Parliament, and removable from Office by His Majesty's representative at his pleasure and especially when they lose the confidence of the people.

* *

21

THE TEST OF THE PRINCIPLE

Since their grandfather's death in 1844, Lawrence Heyden had acted as guardian to the Baldwin children during Robert's enforced absences while attending Parliament. Heyden was Robert's friend and brother-in-law, being the husband of Barbara Sullivan, Eliza's sister. By 1848 the boys had left the seminary at Quebec and were attending Upper Canada College in Toronto under the stern eye of Mr. Barron. Morgan Baldwin, the youngest son of John Spread, was also at the college; he was the same age as young Bob although he was actually a first cousin of Robert's and the boys were great friends.

At his rooms on St. Antoine Street in Montreal a letter from his elder son Willy, dated May 9, 1848, was delivered to Robert. It unfolded a little domestic drama.

Dear Father,

. . . . I wish I could spare you the pain that reading this will cause you . . . Yesterday Bob did not appear at dinner, and immediately after dinner Edmund [Morgan's elder brother] came and asked me if Bob had been home since College. I told him, "no", and he said that he feared that Bob and

> Morgan had gone off, and that Morrice had brought home Morgan's books which he had found at Mr. Scadding's . . . We then went to the College to see if they had been there in the afternoon, and found that they had been absent, and we thought that they might have gone down to Kingston, for a day or two before, Mr. St. George* said to Morgan, "So you intend to be a sailor?" Morgan answered "Yes", and Mr. St. George said, "But your mother will never allow you," to which Morgan answered, "I will then go of my own accord." We did not think they would have attempted to take Mr. St. George's sail-boat, as they neither of them understood how to manage it . . . [But the sail-boat, Willy tells his father, was found to be missing and was seen in the bay trying to put back, but unable to do so owing to lack of wind.] So Edmund went with two men in a skiff, and to his astonishment, found the two boys trying to come home.

Having got Bob home, Willy and Maria were rather at a loss, so Willy went to "Uncle Heyden," who said, "Send him back [to the college] in the morning." But apparently Bob was so fearful of the disgrace of being publicly punished that it was not until Heyden had gone and spoken to him that he "no longer objected, I went with him to tell the reason why he was not there earlier. Morgan had been punished in the morning, so they punished Bob in the afternoon." Willy goes on to say that while out in the boat Bob realized that he could not leave his grandmama (Phoebe Baldwin) and so he and Morgan had tried to return.

This incident was to have a happy sequel, for Robert appears to have been a wise as well as an affectionate father, and by 1849 he had made it possible for Bob to realize the great ambition that he shared with Morgan, to sail before the mast.

Although it was to be nine months before the next session began on January 18, 1849, a prodigious amount of legislation was planned. Before the session ended on May 30, 1849, about 190 bills had been introduced and enacted and had received royal assent.

* This was Henry, the son of Quetton St. George, the great friend of William Warren. He had been born in Montpellier, France, but had come to Canada and lived for a time at Oak Ridges, where his father had extensive properties.

This ambitious program was made possible, not only by the unanimity of a solid majority in Parliament, but more especially by the teamwork of LaFontaine, Baldwin and Hincks in dividing the work load and being responsible for the legislation in their own particular fields. LaFontaine busied himself with matters dealing with Canada East, specifically the reform of the judicial system and political measures such as the amnesty Bill; a Court of Queen's Bench was established and the Superior Court was revised.

Francis Hincks dealt with fiscal matters, trade and transportation. He was in his element with the coming of the railroads, and materially stimulated their expansion by his measure guaranteeing, at 6% interest, half the bonds of any railway more than seventy-five miles long, once half the line had been built. Canals were completed on the upper St. Lawrence, and the country, which had been in a depression in 1848 and 1849, began steadily to improve.

Robert's name is particularly associated with two Bills, the University Act to amend the charter of the university established at Toronto, and the Municipal Act, often called the Baldwin Act. The final settlement of the school system under Ryerson owes a good deal to Robert as well.

Ever since 1842 Robert had wished to extend higher education to Canadians, irrespective of creed. Up until this time there were a number of sectarian colleges, notably King's College in Toronto, Queen's University, and the Upper Canada Academy, later Victoria University. The University Act was to achieve its purpose, although certain parts dealing with administration were later amended. John Strachan, Bishop of Toronto, raised his voice in violent protest, along with others of the old Family Compact party such as W. B. Robinson and W. Boulton. In spite of strong opposition and the *Globe*'s report of April 21, 1849, that Bishop Strachan considered it would produce "an infidel College," the Bill was passed by forty-four to fourteen and marked a great advance in higher education.

The School Act of 1849, which was drafted by Malcolm Cameron, was so formed that it resulted in the resignation as Superintendent of Schools of Egerton Ryerson, to whom Cameron and other Reformers were deeply opposed.

Ryerson's letter of objections to the Bill was suppressed by

Cameron in submitting the proposed legislation to Baldwin and LaFontaine. When the matter was brought to Robert's attention, although he had more reason than Cameron for disliking Ryerson for his political actions in 1836 and 1844, still in fairness to him and his valid objections to the Bill, he took the extraordinary step of suspending the school legislation. This demonstrates Robert's great interest in education at all levels, as well as the fact that he was not swayed by rancour. It also resulted in an excellent school Bill by Ryerson in 1850.

With regard to the Municipal Act, the Upper Canada Law Journal noted: "Had Mr. Baldwin never done more than enact our municipal and jury laws, he would have done enough to entitle his memory to the everlasting respect of the inhabitants of this province. Neighbouring provinces are adopting the one and the other almost intact . . . equally noted for simplicity and for completeness of detail not to be found elsewhere." It was only to be expected that the man who had fought so long for responsible government would be almost equally interested in seeing that the province acquired local municipal government and local autonomy. In essence this Act abolished the districts, which in earlier times had been the units of rural government under magistrates as in the days of Robert's grandfather, and recognized: the police villages, with very limited powers; the incorporated villages; and the townships, with their own elected officers, five councillors and a reeve (the latter also a member of the County Council). Towns were to enjoy wider powers of self-government, while the three cities, Hamilton, Kingston and Toronto, were to be treated as counties, with additional powers.

This statute was a fairly massive document of some sixty-eight pages, but its ideas were clear and logical and they stood the test of time. Needless to say, modern problems of local improvement and rural development have introduced new dimensions in municipal government, as Robert foresaw when he made the Act as flexible as possible.

But the Bill over which there was the greatest controversy and which threatened to bring down the Government was LaFontaine's Act of Indemnification, generally referred to as the Rebellion Losses Bill. It is also the statute over which there has been the greatest misconception.

The Act itself was for the purpose of compensating those

in Canada East who had suffered property loss or damage during the suppression of the Rebellion of 1837. In the minds of many Canadians, and of some people in Britain, it was a scheme to indemnify rebels, but in fact the Act specifically excluded all those convicted of treason or who had been sentenced to transportation. What the Act proposed was simply to do for those in Canada East what had already been arranged for by enactment for those in Canada West. In October 1840, before the Union, a statute had been passed in Upper Canada giving compensation for damage suffered in the uprising to the tune of £40,000 sterling. This, however, had not been implemented at the time because no mention had been made as to the method by which the money was to be raised. But in 1845 an Act was passed by Draper and his Tory Government making the Act of 1840 operative, and setting aside the receipts from the tavern licences in Canada West for this purpose. The amount so collected from 1845 to 1849 was approximately £38,000.

Naturally there had been a great outcry from Canada East for similar legislation, and Metcalfe had set up a commission of five members to look into the question of indemnification for that province, but with very restricted powers. And, since no satisfactory amounts of compensation could be arrived at, the matter had rested.

Now with the LaFontaine-Baldwin Ministry this was a matter obviously needing attention. LaFontaine gave very careful thought to drafting the Bill and arrived at the figure of £100,000 as the limit of compensation. Ten thousand pounds of this had already been covered by claims which had been certified, leaving some £90,000 to be covered by the Rebellion Losses Bill.

Although LaFontaine's Bill, which had been preceded by seven resolutions, was vigourously debated, and though Sir Allan MacNab and W. H. Blake nearly came to blows on the floor of the House, still it passed by a comfortable majority of forty-seven to eighteen.

The Bill received royal assent by Lord Elgin and this was the signal for the most violent protests and mob scenes ever staged in Canada. All through the debates on the Bill, meetings, petitions and violent articles in the Tory press had built up the issue as one of loyalty on the part of the Tories, who opposed the Bill, against a so-called rebel majority that supported the measure. In both Toronto and Belleville there had been ugly riots and on March 22 mobs in Toronto had burned the effigies of Baldwin and Blake and stoned houses. With the signing of the Bill violence broke out in Montreal.

On the afternoon of April 25, 1849, Lord Elgin visited the Parliament Buildings and gave his assent to this and other measures in the ordinary manner. This was the last straw as far as the Tory mob was concerned. As the evening drew in, crowds gathered and were incited by speeches; the coach of the Governor-General was stoned as he returned to his residence, and by eight o'clock the mob had taken control and surged to the Parliament Buildings. They burst into the Assembly and fired the Houses of Parliament, holding back the fire brigade and burning the buildings to the ground, including the valuable library of some twenty thousand books.

The Montreal mob remained in control for two days, and even on the third day the Governor-General's coach was again attacked as he drove to and from the Chateau de Ramezay. Lord Elgin escaped harm, but some members of his escort were injured. Nor did the mob neglect the leaders of the Government. LaFontaine's new house was wrecked (he was not in residence at the time) and his stables burned, and the rooms in St. Antoine Street occupied by Robert and the Commissioner for Crown Lands, Mr. Price, were stoned.

But, to his eternal credit, Lord Elgin did not flinch from carrying through his constitutional responsibilities during this dangerous and inflammable period. He could have reserved the Bill, but he did not do so because, as he said, "By reserving the Bill, I should only throw on Her Majesty's government a responsibility which rests, and I think ought to rest, on me." He did not dissolve Parliament either because this could have resulted in out-and-out rebellion, and would not have resulted in a change of ministry. And finally he was determined at all costs to shed no blood as a result of these unruly scenes and disturbances, realizing that violence would beget more violence. And his decisions in handling this matter were fully justified.

Fortunately the Whigs under Lord John Russell and his Colonial Secretary Lord Grey supported Lord Elgin, thus setting the seal of their acceptance on the principle of party rule and recognizing colonial self-government in internal matters even of this magnitude.

This did not mean that vigorous debates did not rage in the Imperial Parliament on the Canada question and the Rebellion Losses Bill. Gladstone was of the opinion that colonial policy had gone too far and that the honour of the Crown was at stake. "That advice should not be delayed until a measure assumed the form of a statute . . . and before public opinion was appealed to in the country."

This was the time when Francis Hincks had his finest hour in defence of responsible government. Shortly after the passing of the Rebellion Losses Bill he had journeyed to London in order to obtain financial backing for Canadian debentures. He was also acting as a special representative of the Canadian Administration, and as such was received by both Lord John Russell and Lord Grey and had an interview with Mr. Gladstone. But most important was his series of letters to the papers, the first of which was published in the *Times* on June 20, 1849. In it he refuted statements made by Gladstone and others in the British House of Commons and showed that Baldwin, LaFontaine and his other colleagues in the Canadian Government "have as much true British feeling as any member of that Party which seems to wish to monopolize it."

In support of his financial mission he issued a pamphlet entitled *Canada and Its Financial Resources* and wrote a number of articles for the *Daily Mail* on similar lines. For the hard-headed London business man nothing could have done more to restore confidence in Canada and in the present Administration. Hincks was unique in his intimate knowledge of Canadian financial affairs since 1840, which with his brilliant mind and his ability to write with clarity and conviction made him the man most able to put the facts before the British public.

By 1849 the Reform Party was becoming top-heavy. Its large majority made some of its members less inclined to observe party discipline and more inclined to express their own theories and their more radical ideas. It is ironic that two or three of the old Reformers now returned to politics to spearhead what was to become a radical wing and later a splinter party known as the Clear Grits, so called because they wanted only men of "clear grit."

From a retirement of more than ten years emerged Peter Perry, that crusty battling Reformer who had been so effective in withholding supplies at the time of Sir Francis Bond Head, and in supporting Robert's resignation from the Executive Council then. And with him reappeared John Rolph, who after being implicated in the Rebellion had fled to Rochester. Now they came back into politics to haunt Robert and with their radical ideas to sow consternation among the more numerous, but less aggressive, moderate Reformers.

There is no doubt that Perry and the group that rallied around him had been influenced by the Chartists in England. They advocated, once again, an elected Legislature and the secularization of the clergy reserves, also a fixed date for elections and a biennial Parliament. In addition, to the added consternation of Baldwin, LaFontaine and others, Perry appears to have favoured annexation to the United States. This was a heresy that had just been propounded in the Annexation Manifesto by the English Tories in Montreal to protect their business interests.

In a very outspoken letter to Lawrence Heyden on October 5, 1849, Robert dealt with the United States annexation movement, and in particular Peter Perry's interest in that direction:

> I felt it right to write to Mr. Perry expressing my decided opinions in respect of the annexation question and that I could look upon those only who are in favour of the continuance of the connection with the Mother Country as political friends – those who are against it as political opponents – I felt this to be the more necessary because I had heard within a few days that one of our Parliamentary friends here was said to have given in or to be about giving in his adherence to the annexation movement – The tactics of our opponents are transparent – They want to get some of our supporters of standing to commit themselves and then turn round on them and the whole party and impute the call for annexation to the liberal party generally – I believe that our party are hostile to annexation – I am at all events hostile to it myself – And if I and my party differ upon it it is necessary we should part company – It is not a question upon which a compromise is possible.

After the burning of the Parliament Buildings in Montreal it became apparent that a new location for Parliament had to be selected. It is interesting to note that Sherwood proposed Bytown (now Ottawa), but the obvious choice lay between Toronto and Quebec City. It was finally decided that Parliament would meet alternatively, every four years, in these two cities, starting with Toronto. As Robert pointed out, this would help to expel the idea that the French were dominating Parliament. The next session met in May 1850 at the old Parliament Buildings on Front Street in Toronto.

Robert had been seriously ill during the previous winter but was able to take his seat, despite rumours that he had contemplated resignation.

The Ministry was in a strong position, and one of the first important measures dealt with during this session was the organization of the postal service, and the subsequent lowering of the postal rates. The United Kingdom had transferred this matter to Canadian jurisdiction as another proof of her confidence in Canada's ability to manage her own affairs.

But, by the same token, local differences now came to the surface. Robert, with a number of his former supporters in the Ministry, became the conservative element, whereas the dissenters – Malcolm Cameron, H. J. Boulton and Peter Perry, among others – held radical views. Malcolm Cameron had been dropped from the Government over his school Bill; H. J. Boulton, a former Tory and Family Compact man turned Reformer, was bitterly disappointed at not being raised to the Bench (at one time this had seemed a certainty). These men were the hard core of the Clear Grits.

Also William Lyon Mackenzie had returned to Canada after the Amnesty Bill and in 1851 sought election, as an independent, in a by-election in the County of Haldimand, defeating George Brown, who in the early days was one of the most severe critics of the Clear Grits. In the *Globe* he had castigated them as "A miserable clique of office-seeking, bunkhum talking cormorants, that met in a certain lawyer's office on King Street and announced their intention to form a new party on Clear Grit principles."

Thus it was that Perry, Rolph and later Mackenzie became the *bêtes noires* of the moderate Reform Party and in particular of Robert Baldwin. In like manner, among the French, Louis-Joseph Papineau was the *bête noire* of LaFontaine. Louis-Joseph Papineau was apparently against everything but Papineau and the repeal of the Union. It was in vain that LaFontaine pointed out that, but for the Reformers and his French party, Papineau would still be in exile, and that he was in Canada and in Parliament by virtue of the Amnesty Bill and the fact that the British Government had not disallowed it.

In Canada West William McDougall, a lawyer, spread the views of the Clear Grits and their supporters with his radical paper, the *North American,* while in Canada East Papineau and the radical party were served by the newspaper *L'Avenir.* This radical group in French Canada became known as the Parti Rouge; it was in violent opposition to LaFontaine and his Administration and advocated such measures as the repeal of the Union, the abolition of church tithes, and, like the Clear Grits, an elected upper house. But it went further and in some cases called for annexation to the United States.

A vexed question in Canada East was that of seigniorial tenure. Many thousands of acres in Quebec had been granted to the French seigniors under the old French laws. No change had been made in the tenure since 1825 when enabling legislation had permitted seigniors and *censitaires* (tenants) by mutual consent to terminate the tenure. Now there was a diversity of opinion among the French party, although most were agreed that something should be done. Some felt that the system should be abolished altogether and the land become the property of the tenant in fee simple. Others felt that the seignior should be compensated, while a few like Papineau, himself a seignior, were in favour of leaving matters as they were, or granting the land outright to the seigniors.

This whole question put LaFontaine on the horns of a dilemma. He himself favoured the middle course, that of compensating the seigniors, but whatever he did he stood to divide his party, and this question was referred to a committee of inquiry and held over until the next session.

In Canada West it was the Commissioner of Crown Lands, John H. Price, who introduced the perennial question of the clergy reserves. In 1840 an Act in Canada to settle this question had been disallowed; but an imperial Act had been passed, in the same year, the terms of which differed somewhat from the proposed Canadian Act, and this did not satisfy the majority of the people of Canada.

Price now introduced certain resolutions, among them one stating, "No religious denomination can be held to have such vested interest in the revenue derived from the proceeds of the said Clergy Reserves as should prevent further legislation with respect to the disposal of them." Another asked that the Imperial Parliament should grant the Canadian Parliament power to deal with this matter as it saw fit.

Hincks, who had seconded these resolutions, saw clearly that to have any success the requests should go forward to the British Government without any mention of the intention of the Clear Grits to secularize the clergy reserves. He knew full well that the British House of Lords, containing many bishops, would have little sympathy for secularization.

Unfortunately Baldwin and LaFontaine were divided on this question. And Robert, who for once does not appear to have had very definite opinions, would have been far wiser to abstain from voting. As it was he and LaFontaine found themselves voting against each other, a point which was not lost on H. J. Boulton and his associates. In consequence this measure was also held over, although since the resolutions had been passed, the request to the Imperial Government went forward in the form of an address to "Her Most Gracious Majesty."

* *

22

"I NOW SAY — FAREWELL"

In November 1850, Robert's youngest daughter Eliza became engaged to John Ross of Belleville, a successful lawyer and member of the Legislative Council. He wrote asking for Eliza's hand and here is part of Robert's reply, November 18, 1850:

> Occasions like the present are those on which a widowed father realizes the extent of the chastening which has been laid upon him in the loss of the mother of his children. . . . It is true that in one whom I know to possess many estimable qualities both of heart and head, and who has ever proved himself a good son and a good brother, I have guarantees, perhaps the best that a father can obtain, for the happiness of a daughter. My child, – . . . possesses all the confiding sweetness of disposition of her mother . . . The union of such a woman to be a happy one, must be with an entirely congenial spirit and it would make me more wretched than you may as yet be able to conceive, should I hereafter have the misfortune to find that my child was pining under the absence of that confiding tenderness on the part of her husband so essential to a wife's happiness.

On February 4, 1851 Eliza and John Ross were married, and in the *Examiner,* Toronto, Canada West, Wednesday morning February 5, 1851 appears the following announcement:

> Yesterday, at the residence of the bride's father, the Hon. John Ross L.C. to Miss Eliza Baldwin, daughter of the Hon. Robt. Baldwin Attorney General West. The ceremony was to have taken place at the church of the Holy Trinity, but owing to a slight indisposition of the bride, it was performed at the residence of her father. His Excellency the Governor General was present on the occasion.

A few weeks after Eliza's marriage Willy and Maria decided on a gala event, and they were ably abetted by their Uncle William. Spadina made a splendid setting and the arrival of Lord and Lady Elgin from Hamilton gave the affair that social élan so conducive to success. Robert was still a little doubtful the day before. Writing to the newlyweds on February 27, 1851, he remarked:

> My Mother and Aunt Sullivan are much as when you left us. Aunt Ann has a boil on her face and the rest of us are much as usual. We are to have our Ball tomorrow night – where our guests are all to be stowed I know not, but Willy and Maria, say there will be plenty of room and they have got their Uncle William to pronounce the same opinion. So I suppose it will be all right.

The happiness of the first months of 1851 was to be rudely shaken in May, just before the disturbing political events which lead to Robert's resignation. In the Toronto *Examiner* of May 21, 1851:

> DEATH
>
> At the family residence on Front Street in the City at an early hour on the morning of Thursday 15 last, deeply regretted by a numerous circle of relatives and friends Margaret Phoebe Baldwin relict of the late Hon. William Warren Baldwin of Spadina aged 80. She was the second daughter and

only surviving child of the late William Willcocks Esq. of Cork.

The session of 1851 began on May 20. Robert had again been in very poor health. In fact Blake, during Robert's illness a year before, had written to him protesting the folly of his way of life – his lack of exercise and his ceaseless overwork, for with Parliament now meeting in Toronto, Robert felt it necessary to attend in person to all the legal business of the Crown. But he continued in his old ways and attended the new session, although a sick man.

The Government still commanded a large majority, but in its strength lay its weakness, for with this large majority members felt free to air their diverging views, and were not slow to do so. The session opened quietly; the Speech from the Throne, with no amendment by the Opposition, was disposed of in one day.

In regard to the clergy reserves, the Imperial Government did not pass enabling legislation at this time, but the Colonial Secretary advised the Ministry that the British Government would be willing to do so. Apart from an address of thanks to the Imperial Government, there the matter rested until it was finally settled in 1854.

Robert now introduced a Bill which abolished primogeniture in the case of those dying intestate. This was ironic as Robert's father William Warren had wished to entail Spadina to his heirs in perpetuity. Nevertheless Robert felt that this legislation was proper at this time and his sense of duty overcame all other considerations.

During the final sessions of what has been called "the great Ministry," other political figures began to assume major roles. These were the giants of the future, George Brown, John A. Macdonald, Etienne Cartier, Alexander Tilloch Galt, crowding into the wings for the next great historical drama for, in the history of a country, the show must go on. Men like Hincks and Morin remained with the Government but others, like George Brown, now Secretary of the Penitentiary Commission, were beginning to move away in the direction of the Clear Grits. As lately as 1849, Brown had attacked the Clear Grits savagely in the *Globe,* but by 1850 his vigorously anti-Roman Catholic articles were driving a wedge between him and the Reform Party.

In 1848 a thick-set Montrealer of great energy and ability had been elected to the Assembly. Born in 1814, George Etienne Cartier had been called to the bar in 1835. Like a number of young men in French Canada, he had fled the country in 1837, but he returned after the amnesty to become a first-class lawyer with a particular flair for company law and administration. When he entered politics in 1848 and was elected to the Assembly he became a great admirer and confidant of LaFontaine. But it was not until 1854 that he took his place as a leading member of the Liberal-Conservatives. He and John A. Macdonald were later to attain fame together.

In great contrast to the former was Alexander Tilloch Galt. Born in Scotland, he had come to Canada in 1835 as chief agent and promoter of the British American Land Company, and was soon to become interested in railway construction and promotion. In 1849 he entered politics as the Liberal (Rouge) member for Sherbrooke, but he was so incensed at the Rebellion Losses Bill that he resigned from politics and even signed the manifesto in favour of union with the United States. But by 1853 he had re-entered politics and had become one of the leading spokesmen for the Anglo-Saxon Protestants in Quebec. With his broad vision, he became an ardent federalist.

In 1851 John A. Macdonald saw his chance. His real flair was in the field of political tactics, and he did all he could when in opposition to promote discord and distrust among the ranks of the Reform Party. He now rose to demand a parliamentary inquiry into the Penitentiary Commission. Baldwin opposed the inquiry. LaFontaine defended the Commission, but no mention was made of George Brown, the Secretary. Two days later Macdonald's wily plan succeeded beyond his hopes; Brown launched a most violent attack in his newspaper against both his real enemies and the friends by whom he felt he had been betrayed. He was clearly drifting into the orbit of the Clear Grits.

The ranks of the Clear Grits were often increased by the addition of William Lyon Mackenzie. He was a vindictive man and disliked both Baldwin and LaFontaine. The dislike was mutual. Perhaps Mackenzie envied Baldwin the position of leadership which he himself might have attained. Baldwin may have seen in Mackenzie a reminder of the victims, Lount and Matthews, and those whom he had defended in the courts in 1838 and who had been left to face the music which Mackenzie had orchestrated.

Mackenzie now realized that he could most readily attack Baldwin through the Court of Chancery. This court had been unpopular during the period 1840 to 1849, but Robert had spent a great deal of time and thought on reforming it and these reforms had been instituted in 1849, under the Baldwin-LaFontaine Ministry, and approved.

On June 26, 1851, Mackenzie moved that a committee be set up to "report by bill or otherwise, for the abolition of the Court of Chancery." In his defence Robert pointed out that the Court of Chancery had been working in a much improved manner, that it should be given a fair trial since it had been approved by the present Government, and that by abolishing it now the Government was negating itself.

In the ensuing vote, Baldwin was supported in his defence by thirty-four to thirty, but he had been sustained by the members for Canada East. H. J. Boulton was quick to point out that most of the members from Canada West had voted for Mackenzie's motion, and Robert was particularly sensitive to the fact that seven members of the Bar had also voted for the abolition of the Court of Chancery.

Robert took this as a vote of no confidence from his English-Canadian colleagues, and he handed in his resignation to his friend LaFontaine, who begged him to reconsider his action. Lord Elgin also tried to persuade him to remain in the Ministry. But he was determined to have done with politics. For one thing, he was completely out of sympathy with the radical views of many of the Reformers, particularly those of the Clear Grits, notably Mackenzie. Secondly he felt he had been deserted by his colleagues, who had repudiated his leadership. Finally, having achieved his lifelong aim of responsible government, the driving force for politics had gone. It was perfectly clear that he did not resign on any question of the double majority; this principle he abhorred and he made his actions in this regard quite clear in a letter to his son-in-law John Ross, written at this time.

On June 30, 1851 Robert rose and with considerable emotion gave his reasons for resigning and made his farewell to the

House. However Louis LaFontaine refused to fill the office of Attorney-General of Canada West and, in deference to his friend, Robert stayed on as chief law officer although he no longer attended Cabinet meetings. LaFontaine followed Robert's resignation by announcing his own intention of retiring from politics at the end of the session.

The session finally came to an end on August 30. Even after prorogation LaFontaine had not handed in his or the Government's resignation, so Hincks, as Inspector-General and heir apparent, and the most active member of the Government, decided to speed the parting Ministry by tendering his own resignation; and Morris, the Postmaster-General, also submitted his. This action forced LaFontaine's hand and he and his Government resigned. Lord Elgin now sent for Hincks and Morin to form a new government and a general election was called for the end of the year.

Having taken the decision of resigning, Robert found that the relief of being free of politics precluded the possibility of his changing his mind – with this one exception, that since he had been elected for the Fourth Riding of York, he felt it was now incumbent on him to offer himself as a candidate in the election at the close of 1851. This was to show his constituents that he was still at their call as a private member, should they so desire. It was typical of Robert that he felt compelled to take this action in spite of the fact that he was a very sick and weary man and did not desire office.

By this move Robert again put himself in the middle of the wrangling within the Reform Party. John Rolph had very nearly succeeded in putting a spoke in Hincks's political wheel, so it was in this context that Francis Hincks felt it necessary to write to Robert on December 19, 1851:

> I regret very much to observe a reference in Dr. Rolph's speech in Dundas to the difficulty of my position in the late Administration owing to a supposed difference of opinion with yourself on religious questions.
>
> I have on all occasions of my canvass justified my entire policy of the late Administration and I took first opportunity that was afforded me after reading the speech in question, to declare publicly that I had no difference with you on the

> Clergy Reserves or any other question. My speech was published in the *Hamilton Journal* last Sunday (yesterday). I had, as you would see, a sharp contest owing to the treachery of a certain section of the Reformers. Every effort was used by Mackenzie, Brown and [name illegible] to defeat me and I therefore, think my election [Oxford] a great triumph. I am looking forward most anxiously for your election. I fear Scobie will do mischief. I know not whether the ingratitude or the stupidity of your opponents most encites my disgust. I shall, I presume, be elected for Niagara. If defeated in York would you like to sit for that town, as in that case I would do what I could to pave the way . . . If you have any objection to make a recommendation would you get some supporter of the administration to do so.

However, Robert was not elected. Of course there was regret on both sides and Robert felt keenly this parting from his constituents. In his speech at the close of the election of 1851, he concluded: "To my friends then of the North Riding, gratefully and not without regret; to my opponents without any feeling of unkindness, I now say – Farewell."

Robert lived for seven years after his retirement, and we get a picture of this period from the letters which passed between him and his son-in-law John Ross. Some of these have an added interest because Ross was to become a member in the Cabinets, first of Hincks, and then of the Liberal-Conservative Party.

During these years there were many attempts by Robert's friends and admirers to confer positions of distinction upon him, and to woo him back into public life. To many his refusal of honours and position is inexplicable; and it cannot be attributed to ill health alone. Honours as such did not interest him. Robert's own words perhaps best illustrate his feelings. In September 1851 he wrote to John Ross:

> The relief from mental anxiety which I have experienced since relieved from the responsibilities of office has been so great that without saying that no concurrence of circumstances could induce me again to resume such duties, which perhaps no man strictly speaking, has a right to say, I feel daily an increasing disinclination even to remain in public life at all.

Robert's friendship and correspondence with LaFontaine continued and on November 6, 1851, LaFontaine wrote to him: "What do you say of your friend Brown? Let the Clear Grits, even Hincks, give him the M.P.P. and he will as the case may be, [be] either the first Clear Grit in U.C., or Hincks' best friend – Away with such traders in politics." In 1854, Brown became one of the leaders of the Clear Grit party.

And after Robert's defeat, LaFontaine wrote:

> News has reached me by telegraph, that you have been unsuccessful in the Fourth Riding. As you were willing once more to serve your country in Parliament, I sincerely regret the result of the election. You will, however, allow me to say that, in another respect, I cannot but rejoice at the opportunity given you to restore your health and to enjoy all the comforts and the tranquility of private life. . . . Did you observe also that Dr. Rolph has made use, very improperly, of the name of the Governor General, *le mettant à découvert* as we say in French, by citing a pretended speech of his at the Council Board, which I am sure he never uttered, at least not in the sense conveyed by Dr. Rolph. I was very near taking up the gauntlet, but, on reflection, I thought it was better not to do so, as I have made my adieux to Politics. . . . Mr. Hincks stated that for his part, he had not opposed any one of their [the Clear Grits] candidates. The inference drawn from that statement is that when Parliament meets, Mr. Hincks, alluding to Mr. George Brown will say: "My Honourable Friend", and the latter will reciprocate by calling Mr. Hincks "My intimate Friend, for whom I have always entertained the greatest respect."

Robert would appreciate his friend's feelings and his dry humour about the results of the Lower Canadian elections: "The Red or Papineau Party have been here defeated, horse, foot and artillery. There never was such a complete *déroute* notwithstanding the coalition between them and the (once so called) higher Tory Party."

In 1852 the Convocation of the University of Toronto asked Robert Baldwin to accept the chancellorship of that institution. His relationship towards the university had always been sympathetic; since his University Bill it had been friendly. In fact it amounted to this, that without Baldwin there would not have been a non-sectarian university, at any rate not for a time. It was therefore fitting that he should be so honoured and he was sensible of this mark of recognition. Professor H. H. Croft wrote to him on November 30, 1852: "At a meeting of Convocation held on Saturday last a committee was appointed for the purpose of waiting upon you to explain the wishes of Convocation".

To this request Robert made a curt and, for him, uncivil reply; this is explained by the fact that he felt he had been drafted before being consulted.

> I am not informed of the object of the proposed conference for which you request me to fix a time in your note of this day. I have indeed heard a matter of rumour however, only, that I have been elected Chancellor of the University – such rumour must however, I trust be incorrect as the members must, I think, through one at least of their number, have known that I could not, under any circumstances, accept that honour and such being the case, such an election appears to me so injudicious that I cannot think it can have taken place.

Professor Croft persisted in trying to arrange the interview with the result that Robert sent a formal refusal on December 8, 1852. His reply shows clearly that had he not felt entirely out of sympathy with the Government at the time, the chancellorship was a position he would have enjoyed:

> Gentlemen:
>
> I have in compliance with your request reconsidered the answer which I was prepared to have given to the communication of which you were the bearers – that the Convocation of the University of Toronto had done me the honour of electing me to the high and honourable office of their Chancellor . . . Under the circumstances in which I am placed, I cannot consent to accept a position in regard to that great and important Provincial Institution which might either imply less hostility than I entertain to the course of the present Government in regard to it or impose upon me the obligation of embarking on an active opposition.

The next effort to put Robert into harness was political; Francis Hincks and John Ross were probably at the back of it. W. B. Richards, the Attorney-General for Canada West, wrote to Robert offering him the position on the Bench left vacant by the death of his cousin and brother-in-law, R. B. Sullivan.

Robert was consistent in his refusal to accept office. Although, as he wrote to Attorney-General Richards, he thought himself better, he must have had a premonition, for three days later, on May 3, 1853, he was struck down by a sudden and severe illness, which seemed as if it might be his last.

In August he wrote to LaFontaine:

> I ought, long since, to have acknowledged your kind enquiries for me by telegraph and otherwise during my last severe illness as well as to have reported to you my reply to the offer made me of a seat on the Bench. . . . It is true that I look well, as I am told . . . I am however, seldom free for two consecutive days from the disagreeable rumbling noise in my head and I have frequent returns of headache with occasional fits of giddiness attended with a feeling of confusion in my head that is even more distressing than actual pain to a moderate extent, added to which I find that a very little thing worries and excites me – . . . as respects the Chief Justiceship of Lower Canada I rejoice to find that you felt yourself able to accept it . . . The addition of mine to the universal approbation of the whole Province can be intrinsically of little moment, to yourself however, as that of an old colleague and attached friend, it is I know, not indifferent . . . And now as respects your invitation to accompany you to Europe, if anything could induce me to undertake the trip the pleasure of having you for a companion would certainly do so, and I doubt not I shall be considered obstinate indeed by both friends and relations. Still, there are circumstances in which neither friend nor relative, nay not even a man's physician, can upon the whole judge so well for him as himself and such is, or at least is by myself felt to be the case. [He goes on to describe the shock of Mrs. Henry Sullivan's* sudden death and concludes:] I confess when I think of the

* The wife of Dr. Henry Sullivan, younger brother of Robert Baldwin Sullivan and of Robert's wife.

> suddenness of that event I feel my life hanging by a precarious thread and I have no wish to risk having that thread cut in a foreign or distant land far from my family and home. Were I suffering from a weakness of the lungs requiring a milder climate or from weakness or a derangement of the digestive organs, I could understand the use of a change of air, etc., but in fact, the fault with me is that in these latter particulars at least my organs are too powerful. I am, as Willie says, of the Durham Breed – I manufacture blood and fat too rapidly.

John Morgan had died in 1849, but the two families kept in close touch. Now at the end of 1853 there came sad news of Aunt Elizabeth Morgan. General Dix, her son-in-law, was to have gone to France as United States Ambassador in 1853, but his appointment was rescinded at the last minute due to the Southern Democrats.* However, the General had sent his wife and family on ahead, and Aunt Morgan had gone with Catherine Dix, her adopted daughter. Robert, writing to John Ross on December 1, 1853, reports:

> I have the painful duty of announcing to you and our dear Eliza the death of poor Aunt Morgan. I this day received a letter from Mr. Dix informing me that she had had an attack of congestion of the brain (the third since the commencement of the year) on the halt during the voyage to Havre and had died the morning of the 7th, the day after the arrival of the *Humboldt* at that port. . . . She was in uncommon good health before the fatal attack, ate well, slept well and had no sea sickness and enjoyed more than her usual good spirits. The sea voyage had nothing to do with the cause of her death. . . . had she consented to be parted from Catherine and Lizzie and to have remained with Mr. Dix, he would at least probably have had ere this, the same melancholy event to record. . . . She was in her seventy-second year.

The year 1854 was an extremely full one for Robert and it very nearly saw his return to public life. In February he was asked to serve on a judicial commission regarding the amalgama-

* General Dix became Ambassador to France in 1866 and held the office until 1869.

tion of the laws of both sections of the province. Replying to John Ross on February 15, 1854, he wrote:

> I have received your letter respecting the Commission, I do not, however, feel that I should be equal to undertaking it with any regard to my health. If in the Commission I could not . . . do otherwise than labour at the work in a manner that would at once interfere with my physical regime and tax my mental application. I cannot therefore, take upon me the responsibility of acting on it. . . . Mama [his mother-in-law and aunt, Barbara Sullivan] and Aunt Anne [Mrs. John Spread Baldwin] join in love to you and dear Eliza, whose letter of the 4th I was glad to get. I have had an obstinate cold but am getting better.

During March and April of 1854 there was considerable family news. Eliza and John Ross had telegraphed Robert of the birth of their first son, Robert Baldwin Ross. Maria, who was keeping house for Robert, had written by return; Robert had waited, hoping to hear from his daughter, and so wrote to Eliza on April 17:

> I was, you may be sure, my beloved child, delighted at receiving the telegraphic announcement of your safe delivery. . . . Thank you for the lock of my dear Grandson's hair. I should say it promises to be more like John than your's, but one cannot judge at such an age. You say he is like poor little Mary. [Eliza's first child, who died in infancy.] I always thought she resembled my poor Mother. If like her, he will be like the master-mind of our family, for such was unquestioningly my dear Mother. . . . This is dear Bob's birthday and I selected it on purpose to answer your letter on. We cannot expect to hear from him for some time yet [he was in Hong Kong] and so console ourselves with drinking his health and safe return. Willie is at Larchmere.* I do not consider him as having finally left us yet. . . . My own health is, I think, better, though I have had some spells of very uncomfortable

* Willy (*i.e.*, Willcocks), Robert's eldest son, had inherited property near Oak Ridges, where he built an attractive house beside a small larch-bordered lake.

feeling in my head. Love to John and with love and a kiss to Baby.

Among the Elgin Papers for 1854 is Robert's reply to Lord Elgin.

> Mr. Baldwin has the honour to acknowledge the receipt of the Governor General's Letter of the 5 July instant acquainting him by the Queen's command that Her Majesty has been generously pleased to confer upon him the distinction of Companion of the Most Honourable Order of the Bath.
>
> The additional satisfaction of having received this mark . . . through the hands of His Excellency and to add the assurance that the kind terms in which His Excellency has been pleased to speak of his public service will be ever most gratefully remembered.
>
> Spadina 13 July.

In August Robert was writing to John Ross and again refusing to take office:

> You will, I think, upon consideration, see that . . . it would not be consistent either with my own position or with my duty to the Crown to accept an office, the duties of which I anticipated would prove too much for my health and necessitate an early resignation. . . . In reply to application from friends in five different constituencies I lately declined again entering, at all events, for the present, upon political duties. Duties with which I am somewhat familiar and which . . . are far more capable of being graduated, if I may be allowed the term, to the calibre of one's capabilities, than those of the Bench. . . .
>
> I fully approve of the delicacy which dictated your requesting Mr. Hincks to be the organ of communicating with me on this subject and no one could have done so in kinder or more considerate terms. My answer I have, of course, addressed to him. [John Ross was in Quebec and had left his wife and family at Spadina, so Robert adds:] P.S. Eliza and the child are well. I think the young Attorney General improves under the influence of the air of Spadina.

After the resignation of Hincks and Morin in September 1854 a Liberal-Conservative coalition was formed which was to have important consequences; strange political combines were the order of the day and, during these years prior to Confederation, stable government in Canada was a rarity.

Following the coalition, Hincks wrote to Robert because of the esteem in which Robert was held for his political ethics. He replied on September 22, 1854:

> If therefore, by its being "on all sides said that I would never consent to a coalition," it is meant, in that way to draw a contrast between us to your prejudice . . . I add without reserve, that, in my opinion, you appear to have acted in this matter with judgement and discretion in the interests at once of your party and your country.

The explanation of this comment from Robert to Hincks is given by John Ross in a letter to William Young, Attorney-General of Nova Scotia, written from Quebec, October 27, 1854, of which a copy was sent to Robert:

> My dear Attorney General,
>
> You will be surprised to hear of the Coalition Government here, but not more surprised than I was myself when the events occurred which rendered such a combination necessary.
>
> Although we had a large majority of the members from both sections of the Province returned in the interest of Hincks and his Government, yet their very strength as a party, proved their greatest weakness, and they thought they could safely take any course no matter how factious, believing that no government would be possible except one made up wholly from the ranks of the Reform Party, and believing this, dissensions ensued which led to Hincks's resignation and Sir Allan as the only recognized leader of opposition was sent for and formed his Coalition hereby agree[ing] to take up all the leading measures and policy of his predecessors, Clergy Reserves included.
>
> I am bound to say that he and all my new colleagues have acted in the most straightforward way since we came together and our friend Hincks gives us a cordial support because his

> policy is being carried out. I need not tell you that I only consented to join the new administration with the assent and solicitation of my own party. Hincks pressed it very strongly upon me and a majority of Upper Canada Reformers joined Hincks in tending us [John Ross and Robert Spence] their support. [And then, singling out the Clear Grits:] The disaffected of our party therefore, are thrown into opposition and have little hope of doing much mischief for the present.

Previously, in September 1854, LaFontaine had been created a baronet. A lawyer first, he became an outstanding and distinguished figure on the Bench on retirement from the political scene, and Robert wrote to his friend delighted by the well-deserved honour which had been conferred on Sir Louis LaFontaine.

* *

23

THE END OF THE PILGRIMAGE

By this time Robert, though active in mind, was ailing in body. He had never been strong; now he was, he felt, considerably weaker. Although he continued a Bencher of the Law Society and its treasurer, he had retired from his law practice in 1848; but he had extensive holdings in land, and much family business to attend to. His interest in politics was intense, and it was his constant wish to promote a good relationship between the French and English peoples in Canada. He was constantly in touch with John Ross, his son-in-law, who was now Speaker of the Legislative Council.

Another matter of concern to Robert was the medical profession, in which his father had been prominent, and when this interest and the university were both involved, Robert was quick to take up the issue. In January 1855 he wrote to John Ross:

> Rumour has it that the Ministry have resolved to restore the Medical Faculty in the University of Toronto. But that while Dr. Beaumont is to have his chair again and Drs. King and Herrick are to be offered theirs (as it is said with the under-

standing that they will decline them and be otherwise remunerated for the loss) Dr. Richardson is to be entirely given the go by and another appointed in his place. It certainly appears to me that if it has been found that the experiment of having no medical faculty has not answered the expectation of the Legislature, that in restoring it to the Institution these gentlemen, who for no fault of their own, were thus deprived of their chairs have a fair right to be reappointed to them. . . . Dr. Croft has also requested me to write you on the subject of the applications of himself and Dr. Beaver for an increase of salary. [Robert was continually being approached to use his good offices for assistance.] He assures me that it is with great difficulty that he can manage to get along at all under present circumstances. And there can be no doubt that the increase in the expense of living is enormous. We all feel it.

It was in February that Robert received a most cordial and friendly letter from the Attorney-General John A. Macdonald, urging him to accept the office of Chief Justice of the Common Pleas.

Quebec 13 Feb 1855

My dear Mr. Baldwin

Chief Justice Macaulay only awaits . . . the appointment of his successor to retire from the bench. . . . We are extremely desirous that this eminent judge should be succeeded by one not less competent than himself to perform the high duties appertaining to the office . . . We are satisfied that these requisites are to be found in yourself and that no more worthy successor to Mr. Macaulay could be selected.

I am therefore instructed or rather authorized to offer the Chief Justiceship of the Common Pleas for your acceptance.

I need scarcely assure you of the great gratification I should feel on personal as well as professional grounds at your acceptance of the office. . . .

My dear Mr Baldwin
vy faithfully yours.
John A. Macdonald.

This would have been a cementing of the Liberal-Conservative alliance, but again Robert felt himself obliged to refuse as he did not feel strong enough to fulfil the duties involved in such a position on the Bench.

Robert was happy to supply a home to all members of the family, and in July 1855 Eliza Ross was at Spadina, and her father wrote to her husband:

> Our dear Eliza was this morning safely delivered of a fine little girl. She was in labour between six and seven hours and the child was born at 10 o'clock. She had a much easier time than with either of her former labours and, please God, all will go well. Mrs. Charley it was feared would have to leave sooner than was desirable to attend to her engagement with Mrs. Boulton, but Mrs. B. was out in her reckoning and has been confined last week so that Mrs. Charley will now be able to stay as long as Eliza requires her.

John Ross owned property on Davenport Road, not far from Spadina, and in 1855 that land was being cleared and Robert wrote:

> The stump man refused to undertake the job as he says his machine would not be strong enough. Dunne has been at work with one hand which was all he could get, but evidently not to his own satisfaction. It is new work to him and he did not know what it was to attack one of those stubborn nuisances. A man of the name of McCarthy has offered to take them at 3/9 taking the whole field. Dunne wanted to beat him down to 2/9 and they could not agree. As I understood Dunne he was to come to see Eliza or me on the subject. . . .
>
> [Then a day later Robert reported:] McCarthy has been with me and I have agreed with him at the 3/9 per stump, none but those a foot across half way between the surface of the ground and the top of the stump to be reckoned a stump and stumps under that size to be counted 2 for one. He to take out any that may be required about the house.

Later on at this house of John and Eliza Ross, John A. Macdonald was to spend week-ends and enjoy "Two good nights rest and to spend Sunday lounging in peaceful ease on the sofa."

Bob, the younger son, was still at sea, and in December 1854 had passed the Marine Board as mate; in January 1855 he joined the clipper *Stornoway* sailing for Hong Kong and Wampao, which they reached in July. At this time the *Stornoway* was one of the swiftest of the China clippers. Great financial profits were to be made on the first consignment of teas to reach the English markets, so the trip back was a race.

Early in 1856, Bob passed the Marine Board in England as chief mate and in March he arrived back in Canada; in June he took up his first command, sailing from Quebec as captain of the *Bramley Moore,* bound for Liverpool.

In October 1855, Parliament removed from Quebec to Toronto so that the session which began early in 1856 met in the refurbished Legislative Building fronting on the bay. This change brought John Ross back to Toronto, of course, which accounts for the unfortunate lack of letters between him and Robert; these would have provided valuable comment on the course politics was taking.

The figure-head of the Liberal-Conservative party was the ailing Sir Allan MacNab who seemed incapable of leadership at this time and was looked upon by many as greedy and indolent. John A. Macdonald was emerging as the real head of the uneasy coalition but, in spite of his effort at peacemaking, in April 1856 Ross resigned from the Government, in which he had been latterly president of the Council, and became president of the Grand Trunk Railway. Two other Canadians also connected with the Grand Trunk were George Etienne Cartier, the chief solicitor for the company, and Alexander Tilloch Galt, entrepreneur, railway contractor and promoter. All three men were showing an interest in federalism, that is the union of all the British North American provinces. This union also presented possibilities in railway expansion.

Another political event which would have interested Robert was the making of the Legislative Council elective. He had always been sceptical that this would have any marked effect on Canadian politics – it made hardly a ripple. Also in 1856, George Brown's ever increasing influence in Canada West was becoming apparent; the previous year, the *Globe* had taken over W. McDougall's Clear Grit newspaper, the *North American,* and now George Brown acquired the *Examiner*. His cry of "Rep. by Pop." had a fascinating appeal to many of the anti-French and anti-clerical factions in Canada West.

On October 16, 1856, Robert's elder son Willie, whose wife had died the year before, leaving him with an infant daughter, married Susanna-Mary Yarwood; there were to be three sons and three daughters of this marriage. During the next two years Robert seems to have been occupied with his family. Apparently Maria, his elder daughter, kept house for him, Eliza Ross lived near by (it was in this year that little Robert Baldwin Ross died), Willie and his family were happily settled at Larchmere, and Bob was justifying his father's decision to allow him to go to sea. Robert handled estate matters and evidently interested himself in his garden, for in June 1857 he wrote to John Ross:

> Thank you for the manure and I will gladly accept your offer to draw it next week if not too much interfering with your own operations. But if you would send me an order that if I run short in the meantime I may send for some of it myself I will thank you. Your man when he comes with his first load can learn from Dillon how many, (if any) I had already drawn. I send you the tye.* Love to Eliza and Baby.

But Robert, in spite of having his family around him, was a lonely man. The elder members of the family, who for so long had been part of his life, had died. Robert had never been afraid to die and had always longed for the reunion with his beloved Eliza.

In June 1858, Bob returned to Canada and was taken dangerously ill with what appears to have been an attack of polio; he was confined to bed for many months. In spite of this added anxiety, there were renewed efforts by Robert's friends and supporters to bring him back into politics as a counterweight to the Clear Grits in York, where they wished him to contest a seat for the Upper House, now elective. George Brown and A. A. Dorion (Parti Rouge leader) were in office on August 2 but out of office a few days later, for the political pace was fast and furious. Although Robert accepted and became a candidate,

* A tye was a kind of trough used for cattle, but more usually for washing ore.

he soon realized that his strength was now inadequate to cope with the duties which would be involved, or even with the election. So he wrote to Ross on September 3, and as a result of this letter, which Ross placed before the committee, Robert's name was withdrawn.

In the new Liberal-Conservative coalition which was formed after the fall of Brown and Dorion, Macdonald and Cartier were the leaders, with Cartier as the Chief Minister. It was now decided to send to England three ardent federalists – John Ross and Alexander Galt, led by Cartier himself. The purpose of this was to urge a federal union of all the British provinces in North America, and to obtain financial backing for railroad expansion in Canada, where an intercolonial railway link with the Maritimes was under consideration. Thus John Ross has a claim, along with the others, as an initiator of Confederation. He would have discussed federal union with Robert Baldwin, and there is absolutely no evidence that the elder statesman was in any way opposed to it, now that responsible government had been achieved.

Robert still rose at a very early hour, sometimes as early as four in the morning. Until breakfast time he wrote or read and afterwards busied himself about the place. Everything was ready for the coming of winter. His affairs were in order, he had run his course. Rapidly now he felt life slipping away. Winter was coming, cold and grey; he had finished now that feverish writing and the copying of his wife's letters:

> The letters which I have here transcribed are those which passed between your dear Mother and myself; some of them before, and some after our marriage. I have made this copy of them not only on account of the gratification which I derived from the occupation, but because I was desirous of leaving you this memorial of what your parents were to each other. And having a request to make.

The request was contained in a three-page memorandum headed "Ante-Mortem Directions" which he desired his daughter Maria to carry out. It is a poignant, pathetic but morbid memorial of his devotion to his dead wife. Of the original letters, which were to be buried with him, he writes: "I have never left home for any time without taking one or more of them with me for I ever wished to die with one of them near me." Among the directions were the following: "Let my little pearl brooch, a present from herself, be placed in my bosom, that as she rests with the nuptial ring upon her finger I may rest beside her with this token of her affection on my breast."

The chairs on which his wife's coffin had rested had been marked, and he directed that his own should rest on those same chairs, and that as he lay in his coffin his face should be covered with the handkerchief which had covered her face, and the letters, wrapped in another of her handkerchiefs, placed upon his breast. His coffin was finally to be placed at the right side of hers and "a small iron chain be passed round the two coffins and locked so as to chain them together."

November 1858 came and passed, the end was very near; now and then he would go to his wife's room, where everything lay undisturbed, just as it had been left nearly twenty-three years before. During the first week in December he had an attack of angina pectoris, but there was time to see his children; Bob "was compelled to be lifted to his father's bedside, to receive his last farewell."

Then, on December 9, 1858, death came to Robert Baldwin as a release from years of loneliness, as a reunion. His restless spirit found peace at last beside the one person who had in life meant everything to him.

Among the tributes that were paid to Robert as an outstanding personality were many that revealed a deeper feeling than the usual conventional eulogies. Many such are preserved in Bob's scrapbook, unfortunately unidentified and undated. One reads:

> Mr. Baldwin has left his mark upon the institutions of his country. He was the main spring through which Responsible Government was established in Canada. Our liberal Municipal institutions are evidence of his skill, and of his liberality. To him Canada owes much and, for years passed he has ranked, and justly so, among the most honourable of her sons. A Canadian by birth, education and every feeling of his heart, he was at the same time thoroughly British and thoroughly loyal. Of him it may be said he was beloved, honoured, and respected both at home and abroad. No Canadian statesman

has received such unequivocal praise from the London *Times* and from the English Press generally.

Speaking for the legal profession were the motions of two future prime ministers: that of "Mr. Attorney General John A. Macdonald, seconded by Geo. Ridout Esquire," recording the loss to the whole profession; and that of "the Hon. J. S. Macdonald, Q.C., seconded by the Hon. P. M. Van Koughnet, Q.C.: that the legal knowledge and ability of the late Robert Baldwin secured to him the highest regard of the bar, while his pure love of justice and the unaffected honesty of his character commanded the sincere admiration and esteem of all who knew him."

An editorial in *La Minerve* of December 15, 1858, speaks for the French-Canadians for whose rights he fought so long:

> *Aucun homme public de son temps n'a peut-être mérité autant de respect que l'Hon. Robert Baldwin. Son intégrité, sa probité étaient au-dessus de tout soupçon, et dans sa vie publique il a su à un haut dégré s'assurer l'estime de tous les partis. Digne héritier des principes libéraux de son père . . .*

But perhaps the most vivid and engaging tribute is the following, taken from his son's scrapbook:

> Between his own house and the precincts of Osgoode Hall he sacredly devoted the remaining years of his eventful life. Seldom a term passed that he was not to be found among his brothers of the law, unobtrusively and yet religiously engaged in the exercise of his functions as a Bencher and as Treasurer of the Law Society – offices which he held to the day of his death.
>
> We can ill spare the appearance of that grave and yet good natured man, as he was wont to pass among the students or expectant members of the bar, at once their awe and their admiration. His word among the Benchers was law. Upon his word often depended the reception or rejection of the application of many an anxious aspirant to the glories of the profession. Respected as he was in public life, so respected was he among students and the junior as well as senior members of the bar. How serene and unostentatious did he appear when

introducing to the Court some successful candidates for call to the bar. He would enter the Court, followed by the newly called barristers; and if an argument were pending, or the Court otherwise engaged, he would quietly take his seat and wait the opportunity to introduce his care to the Court. This he would do with his usual unobtrusiveness; and having done it, would bow and retire. No one could witness either the scene or the man without feeling that he was in the presence of a good if not a great man, as unpretending as he was good and great.

BIBLIOGRAPHY

BIBLIOGRAPHY

CONTEMPORANEOUS MANUSCRIPTS AND PUBLICATIONS

While in Ireland we were so fortunate as to be allowed to consult the family letters and documents in the possession of Miss M. G. Baldwin of Bandon, Co. Cork. Our own collection includes one of the copies, written in his own hand, of Dr. William Warren Baldwin's Memorandum of 1816 (another copy is in a notebook in the Baldwin Room of the Metropolitan Toronto Central Library), letters from Dr. Baldwin and the Honourable Robert Baldwin to Lawrence Heyden and other family letters written between 1836 and 1858 which are on loan to the Baldwin Room, letters from the Honourable Robert to his children, and a diary written by Robert Baldwin, younger son of the Honourable Robert, from February 1851 to September 1858. Other sources in our possession are:

KIRBY, WILLIAM. "Notes on Trinity Church Yard Families (1841-1898)" a copy from the archives of the New York Historical Society.

Laws of Upper Canada 1792-1818, Vol. I. York, 1818

Laws of Upper Canada, Vol. II, *Statutes* York, U.C., 1823

(both personal copies of the Hon. Robert Baldwin)

MURNEY, MARIA. *Some Account of the Settlement in Canada of Robert Baldwin, "the Emigrant", by a Granddaughter,* being the recollections of Mary Warren Breakenridge written by her daughter, Mrs. Murney, from her Mother's own words in 1859 and printed for private circulation; reprinted for the Women's Canadian Historical Society of Toronto, *Transactions,* No. 11 (1913). (This is known as the Murney Diary.)

SMITH, CHARLES, M. D. *The Ancient and Present State of the County and City of Cork,* Cork, 1815.

PUBLIC ARCHIVES OF CANADA

Sir Charles Bagot Papers

Sir John Colborne Correspondence

Colonial Office Records

Elgin Papers

Executive Council Correspondence

Hugh Hovell Farmar Papers

Journals of the House of Assembly of Upper Canada, 1815-1840

Journals of the Legislative Assembly of the Province of Canada, 1841-1851, and Appendices

LaFontaine Papers

Letters on Responsible Government by "Legion" (R. B. Sullivan), Toronto, 1844.

Joseph Willcocks Memorandum and Letter Book

COUNTY CORK LIBRARY, CORK.

Deasy Papers

UNIVERSITY COLLEGE LIBRARY, CORK

Caulfield, Richard. "Apprentice Indentures Enrolling Book" (covering the period from January 17, 1756, to December 14, 1801), unpublished manuscript

Cork Directory, 1787

Irish Parliamentary Debates, Dublin, 1780

Tithe Allotment Book for the Parish of Magourney, Co. Cork

Volunteer Journal or Independent Gazeteer, 1782 to 1785

NATIONAL LIBRARY, DUBLIN

Charlemont Papers

Shannon Papers

"Freemen & Freeholders who Voted on the Election for two Members to Serve in Parliament for the City of Cork which commenced the 13 of August 1783", Cork (printed by J. and R. Baldwin).

REGISTRY OF DEEDS, DUBLIN

Baldwin Deeds and Leases

PROVINCIAL ARCHIVES OF ONTARIO

Baldwin Papers

Macaulay Papers

Minutes of the Court of the General Quarter Sessions of the Peace for Newcastle District

METROPOLITAN TORONTO CENTRAL LIBRARY

Baldwin Papers

James Lesslie's Résumé of Events

Elizabeth Russell Papers
Peter Russell Papers
Sir Charles Metcalfe Defended Against the Attack of His Late Councillors by Egerton Ryerson (pamphlet), Toronto, 1844
St. George Papers

BOOKS AND PUBLISHED DOCUMENTS

BOUCHETTE, JOSEPH. *The British Dominions in North America or a Topographical and Statistical Description of the Provinces of Lower and Upper Canada.* London, 1832

BULLER, CHARLES. *Responsible Government in the Colonies.* London, 1840

CAULFIELD, RICHARD. *Council Book of the Corporation of Cork,* Cork, 1826.

DAVIN, NICHOLAS FLOOD. *An Irishman in Canada,* London and Toronto, 1877

DOHING, MICHAEL. *History of the American Revolution and the Volunteers,* Dublin, 1846

DOUGHTY, ARTHUR G. AND STORY, NORAH, editors, *Constitutional Documents 1819-1829,* Ottawa, 1935

EDGAR, M. *Ten Years of Upper Canada in Peace and War, 1805-1815; being the Ridout Letters.* Toronto, 1890

GRATTON, HENRY. *The Speeches of the Rt. Hon. Henry Gratton,* Daniel Owen Madden, editor, London, 1845

GRATTAN, HENRY JR. *Memoirs of the Life and Times of Henry Grattan,* Vol. III, London, 1849

HEAD, SIR FRANCIS BOND. *A Narrative,* London, 1839

HINCKS, FRANCIS. *The Reminiscences of his Public Life,* Montreal, 1884

JACKSON, JOHN MILLS. *A View of the Political Situation of the Province of Upper Canada,* London, 1809

KAYE, J. W. *Life and Correspondence of Charles, Lord Metcalfe,* Vol. II, London, 1854
– editor, *Selections from the Papers of Lord Metcalfe,* London, 1855

MACNEVIN, THOMAS. *History of the Volunteers of 1782,* Dublin, 1846

SCROPE, GEORGE POULETT. *Memoirs of the Life of the Right Hon. Charles Lord Sydenham,* London, 1843

TUCKEY, FRANCIS H. *The County and City of Cork Remembrancer,* Cork, 1837

NEWSPAPERS

The Advertiser, Markham
L'Aurore des Canadas, Montreal
The British Colonist, Toronto
The Canadian Freeman, Toronto
The Colonial Advocate, Toronto
The Cork Chronicle, Cork
The Cork Evening Post, Cork
The Examiner, Toronto
The Globe, Toronto
La Minerve, Montreal
The North American, Toronto
The Montreal Gazette
The Pilot, Montreal
The Quebec Gazette, Quebec City
The Upper Canada Gazette, Niagara, York and Toronto

SECONDARY SOURCES

ARTHUR, ERIC. *Toronto No Mean City,* Toronto, 1964

BENNET, GEORGE. *History of Bandon,* Cork, 1869

CANNIFF, WILLIAM. *The Medical Profession in Upper Canada,* Toronto, 1894

CARELESS, J. M. S. *Brown of the Globe,* Vol. I, Toronto, 1959

– *Union of the Canadas 1841-1857,* Canadian Centenary Series, Toronto, 1967

CHADWICK, E. M. *Ontarian Families: Genealogies of United-Empire-Loyalist and Other Pioneer Families of Upper Canada,* Toronto, 1894-1898

COLQUHOUN, A. H. U. "The Career of Joseph Willcocks", *Canadian Historical Review,* Vol. VII, 1926

COTE, J. O. *Political Appointments and Elections in the Province of Canada, 1841 to 1865,* Ottawa, 1866 and 1918

CRAIG, GERALD M. *Upper Canada, the Formative Years, 1784-1841.* Toronto, 1963

CREIGHTON, DONALD. *John A. Macdonald.* Vol. I. Toronto, 1956

D'ALTON, REV. E. A. *History of Ireland.* Vols. IV & V. Dublin and Belfast, [1920?] 1925

DENT, JOHN C. *Canadian Portrait Gallery.* Toronto, 1880.

DUNHAM, AILEEN. *Political Unrest in Upper Canada, 1815-1836.* Reprint, Toronto, 1963

EDGAR, M. *Ten Years of Upper Canada in Peace and War, 18o5-1815; being the Ridout Letters.* Toronto, 1890.

FIRTH, EDITH G. *The Town of York, 1793-1815,* Toronto, 1962

– *The Town of York, 1815-1834,* Toronto, 1966

GUILLET, E. C. *Early Life in Upper Canada.* Toronto, 1933

HANCOCK, W. K. *Survey of British Commonwealth Affairs.* Vol. II, Part 1. Oxford University Press, 1937

HARLOW, VINCENT T. *The Founding of the Second British Empire, 1763-1793.* Vol. I. London, 1952.

HODGINS, J. G. *Documentary History of Education in Upper Canada.* Toronto, 1894.

INGLIS, BRIAN. *The Freedom of the Press in Ireland, 1784-1841.* London, 1954.

JOHNSON, J. K., editor. *Letters of John A. Macdonald, Papers of the Prime Minister,* Vol. I, Ottawa, 1968

KENNEDY, W. P. M. *Constitution of Canada.* Toronto, 1922

KILBOURN, WILLIAM. *The Firebrand.* Toronto, 1956

LEACOCK, STEPHEN. *Baldwin, Lafontaine, Hincks,* Makers of Canada Series, Toronto, 1907

LECKIE, W. E. H. *A History of Ireland in the Eighteenth Century,* Cabinet Edition, London, 1892

– *Leaders of Public Opinion in Ireland, 1763-1793,* London, 1903

LOWER, A. R. M. *Colony to Nation,* fourth edition, Toronto, 1964

LUCAS, C. P. *Lord Durham's Report on the Affairs of British North America,* Oxford, 1912

MACCARTHY, JOHN GEORGE. *Henry Gratton: an Historical Study,* Dublin,1816

MANNING, HELEN TAFT. *The Revolt of French Canada 18oo-1835,* Toronto, 1962

MCDOWELL, R. B. *Irish Public Opinion 1750-1800,* Studies in Irish History Series, London, 1944

– *Public Opinion and Government Policy 1801-1816,* Studies in Irish History Series, London, 1944

MCNEIVE, J. *Concise Economic History of Ireland,* Dublin, n.d.

MIDDLETON, J. E. *The Municipality of Toronto,* Toronto, 1923

MOCKLER, REV. JAMES. "Mallow and Neighbourhood 1775", a Report for the Dublin Society, *Journal of the Cork Historical and Archaeological Society,* Nos. 27 and 28, 1921-1922

MORGAN, HENRY J. *Sketches of Celebrated Canadians.* London, 1862

O'BRIEN, GEORGE. *Economic History of Ireland in the Eighteenth Century.* Dublin, 1918.

O'CONNELL, M. J. *Last Colonel of the Irish Brigade.* London, 1892

O'CONNELL, MAURICE R. *Irish Politics and Social Conflict in the Age of the American Revolution.* Philadelphia, 1965

READ, DAVID B. *Lives of the Judges of Upper Canada and Ontario.* Toronto, 1888

RIDDELL, W. R. "Joseph Willcocks", *Ontario Historical Society Papers and Records,* Vol. XXIV, Toronto, 1927

ROBERTSON, J. ROSS. *Landmarks of Toronto,* Vol. I, Toronto, 1894

RUSSELL, PETER. *Correspondence,* E. A. Cruikshank, editor, Toronto, 1932-1936

SCADDING, HENRY. *Toronto of Old,* Toronto, 1873

SENIOR, HEREWARD. *Orangeism in Ireland and Britain 1795-1836,* London and Toronto, 1966

SHORTT, ADAM, editor. *Canada and Its Provinces,* Vol. III and Vol. V, Toronto, 1914

SIMCOE, JOHN GRAVES. *Correspondence,* E. A. Cruikshank, editor, Toronto, 1923

WILSON, GEORGE E. *The Life of Robert Baldwin,* Toronto, 1933

INDEX

INDEX

LAKE HURON
The Projected District of Newcastle
The HOME
County of Simcoe
Gloucester
Penetanguishene
Matadosh B.
The County of Lake Simcoe
The District of LONDON
The Western District
River St Clair
County of West Riding
Missisagua's Land
Reserve
York East Riding
Peninsula
Gibraltar Pt
County of Durham
Outlet of Burlington Bay
Beach
Dundas Street
The DISTRI NIAGARA
Haldimand
Niagara
Falls
Thames
County of Middlesex
County of Norfolk
The Promontory of Long Pt or the North Foreland
Lake St Clair
County of Essex
Kent
The Straits
Pte Pelée or South Foreland
LAKE ERIE
Scale 20 Miles to an Inch